Critical Reflections and Explorations in Regional Development

Critical Reflections and Explorations in Regional Development:

Insights from North West India

Edited by

Dr. Effat Yasmin

Dr. Javaid Iqbal Khan

KALPAZ

First Published, 2018

Published by

Kalpaz Publications
C-30, Satyawati Nagar,
Delhi – 110052
E-mail: kalpaz@hotmail.com
Ph.: 9212142040

Printed at: G. Print Process, Delhi

Cataloging in Publication Data—DK
Courtesy: D.K. Agencies (P) Ltd. <docinfo@dkagencies.com>

National Seminar on "Growth and Development in North-Western Region: Issues and Perspectives" (2016 : University of Kashmir)
Critical reflections and explorations in regional development : insights from North West Indian / edited by Dr Effat Yasmin, Dr Javaid Iqbal Khan.
pages cm
Papers presented at a two day National Seminar on "Growth and Development in North-Western Region: Issues and Perspectives" held at the University of Kashmir in 2016, sponsored by Indian Council of Social Science Research, organized by Department of Economics, Kashmir University.
Includes bibliographical references.
ISBN 9789386397744 (HB)

1. Economic development—India, North--Congresses. 2. Sustainable development—India, North—Congresses. 3. Community development—India, North—Congresses. I. Yasmin, Effat, 1965- editor. II. Khan, Javaid Iqbal, editor. III. University of Kashmir. Department of Economics, organizer. IV. Indian Council of Social Science Research, sponsoring body. V. Title.

LCC HC437.I5N38 2016 | DDC 338.954 23

Contents

Preface

This volume owes its origin to an academic event of seminal significance when we had a two day national seminar on "*Growth and Development in North-Western Region: Issues and Perspectives*", sponsored by Indian Council of Social Science Research. It coincided with the Golden Jubilee celebrations of department of Economics at University of Kashmir. The event saw civic and sober discussion on varied issues viz, growth and structural development, gender and development, infrastructure development, energy, environment; human resource development, health, education and employment with special reference to Northern States of India.

The seminar provided a platform for scholars- native and from outside to share their research experiences with a wide spectrum of people consisting of academics, policy planners and civil society. The book contains select papers presented in the seminar. We are grateful to all who contributed in one way or other to make this academic endeavor possible. We hope that the students, scholars and all others who are interested in development of North western region will find this book useful.

Dr. Effat Yasmin

March 2018 **Dr. Javaid Iqbal Khan**

List of Contributors

1. Sucha Singh Gill is Professor and Head, PRI Unit, CRRID, Chandigarh
2. R.L Bhat is professor and Head Department of Economics, Central University of Jammu
3. Mudasir Afshan is Associate professor of Economics in Department of Higher Education Government of Jammu and Kashmir
4. Aijaz A Bhat is PhD research scholar at department of Economics, University of Kashmir
5. Fayaz Ahmad Bhat is Assistant Professor of Economics in Department of Higher Education Government of Jammu and Kashmir
6. Javaid Iqbal Khan is Sr. Assistant Prof. at department of Economics, University of Kashmir
7. Sheikh Aftaab-ul-Maroof is a PhD scholar at the department of Business and financial studies University of Kashmir
8. Mohi-ud-Din Sangmi is professor at the department of Business and financial studies University of Kashmir
9. Dr. Mohammad Shafi Bhat is Sr. Assistant Professor, Department of Geography and Regional Development, University of Kashmir
10. Falendra Kumar Sudan is Professor and Head, Department of Economics & Director, Regional Centre of Expertise on Education for Sustainable Development, University of Jammu, Jammu, Jammu and Kashmir.
11. Mohammad Younus Bhat Adjunct Faculty, Jamia Millia Islamia, Jamia Nagar, New Delhi-110025

11. M.S. Bhatt is Professor (Rtd.) of Environmental Economics, Jamia Millia Islamia, Jamia Nagar, New Delhi
12. Sajad Padder is Assistant Professor of Political Science in Department of Higher Education Government of Jammu and Kashmir
13. Prof. Gull Mohammad Wani is a political Scientist and is presently Dirctor UGC – HRDC University of Kashmir
14. Ishtiaq A. Mayer is Professor, Department of Geography and Regional Development, University of Kashmir
15. Bashir A. Lone is PhD Research Scholar, Department of Geography, and Regional Development, University of Kashmir
16. Sheraz A. Lone. is PhD Research Scholar, Department of Geography, and Regional Development, University of Kashmir
17. Manzoor A. Wani is PhD Research Scholar, Department of Geography, and Regional Development, University of Kashmir-India

Abbreviations

AFCs : Annual Fixed Charges

AOA : Agenda of Alliance

BOOT : Build, Own, Operate and Transfer

BPL : Below Poverty Line

CEA : Central Electricity Authority

CGWB : Central Ground Water Board

CPSUs : Central Public Sector Undertakings

CSO : Central Statistical Organization

DALYs : Disability Adjusted Life Years

DNP : Dachigam National Park

GIS : Geographic Information System

GSDP : Gross State Domestic Product

HDI : Human Development Index

HOI : Human Opportunity Index

HUF : Hindu Undivided Families

ICB : International Competitive Bidding

IHD : Ischemic Heart Disease

IMR : Infant Mortality Rate

IPPs : Independent Power Producers

ITCM	:	Individual Travel Cost Method
IVS	:	Indian Version of Socialism
IWT	:	Indus Water Treaty
JAKEDA	:	Jammu and Kashmir Electricity Development Authority
LADF	:	Local Area Development Fund
LEB	:	Life Expectancy at Birth
MDPI	:	Multidimensional Poverty Index
MHI	:	Micro Health Insurance
MMR	:	Maternal Mortality Rate
MMRP	:	Modified Mixed Reference Period
MNREGA	:	Mahatma Gandhi National Rural Employment Guarantee Act
MPCE	:	Monthly Per Capita Consumption Expenditure
MRP	:	Mixed Reference Period
NCDs	:	Non Communicable Diseases
NEF	:	National Electricity Fund
NHPC	:	National Hydroelectric Power Corporation Limited
NPG	:	National Power Grid
NRRP	:	National Rehabilitation and Resettlement Policy
NSDP	:	Net State Domestic Product
NSSO	:	National Sample Survey Organization
NTPC	:	National Thermal Power Corporation
NWH	:	North Western Himalayan
NWR	:	North Western Region
PCY	:	Per Capita Income
PDD	:	Power Development Department

PGCI	:	Power Grid Corporation of India
PMLE	:	Pseudo Maximum Likelihood Estimation
PPA	:	Power Purchase Agreement
PQLI	:	Physical Quality of Life Index
REA	:	Regional Energy Accounts
RGGVY	:	Rajiv Gandhi Grameen Vidyutikaran Yojana
RLDCs	:	Regional Load Dispatch Centres
RPCs	:	Regional Power Committees
RSBY	:	Rashtriya Swasthya Bima Yojana
SCDP	:	Srinagar City Development Plan
SEBs	:	State Electricity Boards
SER	:	School Enrolment Ratio
SERCs	:	State Electricity Regulatory Commissions
SGWB	:	State Ground Water Board
SHIEF	:	Social Health Insurance with an Equalization Fund
SPU	:	State Power Utilities
SWRRA	:	State Water Resources Regulatory Authority
TFR	:	Total Fertility Rate
TGF	:	Trip Generation Function
TPRM	:	Truncated Poisson Regression Model
UNDP	:	United Nation Development Programme
URP	:	Uniform Reference Period

Introduction

— Effat Yasmin & Javaid Iqbal Khan

Socio-economic performance of a country largely depends on collective as well as individual performance of its constituent states. The 1956 Industrial Policy Resolution of the Government of India proclaimed that 'the country can accomplish higher standards of living only by securing a stable and synchronized development of the industrial and agricultural economy in each region,' Akin to it, the 1961 National Integration Council made it clear that rapid development of the economically backward regions in any state should be given priority in national and state plans, at least to the extent that the minimum level of development was reached for all states within the stated period . There is an increasing recognition of the importance of intrinsic, sustainable and localized growth of the federations for overall performance and sustainable growth at the national level. However, in practice an unbalanced growth strategy has been followed in the post-independence era. This approach has been dictated both by circumstances and realism. Given the fact that inter-state and inter-regional disparities were a colonial legacy, the same was carried forward with the policy of '*one size fits all*'. In essence special needs of backward regions hardly got any focused attention. Received literature on regional development has no pointers towards region specific development initiatives. Instead following the Indian Version of Socialism (IVS) championed by Jawaharlal Nehru, based on Russian model *"All India level"* approach was adopted. This approach culminated into an unbalanced growth strategy. The successive governments at the center followed this approach as a policy to push up the macro aggregates especially the growth of Gross Domestic Product (GDP). Such an approach emanated from the belief of '*trickle down* 'effect which was a policy prescription in India's development approach till the eleventh five year plan. With this approach in place inter- sectoral as well as inter-regional disparities remained glaring. These approaches to growth have compounded the issue of linearity and uniformity across states and regions. Southern states have done exceedingly well on major socio-economic indicators, especially in the post- reform period. With certain qualifications the same is true of the western region. On a relative frame and in respect of Central, North and the North- Eastern states one cannot vouch for major strides to have been made. Each of these regions as well as the states located in them has a history of its own. While political instability, adverse topography and geostrategic positioning are shared by some North and North- Eastern states as a hallmark, antagonistic colonialism and conquests define the Central India. All these regions as such have faced profane detriments to growth and prosperity. Development lag which Central India has had seems to be narrowing down over the next few decades. This is primarily due to extension in public services, expansion of the private sector and provision of merit goods, especially in the post reform period. Inhibitions to growth and development in the extreme North and North-East seem to be reinforcing. Historical specifics and geographical veracities unique to these regions breed unscrupulous growth inhibitors for them. Even within these regions different states have variedly responded to growth stimuli and policy interventions. Each constituent state within Northern India has its own specificities. On the whole this region is among the largest in India. It comprises of eight states: Jammu and Kashmir, Himachal Pradesh, Punjab, Uttrakhand, Haryana, Delhi, Rajasthan, Uttar Pradesh and Union Territory of Chandigarh. Accounting for nearly 30.7% of the total area of India and 31% of its population (census 2011) this region has unique strengths. Abundance of natural resources, availability of skilled/ (un)skilled labor, growing infrastructure, rising consumer demand backed by increasing income per capita make this region a potential growth center. This region is also a viable investment destination for the same reasons. As already flagged above, within this region some states have made significant progress. However, it does not hold true for a set of states, especially those located in the North-West. Both at the inter-regional as well as at intra-regional levels and interestingly within the state level comparisons, on various social and economic indices these states fall somewhere in the lower-middle level. States located in the northwest region have been taken up for understanding and analysis in this volume. A focused analysis of various socio-economic indicators for the states of Punjab, Haryana and Himachal Pradesh has been carried out with added emphasis on Jammu and Kashmir.

The two states of Jammu and Kashmir and Himachal Pradesh offer immense potential for hydro power generation due to their abundant water resources. With an installed hydro power capacity of 19423.77 as on 30 November, 2017,[1] this region accounted for more than 45% of India's total hydro power capacity. Further the geographical terrain, soil and climatic conditions of these states is suitable for production of several fruits. In fact Jammu and Kashmir is the leading producer of almond and walnuts in India. The state along with Himachal Pradesh leads all other states in the production of apple. This not only highlights the potential for horticulture sector but also provides huge opportunities for foundation of agro-processing industries engaged in manufacture of pulps, Jams, jellies, juice. High agricultural produce and potential in other two states of this region viz, Punjab and Haryana support the case for growth of agro-processing industries on one hand and power generation on the other, as the agri- residual can be used for the same. These complementarities within this region outweigh the heterogeneity which otherwise is rampant both in this region and across. This synoptic view of economic diversity and potential of this region is to appreciate its importance in the broader context of the socio-economic development of India.

North-Western states have historically remained important from the point of view of resources, culture, travel, trade and primitive political culture. The 1947 partition disrupted old linkages of economies and trade and the two major states of the region viz, Punjab and Jammu and Kashmir for different reasons, suffered social dislocation and economic decay in the post-independence era. These states have posed challenges to the project of nation-building in India. In present day world concepts like knowledge economy, free trade of ideas, soft power etc has changed the basis of state power. In a globalized scenario *'liberal economy' and 'illiberal politics'* are not the ideal combination of sorts for economic advancement. However, in the post reform India in general and in the extreme North and North-Eastern states in particular the *'liberal economy'* has been overshadowed by *illiberal politics, regional identity, 'mainstreaming'* and *'othering'*. It is not possible to touch upon all core economic concerns of any region and least of the all, the North-Western region in one book. However, a broad brush of the macro economic variables of this region makes one to state that the development process has been uneven across states. The issue of regional disparity is increasingly becoming a serious policy issue with deeper socio-political implications. During last three decades while advanced states have tended to leapfrog in reform period, historically disadvantaged, geo-strategically important and politically unstable states have lagged behind.

The selected states, as discussed above are heterogeneous but complementary. Their heterogeneity emanates from variety in culture, politics and history. Identity politics of each of the states derives from its remote history. Yet, they are complimentary in terms of geographical proximity and shared resource base. They are diverse but still unique. Punjab and J&K share a history of sorts. Himachal Pradesh shares agro-geographical similarities with J&K. Social structures are comparable between Punjab and Haryana as are their agro-climatic zones. Complementary resources bases, shared histories, potential for growth with diversity make a study of this region both interesting and challenging. It is against this backdrop that the present volume has been conceptualized. This book deals with core issues pertaining to growth and Development of North- Western Region. Each author within his area of specialization and interest has tried to analyze the attributes of the region.

S.S Gill and R.L Bhat in first and second chapters of this volume set the stage for deliberations as carried out in the ensuing chapters. S.S. Gill succinctly documents the shared history of the North-Western region and makes inter-state comparisons on various socio-economic indices. A comparison on Physical Quality of Life Index (PQLI), Human Development Index and their relationship to per capita and growth of per-capita income across the states has been carried out. Nuances of the correlation between per-capita income and the HDI have been deliberated upon in the last section of this paper. This analysis is presented for the selected states and their relative position vis-à-vis other Indian states has been brought to the fore. It is beyond doubt that development is multidimensional. One of the major dimensions that traditional literature on economics in general and development economics literature in particular has under-rated is the role of political stability and social harmony. The author touches upon this aspect of development and underlines the role it has played in the sluggish development of the North-Western region, especially in case of the states of Jammu and Kashmir and Punjab. Insecurity and social strife affects economic development through various channels. Capital flight on the one hand and migration of skilled labor force alongside lack of initiative from the private sector create a vicious circle of uncertainty and a downward spiral of economic gloom. The inability of public administration within the limiting security situation compounds the problem of ushering economic development. S.S. Gill indeed refers to this issue but has not taken this argument forward. He also deliberates upon the issue of climate change and its relationship to economic development. Given the fact that the North-Western region is one of the most fragile geographical entities, such dimension could hardly be ignored. In this line of thought he maintains that "North-West India and Pakistan are regions which are likely to be affected seriously by climate change and failure of the monsoons". For mitigation of the same it is important for all the states in the region and also Pakistan to jointly work in this direction. He lays emphasis on increase in the area under forests, judicious and efficient use of water resources and shift from the fossil fuel to renewable sources of energy. He justly underlines the complementarities of development dividend by asserting that an increase in the area under forests and their maintenance in J&K and Himachal Pradesh, which are better suited to the same, will benefit Punjab, Haryana and Rajasthan and also Pakistan. Cooperation leads to collective prosperity (Krishan 2008)[2]. The author through instances refers to this notion of collective cooperation and complementarily between the states of this region and beyond. In summary, S.S. Gill provides an excellent review of various development paradigms in the region. Issues like social harmony, peace and development are discussed at length. The issues of migration of capital and entrepreneurial skills outside the region and creation of opportunities for income and employment of the youth are also broadly deliberated upon. The chapter reflects upon need for cooperation between different states in the region to achieve sustainable development.

Carrying forward the same line of thought R. L. Bhat in chapter two brings to light other regional development issues faced by North-Western India. The author extends his analysis of North-Western region to include five states of Jammu & Kashmir (J&K), Punjab, Haryana, Himachal Pradesh and Rajasthan. A selected set of socio-economic indicators of development have been taken up for analysis in this chapter. An attempt has been made to broaden the reader's understanding of the relative positioning and performance of the states within the North-Western region. Economic growth, sectoral Composition and Growth of the GDP, poverty' Per Capita GSDP, Unemployment, Population Growth, Vital Statistics, Literacy rate, Human Development and Financial Health are dealt with statistical support. As regards economic growth the physiographical heterogeneity of the region gets translated to differentials in economic growth. While analyzing data from various secondary sources he establishes that notwithstanding relatively poor financial health, development performance of Himachal Pradesh is the best in the region. The relationship between HDI and economic performance of a state is indeed peculiar. There exists no unique correlation between the two in the received literature. Economic performance may be related to HDI in numerous ways, but in isolation, economic growth does not guarantee human development. While Haryana shows better performance in economic variables its human development status doesn't commensurate with its economic attainments. In case of Rajasthan lower GSDP, GSDP per capita, and consequent poverty translates into lower values on human development parameters. State of Jammu and Kashmir has its own, unique socio-political and geo-strategic standing in the region. J&K has a history that can barely be ignored in any informed discussion on the growth trajectory of this state. A past fractured by identity politics and an uncertain future alongside a conflict ridden present, this state performs badly on economic as well as social indicators. The author finds the state's performance in indicators like Economic Growth, Per Capita Income, Unemployment, Literacy and Human Development as dismal. Internal mobilization of resources as for as the fiscal scenario of the North-Western region in general and that of the state of J&K particular is concerned is relatively low. Interestingly, both S .S. Gill and R.L Bhat argue that the state of Jammu and Kashmir and Punjab are not moving on at a desired pace, in terms of Economic and Human Development. Punjab indeed has performed well in agriculture both in the pre reform as well as the post reform period. It also has had its tryst with early industrialization. S.S. Gill is candid to sketch, underline and appreciate the role of political stability and social harmony in realization of economic and human prosperity. R.L. Bhat, on the other hand has not dealt with any such straightforward relationship between political stability and social harmony with economic and human prosperity. However, conclusions drawn by R.L.Bhat in light of the available data on the selected variables lend support to the assertions made by S.S. Gill in the first chapter. The two authors establish perpetual interstate disparities on various socio-economic variables in the North-Western states. To put these disparities into a historical context an attempt has been made by Mudasir Afghan in chapter three to study the structural change in this group of states. Structural change in the received literature generally refers to long term and persistent shift in the sectoral composition of economic systems (Chenery& Others 1986, Syrquin 2007)[3]. It is associated with modifications in the relative importance of different sectors over time, measured by their share of output or employment. Growth is inconceivable without structural shifts, contends Simon Kuznets, the pioneer of the structural change literature (Kuznets, 1955; 1971)[4]. To him structural change is a socio-political as well cultural phenomenon apart from having its linkage in economics. "High rates of growth are closely associated with, and indeed require, changes in economic structure; the later require shift in production structure and legal and political institutions and in social ideology" writes Kuznets (Kuznets, 1971; p 348). To elaborate upon the phenomenon of structural change, Kuznets argues that, "it does mean that some structural changes, not only in economic, but also in social institutions and beliefs, are required without which modern economic growth would be impossible". It is in this backdrop that the study carried out by the author becomes important. It underlines the pace of and divergence in structural transformation within the North-Western states. Interstate comparisons of the temporal variation in the composition output and employment are reported in the emergent chapter. While conducting a sectoral analysis of NSDP of the northern states the author argues that the secondary and tertiary sector have higher and continuously growing share in all the states of the region with slight changes. However, in case of Himachal Pradesh secondary sector has shown a tendency to grow faster than the primary and secondary sectors.

The chapter four by Aijaz Ahmad Bhat and Javaid Iqbal Khan provides more empirical support to arguments made by Gill and Bhat in the realm of inter-state and inter-regional disparities. It also builds on the assertions propounded by Mudasir Afshan in the preceding chapter. Linking the current state level development scenarios back to the era of colonialism and unbalanced growth strategy followed by the British the authors argue a persistence of inter-state disparities in socio-economic indicators. Analyzing secondary data from the Central Statistical Organization (CSO) and the National Sample Survey Organization (NSSO) the authors evaluate interstate differentials in Per capita Income, Human Development Index, Poverty and Unemployment. The authors trace the genesis and continuation of inter-regional and interstate disparities and have attempted to link them to a variety of factors. Prominent among them, especially in the post liberalization period has been the flow of private investment to such states where investors earned more returns on their projects. These were naturally the states that had better infrastructure facilities, socio-economic peace and better governance. This further added to the increase in income disparities. Consequently per capita income differentials have been further widening. Such developments, among others as the authors argue have accentuated the economic development prospects in many states. Hence, the situation is no different in North-Western states.

One can decipher inter-state disparities within the North Indian states on different parameters. In the received literature regional disparities are bound to give rise to inequalities at the disaggregated level. As argued above there exist disparities in per-capita income as well as the development indices. Literacy rates also vary across the North Indian states as does the extent and intensity of poverty and unemployment. Explication of regional disparity led income inequality which farms the subject matter of chapter five. In this chapter Fayaz A Bhat and Effat Yasmin highlights pervasive Income Inequality in India in general and within the North-Western in particular. Based on unit level monthly per capita expenditure (MPCE) data of NSSO the authors calculate and compare interstate income inequality on three different measures. The Gini Coefficient, Generalized Entropy measures and Atkinson's measure of inequality are operationalized to realize the objective(s) of the study. It is argueed that for all calculated measures highest values of income inequality are reported from Himachal Pradesh followed by J&K and Punjab. Empirical estimation of income inequality on accepted measures lends support to perpetuation of inequality in the post reform period. However, income inequality necessarily, is not the only issue concerning the development design of a developing nation. In the Indian context, especially in the post reform period consistent withdrawal of the public sector as mass employer has given rise to multiple issues. The employment elasticity in the public sector has continuously been falling. Same is true of the private sector. Latest employment – Unemployment surveys of NSSO point to a perpetual fall in the labor force participation in India between 2004 – 05 and 2011 – 12. Magnitude of this decline has been worked out to be 8.1% for the age group of 15 – 64 years. Reasons for the same seem to be retraction of female labor force from agriculture and an appreciable increase in the School Enrolment Ratio (SER). Is this retraction of labor force from participation a universal phenomenon? How has the North Indian region responded to such a change in labor market at the national level? What are the internal dynamics of labor markets in North Indian states? These issues are dealt within chapter six authored by Javaid Iqbal Khan. The chapter deliberates upon the concept of opportunities in the labor market. While operationalizing the Human Opportunity Index (HOI) the chapter delineates the available opportunities of employment and access to them across the North Indian states. The states have been ranked on the Index and relative positioning has been explored in terms of the underlying explanations. This chapter links with and extends the debate of income inequality to inequality of opportunity. There might be a strong link between these two concepts and approaches to explication of inequality and both might be reinforcing each other. However, to develop an understanding of the underpinnings of this relationship is beyond the scope of present book.

The received literature is decisive about the determinants and indicators of human development. Development in general and human development particularly is a function of variety of outcomes. The Human Development Index (HDI) as well as the Multidimensional Poverty Index (MDPI) captures important determinants of development. Both these indices have been benchmarks for measuring progress of societies towards better socio-economic outcomes since their inception. One of the major dimensions of both these indices has been health outcomes of nation states. Although, for HDI indicator for health is life expectancy at birth, MDPI captures nutrition and child mortality under the dimension of health. The underlying dynamics involved in both these indicators is access to health services generally determined by affordability of health care at the individual level. Affordability gets directly linked to purchasing power. Lower affordability in case of health services is bound to have profound impact on life outcomes of individuals.It is in acknowledgement of this basic preposition that the modern nation states which have a welfare agenda roll out a variety of public policies aiming at universal affordability of basic services, primarily health services. A Universal Health Coverage Program Rashtriya Swasthya Bima Yojana (RSBY) was launched by the Government of India in 2008, to cover in-patient healthcare expenditures of below poverty line households. It intended reducing the financial constraints for and improving healthcare utilization by the poor. The major objective of RSBY is to protect below poverty line (BPL) households from major health shocks that require hospitalization. This protection aims at making treatment more affordable so as to increase the amount of health care that a household can consume and also to limit the disastrous financial impact that households often experience due to out of pocket spending. The authors argue that RSBY is a classic demand side intervention using a sophisticated version of a voucher system combined with targeting. Benefits covered under RSBY involve cost of hospitalization for 725+ procedures at empanelled hospitals up to 30,000 rupees per annum per household plus 100 rupees transport cost per visit up to 1000 rupees. In order to avail the benefits, a household must be on the official state 'Below Poverty Line' (BPL) list. Benefit is limited to five members of the household including household head, spouse and three dependents. In order to get enrolled a household has to pay Rs 30 per annum as registration fee. The scheme is financed to the tune of 75% by Government of India and 25% by respective state governments. In chapter seven Sheikh Aftaab-ul-Maroof and Mohi –ud- din Sangmi evaluates the progress and interstate disparities within the North-Western region on various parameters of this program. The study finds that most of the households under coverage are utilizing the healthcare from the empanelled hospitals. It has been observed that the program has a positive impact on the out-patient treatment domain. People have been found avoiding the informal means of treatment. The authors argue that Health micro insurance is an efficient way of improving healthcare utilization by the poor. On interstate comparison the program has been found more successful in the state of Himachal Pradesh in comparison to Punjab and Haryana, in improving the healthcare utilization. Overall RSBY has been found contributing positively in reducing delay in treatment. Himachal Pradesh reports more positive results with mean score of 0.04 for treatment group in comparison to 0.12 and 0.14 for Haryana and Punjab respectively.

No contemporary work on development perspectives can overlook or undermine the inevitability of discussions on climate and climate change. Climate change is a reality. This reality has manifested itself in myriad ways. Over the past century both mean maximum and mean minimum temperature has considerably increased. Precipitation has witnessed a significant decline at local, national and international levels. Water tables have fallen across India. Decline in water level of more than 2 m, which is considered to be significant has been witnessed in parts of Rajasthan, Haryana, Punjab, and western Uttar Pradesh, western Andhra Pradesh and North West part of Tamil Nadu. Out of 5842 numbers of assessed administrative units (Blocks/Taluks/Mandals/

Districts), 802 units are Over-exploited, 169 units are Critical, 523 units are Semi-critical across the country. This situation is alarming. In case of the North-Western region as argued in the chapter eight authored by Mohammad Shafi Bhat major rivers flowing in the region like Ravi, Beas and Satluj have registered a study decline as per the available discharge data. This decline in river discharge is bound to inflict a negative impact on the irrigation facilities for agricultural operations in this region. This region is one of the most fertile regions of the country. Declines in river discharge and depletion of ground water is a pointer towards an inevitable crisis in the agricultural sector. As argued by Barnett, Adam and Lettenmaier climate change concerns in the Himalayas are multifaceted encompassing floods, droughts, landslides, human health, biodiversity, agriculture livelihood, and food security. This chapter presents an interstate comparison on major indicators of climate variability and its impact on cropping pattern and food security scenarios. The study presents empirical results of climate change and variability upon rainfall, mean minimum and mean maximum temperature, volume and discharge of rivers and exploitation of Ground water resources. Indian irrigation system in general and that of the Northern plains particularly is seasonal in nature. Monsoons are the major feeding channels. Watershed development programs as a means of conservation and preservation of monsoon waters play an important role in meeting irrigation demands of large tracts of agricultural lands. It is in line with the study conducted by M,Shafi that F. K. Sudan also states in chapter nine that the retention capacity of water in the Northern plains is perilously low. This phenomenon is more rampant in Punjab and Haryana. In these states level of exploitation is already at around 98 per cent and 80 percent respectively. As argued by F.K. Sudan groundwater has traditionally been dealt in North Indian states within a laissez-faire mode. The groundwater has been used to irrigate crops typically without attention to the sustainability of the resource and as such no institutional arrangements in this regard have evolved since the 1960s. It is in this backdrop that the study sets out to examine the groundwater scenario and the institutional arrangements and instruments available for groundwater governance in selected North Indian states. The study proposes some key policy options regarding the way forward in groundwater management for the future. State level groundwater legislation and institutional arrangements have been discussed at length. In the Indian context the study contends that groundwater institutions remain legally weak, functionally disjoint, sectorally biased, and regionally uncoordinated. While physical stress and financial crisis have exposed the legal, policy, and administrative weakness of water sector, myopic political issues and administrative resistance have impeded institutional change. Similar is the situation of selected North Indian States. Knowledge dissemination and awareness with respect to an issue of socio-economic development is a key to unlock the potential ways of addressing the same it is in this regard that effective groundwater governance as a pre-requisite requires awareness of the status of groundwater, both its quality and the quantity available and monitoring is a prerequisite in order to identify whether problems are occurring or are likely to occur. Equally important is understanding of the aquifer sufficient to be able to identify options (and targets) to remedy a problem situation. The study suggests proper surveillance, monitoring and adherence to regulatory measures or response to incentives/disincentives and institutional intervention in water conservation and management.

One of the distinctive features of the North as well as the North-Western states of India is their abundant perennial river water resources. This resource provides these states with leverage in generation of hydropower. Nearly 70.6% of the installed capacity of hydropower is generated in these regions F.K. Sudan in chapter ten of this volume touches upon important aspects of hydropower generation in India. The study is focused upon hydro-power development and it's pricing in North Indian States. The issues at hand are multilayered. They are a blend of policy inadequacy and institutional inability. The author aptly revisits various legislative and institutional developments aimed at reviving the power generation and distribution sector both at the national as well as at state levels. Detailed analysis of laws related to reforms in the power sector with a special focus on Jammu and Kashmir has been provided. The author argues that hydro resource and power development scenario at the national level indicate the need for early development of the Northern Region's hydro potential in order to meet the future electricity needs of the country. Alongside, issues of economic feasibility, financial prudence and distributional justice within and across North Indian states are presented in a detailed manner. To overcome the increasing power deficits and revenue losses associated with the hydropower sector within the North Indian states author suggests robust power reforms in T&D through its regulatory authorities and concerned departments. He lays emphasis on the need to reduce tariff subsidy and power sector losses by setting up performance standards for Power Development Department (PDD) and complete re-structuring of PDD in order to enable it to function on commercial lines. Further, need to develop a long-term transmission plan, strengthening T&D infrastructure has also been stressed upon. For overall growth and sustainable development of North- Western region, preservation and conservation and of natural resources be it land, water, forests, minerals or any other resource there is need for a holistic approach to be followed by all stake holders. It is in this backdrop that chapter eleven attempts to make an economic valuation of Himalayan Biodiversity. Conservation and sustainable use of biodiversity have always been an essential part of Indian ethos. India possesses almost 11% of the world's known floral diversity. The Himalayan region is home to nearly 100 million people from a huge diversity of ethnic and linguistic backgrounds, 80 per cent are subsistence farmers and pastoralists whose lives are heavily dependent upon natural resources. However, the region is facing enormous environmental challenges and the loss of habitats, biodiversity, and traditional knowledge, and these problems are being aggravated by the policies of the governments concerned.

Given that the Himalayan regions are endowed with rich biological diversity in the form of forests, wetlands, and aquatic environments. It is the home of four of the world's 34 biodiversity hotspots and two medicinal systems (Ayurveda and Tibetan medicine) based on local resources and associated knowledge, and that many areas in the Himalaya region are still beyond the reach of modern industrial farming and under threat due to demographic and economic pressures, faulty incentive mechanisms and policies. Authors of this chapter have attempted to answer an obvious question that why is valuation of biodiversity needed? A basic premise is that if proper economic values are assigned to biodiversity, then rational decisions are possible, especially in the case of resources such as forests, which have alternative land use options. Valuation helps society to make informed choices about the trade-offs. Decisions on logging, management or conversion of forestlands are most frequently determined on economic criteria such as the demand for timber, for agricultural land or the need to export forest products to earn foreign exchange. But market transactions provide an incomplete picture of the total economic value of biodiversity and the benefits which are not normally exchanged in markets are generally ignored in decision making. Undervaluation of these welfare-enhancing services introduces inherent distortions in efficient resource allocation. Estimating the appropriate (shadow) prices of non-marketed or partially marketed forest functions and developing appropriate mechanisms to capture the estimated economic values required to improve the efficiency of resource allocation was the first objective of this study. To this end, the value of the economic benefits generated by sustainable management of Dachigam National Park in Jammu and Kashmir (North India) has been estimated using data from 301 visitors from different parts of the country. The results reveal that travel cost method is suitable for valuation of various use values generated by environmental resources such as national parks. The second objective was to provide policy makers with much needed information for efficient, effective and sustainable management of this park. Consequently, the estimated economic benefits (only use values) generated out-weight the costs. Moreover, with the use of the benefits transfer method, this case study has made an attempt to provide policy-makers with useful information for the conservation of biodiversity particularly in the Himalayan region.

The issues related to interstate disparities within the North - Western region on majority of socio-economic indicators have also been taken up in this volume. The discrimination and disparity of any type is a detriment to growth and development of any of the state and the state of Jammu and Kashmir is no exception. Among many other reasons, a distinctive feature that is inhibiting growth and development in the context of J&K, is the absence of socio-political peace both within and across. As highlighted above, the geostrategic location of the state of

J&K has got to be accounted for, in any debate of and its relative positioning on socio-economic indicators. Its proximity to Pakistan and China in an evolving south Asia and an emerging India can hardly be ignored as important determinants of prosperity. Political stability and mutual cooperation among the states located in the North-West and beyond as argued by S.S. Gill would yield a growth dividend. He has consciously included Pakistan within this line of thought in general and in case of trade and climate change particularly. It is in line with this argument of significance that Sajad Ahmad Padder analyses the context, content and composition of trade with Pakistan from 1947 to 1965. This chapter sheds light on the relationship between political peace and social harmony between two sovereign neighboring nation states and economic interdependence within the realm of trade and commerce. The study is historical in nature but contemporary in significance. It serves as a case study of how power relations and political structures can influence trade and other economic activities. Even in the backdrop of extreme hostility, immediately after partition volume of trade between India and Pakistan was quite high. The author argues that this was possible due to a high level of people - to- people contact, a shared history, cultural similarities, geographical proximity, relatively open and accessible land routes to cross either side of the border and relatively low accessibility to foreign markets. *Social capital* as we may call it played a very important economic role even in extremely hostile political environment. Tracing the developments in bilateral diplomacy aimed at trade and commerce the author documents multiple agreements and negotiations at different levels between 1947 and 1965. One of the major observations made in this chapter point towards the importance of socio-cultural and political factors in bilateral trade. Economic rationale is subservient to such factors. As the author argues with evidence majority of the trade agreements were not implemented nor was economic prudence given preference over political aspirations. Such an approach played a major role in inhibiting the expansion between Indo-Pak trade during1947-1965. This has become a legacy. The major economic impact of this hostile political relationship between the two neighbors has been the North - Western region in general and the states of J&K and Punjab particularly. In case of J&K this impact has been more profound. This state, otherwise land locked has a tradition of being linked to and getting benefited from the extended market of central Asia and rest of the world through the Jhelum valley road. This road was closed till 2008. Economic costs of such a blockade are difficult to gauge. However, it indeed has prevented growth of important economic activities within the state of Jammu and Kashmir that were, erstwhile directly linked to the demand in central Asia. Shawls and handicrafts are an example. It is in this context that the author aptly argues for restoration of trade between India and Pakistan through the North-Western region. Half-hearted attempts in this direction, as have been done in the past are not going to yield prosperity. A policy of confidence building based on mutual trust free of prejudice has got to be adhered to. Spill-overs and positive externalities associated with well-established trade links between the two countries indeed will pave ways and means for confidence building and resolution of other contentious issues as well. The immediate and major beneficiary of any such arrangement is going to be the North-Western region in general and the state of J&K in particular. As flagged above political instability and an environment of hostility breeds multiple development challenges. These range from depravity of general population from basic amenities to institutional failure. From issues related to livelihood to migration an unstable socio-political environment envelops all walks of life across time and space. Governance in general and humane governance in particular is the worst hit. Planned economic development gets replaced by crisis management. Maintenance of law and order takes priority over development projects. The opportunity cost of development turns out to be minimal but of safeguarding of state supremacy mammoth. Evidence to the same is provided in chapter thirteen authored by Gull Mohammad Wani. A case study of urban development and planning within a political economy framework has been taken up in this chapter. Inferences are drawn from observation and real events. A classic case for easing out the high conflict paranoia has been made by the author. He states that the environment of mistrust needs to be replaced by creation of social spaces that enable individuals to live, work and play in a free atmosphere. While tracing the origin of urbanization author has linked it with the deliberate movement of people from rural to urban areas on different pretexts. Fear and safety included! With institutions of governance facing a trust deficit and engaged in investing into the same high speed urbanization and spread of urban sprawl end up into extensive growth of slums and consequent poverty, unemployment, exploitation, inequality, misery and low quality of human life. This study pleads for focused urban governance taking into account local sensitivities, geographical compulsion historical realities and social heritages. This will go a long way as a sort of relief and investment into peace and tranquility. Governance, the subject matter of this study is all encompassing in a welfarist- democratic set up. Health and extension of health facilities to general public is a merit good. It used to be a pure public good at a point in time. However, in the post reform Indian economy not much appreciable strides have been made in the social sectors, barring an increase in literacy rate. Health indicators are of India are poor even in comparison to immediate relatively poor neighbors like Pakistan, Bangladesh and even Sri Lanka. Within the disease categories, it is true that huge strides have been made in addressing the communicable disease intensity and spread. This is in line with the global effort to reduce the impact and incidence of communicable disease. However, the extent and incidence as well as mortality due to non – communicable diseases (NCDs) have been on a rise. It is in recognition of this latest phenomenon that a study examining the spatio-temporal distribution of non communicable disease across Kashmir Valley forms the last chapter of this volume. Though the subject matter of this chapter may seem remotely connected to the theme of this volume, but it garners relevance from the fact that health infrastructure in the state of Jammu and Kashmir as in other parts of North Western region is relatively poor. The same has been discussed at length in earlier chapters of this volume. In this chapter an attempt has been made to study district level health conditions of the people with respect to NCDs in the valley of Kashmir. Diseases like rheumatic fever, hypertension, Ischemic heart disease (IHD), Diabetes (type I & II), Cancer, Bronchitis and asthama are taken up for an analysis of their prevalence and geographic spread. A detailed district level intensity mapping for the same is done. Interesting to note is the fact that on average districts with lower levels of health infrastructure exhibit higher incidence of majority of the NCDs. Although the authors maintain that "The prevalence of non-communicable diseases have been reported from all the districts of Kashmir valley but the incidence rate is observed high in developed districts (in terms of socio-economic conditions) and low in under developed districts".

References

1. Electricity Board of India Official website
2. Krishan Gopal (2002) "Imperative of Co-operation among Indian States", in S.K. Bhaumik (Ed). Reforming Indian Agriculture: Towards Employment Generation and Poverty Reduction, Saga Publication.
3. Chenery et.at (1986), "Industrialisation New Delhi and Growth, A comparative Study" p. 467-87.
4. Gosh, B (1998), "Economic Growth and Regional Divergence in India, EPW 33, (26), pp. 1623-1630.

Chapter - 1

Development Issues in North West India

— Sucha Singh Gill

Introduction

North-West India consists of Punjab, Haryana, J&K, Himachal Pradesh and Rajasthan. The region also includes Chandigarh Union Territory, the joint capital of Punjab and Haryana. This region is geographically diverse. There are hill states of J&K and Himachal Pradesh on the North, desert state of Rajasthan on the South and alluvial plains of Punjab and Haryana in between. This makes resource base different in hill states compared to flood plains of Punjab, Haryana and Rajasthan. The hill states have plenty of forests and resorts attracting large number of tourists especially in the summer season. The flood plains of Punjab and Haryana are known for rich lands which are irrigated by perennial canals carrying waters from rivers emerging from upper Himalayas. This region is known as a food basket of the country specializing in wheat, rice and dairy products. The Rajasthan's major area is covered by Thar desert but northern districts of Ganganagar and Hanumangarh are irrigated by canals producing a large quantity of cotton and wheat. The dry areas are known for production of oil seeds and pulses. It is because of the difference in geography which makes building of infrastructure and its maintenance costly in the hill areas. The States of J&K and Himachal Pradesh have been designated as Special Category States for Central Transfers under various Finance Commissions. The other three states belong to the General Category States. In spite of geographic differences and differences in the category of states, the region of North-West India is closely connected economically through exchange of goods and services, culture and history. This region has a long border with Pakistan but with very limited exchange of goods, services and other resources especially after partition of the country. Except for Himachal Pradesh and Haryana all other North-Western states have a border with Pakistan on their western sides. This paper makes an attempt to concentrate on development issues in the region drawing on the development experience of different states. The concept of development paradigm is also viewed slightly differently from the traditional way of looking at it. In view of development experience in the region the issue of social harmony and peace is raised from the economic perspective and inter-state regional cooperation. This is significant from the perspective of sustainability of development in view of climate change which is expected to affect this region much more. The paper is organized into four sections. Section one deals with development paradigm in light of changes during the last two and a half decade and also covers performance of different state in terms of different parameters of development. The section two deals with the issue of social harmony, peace and development. Section three reflects on the sustainability of development and need for cooperation between different states. The last section sums up the discussion.

The Development Paradigm

Development Economics has covered a long distance over the period of time. Economic progress was measured erstwhile in terms of real per capita Gross National Product/income (GNP/GNI). But soon a serious dissatisfaction developed against this measure. The main objection was that GNP can measure quantitative aspect of economic growth, it is not a measure of qualitative aspects such as social, political and economic processes which sustain development. It was also pointed out that this measure overlooks distribution of income. A highly skewed distribution of income can deprive a majority of population from the fruits of economic progress. This measure was also considered problematic for international comparison in view of host of difficulties related to conversion of GNP of different countries in US dollars at official exchange rates. As an alternative to real GNP a measure in the form of Physical Quality of Life Index (PQLI) was developed in the latter half of 1980s (Morris and McAlpin, 1982). This measure emphasized on social indicators of economic progress especially infant mortality rate, life expectancy at the age of one year and literacy rate. But this measure completely ignored the role of income in measurement of economic development. The past efforts made a major mistake to construct a separate measure for economic progress (GNP) and social progress (PQLI). This was corrected by developing a composite index including both GNP and as well as social indicators of development. This index was given the name of Human Development Index (HDI). It was based on life expectancy at birth, knowledge measurement (literacy rate with 2/3rd weightage and mean years of schooling 1/3rd weightage) and Purchasing Power Parity in dollar income (Haq, 1996). HDI has now been adopted internationally as an accepted measure of economic development. UNDP brings out annually the Human Development Report since 1990. Continuance of this publication is an indicator of the global acceptance of this measure both for making historical as well as inter country and now interstate (within countries) comparison of economic development. The recent research on this theme in India brings out a positive relationship between human development and economic growth measured in terms of per capita income. This relation is not straight but a complex one and is influenced by a variety of factors (Mukherjee, Chakraborty and Sikdar, 2014).

Applying the HDI on the Indian states brings out that Kerala has remained on the first position among the states between 1983 and 2011-12 in the level of development. In the North-West region Punjab occupied this position till 2004-05 although at national level its position varied between third and fourth. Himachal Pradesh remained at the second rank during this period and its rank at national level remained between 4th to 7th. Haryana remained at the third position with national ranking of 5th to 7th. J&K state has remained at the fourth position with its rank at national level varying between 9th to 13th. Rajasthan has remained at the fifth (last) position among the North-Western states with national rank ranging between 16th and 21st. In the period after 2004-05 Punjab has been displaced from the first rank in the region by

Himachal Pradesh. The rank of other states has remained the same i.e. Haryana at third, J&K at fourth and Rajasthan at fifth position. At national level Himachal Pradesh now (2011-12) holds 3rd rank in HDI, Punjab 6th rank, Haryana 7th rank, J&K 9th rank and Rajasthan 16th rank (Table I). In per capita income Haryana ranks first position in the region followed by Punjab, Himachal Pradesh, Rajasthan and J&K. The difference between per capita income rank and HDI rank is explained by differences in performance of states in social indicators such as life expectancy at birth and educational attainments. Himachal Pradesh which ranks at the first position in HDI is ranked third in per capita income. Haryana which ranks at first position in per capita income but ranks at third position after Himachal Pradesh and Punjab due to relative poor performance in social indicators. Jammu and Kashmir which occupies fifth position in per capita income after Rajasthan is at fourth

Table 1: State-wise Human Development Index (HDI) Scores and Ranks: 1983 to 2011-12 (Rural & Urban Combined)

State	*1983*	*1987-88*	*1993*	*1999-2000*	*2004-05*	*2009-10*	*2011-12*
Andhra Pradesh	0.290 (14)	0.185 (16)	0.217 (18)	0.288 (14)	0.298 (16)	0.286 (16)	0.309 (17)
Arunachal Pradesh	0.116 (24)	0.066 (24)	0.110 (22)	0.168 (21)	0.234 (21)	0.175 (23)	0.124 (27)
Assam	0.242 (17)	0.123 (20)	0.147 (21)	0.144 (25)	0.234 (22)	0.176 (22)	0.138 (26)
Bihar	0.071 (27)	0.024 (27)	0.061 (27)	0.074 (28)	0.050 (28)	0.050 (28)	0.158 (25)
Chhattisgarh*	0.129 (22)	0.077 (22)	0.069 (23)	0.155 (23)	0.142 (27)	0.114 (27)	0.180 (24)
Goa	0.774 (2)	0.540 (2)	0.700 (2)	0.701 (2)	0.781 (2)	0.796 (2)	0.803 (2)
Gujrat	0.502 (8)	0.301 (12)	0.362 (10)	0.390 (11)	0.429 (12)	0.461 (8)	0.477 (10)
Haryana	0.556 (5)	0.415 (7)	0.396 (8)	0.490 (7)	0.544 (7)	0.516 (7)	0.493 (7)
Himachal Pradesh	0.622 (4)	0.461 (5)	0.430 (7)	0.550 (5)	0.605 (4)	0.655 (3)	0.647 (3)
Jammu & Kashmir	0.443 (9)	0.289 (13)	0.316 (13)	0.406 (10)	0.493 (9)	0.443 (11)	0.479 (9)
Jharkhand*	0.071 (27)	0.024 (27)	0.061 (27)	0.077 (27)	0.145 (26)	0.160 (26)	0.222 (21)
Karnataka	0.416 (10)	0.342 (10)	0.326 (12)	0.379 (12)	0.436 (11)	0.457 (9)	0.420 (12)
Kerala	0.818 (1)	0.722 (1)	0.805 (1)	0.815 (1)	1.000 (1)	0.963 (1)	0.911 (1)
Madhya Pradesh	0.129 (22)	0.077 (22)	0.069 (23)	0.152 (24)	0.182 (23)	0.172 (24)	0.186 (23)
Maharashtra	0.504 (7)	0.408 (8)	0.446 (5)	0.506 (6)	0.583 (6)	0.602 (5)	0.629 (5)
Manipur	0.305 (13)	0.205 (14)	0.259 (15)	0.271 (16)	0.256 (19)	0.217 (21)	0.199 (22)
Meghalaya	0.215 (18)	0.124 (19)	0.225 (16)	0.260 (18)	0.340 (14)	0.259 (18)	0.246 (20)
Mizoram	0.547 (6)	0.449 (6)	0.613 (3)	0.576 (4)	0.529 (8)	0.449 (10)	0.408 (13)
Nagaland	0.272 (15)	0.476 (4)	0.438 (6)	0.467 (8)	0.403 (13)	0.262 (17)	0.257 (19)
Odisha	0.187 (20)	0.141 (18)	0.159 (19)	0.175 (20)	0.174 (24)	0.248 (19)	0.261 (19)
Punjab	0.691 (3)	0.519 (3)	0.562 (4)	0.578 (3)	0.640 (3)	0.584 (6)	0.538 (6)
Rajasthan	0.181 (21)	0.081 (21)	0.155 (20)	0.265 (17)	0.278 (18)	0.240 (20)	0.324 (16)
Sikkim	0.211 (19)	0.160 (17)	0.217 (17)	0.236 (19)	0.299 (15)	0.377 (15)	0.324 (15)
Tamil Nadu	0.359 (11)	0.345 (9)	0.387 (9)	0.462 (9)	0.587 (5)	0.621 (4)	0.633 (4)
Tripura	0.258 (16)	0.205 (15)	0.280 (14)	0.285 (15)	0.288 (17)	0.421 (12)	0.354 (14)
Uttar Pradesh	0.102 (25)	0.058 (25)	0.066 (25)	0.142 (26)	0.167 (25)	0.168 (25)	0.122 (28)
Uttarakhand*	0.102 (25)	0.058 (25)	0.066 (25)	0.162 (22)	0.247 (20)	0.378 (14)	0.426 (11)
West Bengal	0.324 (12)	0.318 (11)	0.353 (11)	0.371 (13)	0.462 (10)	0.409 (13)	0.483 (8)

Note: Figure in the parenthesis shows the ranks;*: prior to 2004-05, HDI score and rank is same as the mother state.

Source: Sacchidananda Mukherjee, Debashis Chakraborty and SatadruSikdar (2014), Three Decades of Human Development across Indian States: Inclusive Growth or Perpetual Disparity, Working Paper No. 2014-139, June, NIPFP, New Delhi.

position in HDI and ranks above Rajasthan due to relative better position in relative social indicators. All the states which have low incidence of poverty demonstrate better performance in social indicators. The states of Himachal Pradesh and J&K show very low proportion of landless households in rural areas and also very low incidence of poverty. This is particularly due to better implementation of land reforms in both the states in 1950s.

Social Harmony: Peace and Development

There is a close connection between economic and social development and sustained peace and harmony in the society. A prolonged period of violence and disturbance in particular geographical location disrupts development process by creating insecurity. It also puts high cost on the society in the form of loss of life and property. Capital formation lays foundation for modernization of production processes by bringing new technology which is more productive, safe and time saving. In the absence of capital formation or its slow down the process of modernization of primary sector (agriculture, mining, forestry, horticulture etc) and industrialization suffers and economy remains entrapped in low efficiency production process. Capital formation is very sensitive to insecurity caused by violence, social strife and disharmony in the society. As soon as insecurity develops capital takes a flight to safe locations. This happened in 1980s in Punjab. Two industrial towns of Punjab Amritsar and Batala were de-industrialized in the wake of heightened violence in the state. J&K has not and is not experiencing sizeable private capital formation in the liberalized phase of Indian economy. This has coincided with the rise of disturbances especially since 1987-88.

Social strife and violence not only lead to capital flight it also leads to flight of skills and entrepreneurial persons. The entrepreneurs assemble all other factors and organize the new productive activities. They are capable of taking risks of new experiments, which also include market risk. Any insecurity discourages such persons to start new enterprises or expand existing enterprises at locations infested with violence. This becomes a barrier to expansion of economic activities. The lack of initiatives by investors reduce opportunities for the skilled workforce at the locations which are violence prone. They also start moving out of the region in search of employment. The absence of entrepreneurial initiatives and emigration of the skilled and gifted workforce to other places create a vicious circle of low income economy. This circle can be broken by innovative efforts of the state administration. But an area which remains disturbed for a long time, the orientation of administration also becomes distorted. The orientation of the administration is transformed from promotion of economic and social development towards maintenance of law and order. Such an administration cannot create an environment conducive either for investment or retention of skilled workforce. There is development dividend of peace (Gill, 2014). The slow pace of economic development of J&K in the post reform period can be explained by lack of peace and harmony in the state. J&K has slipped from the status of high income state in 1980s to low income state since 2009-10 and continues in this position afterwards. Disruptions in peace also explain the loss of Punjab's first position in HDI and per capita income at specific points in time. The experience of this region brings out an important lesson, that peace brings dividend in the form of development. Himachal Pradesh is one such example, which has surged ahead both in social as well as economic development indicators. In spite of being a hill state and difficult terrain the state has demonstrated a fast development trajectory. Thus on a relative basis, even within the North-Western region, it is obvious, that peace creates conditions for security of life and property and creates confidence in the entrepreneurial skills and other economic agents to perform better. It also creates possibilities that the administration becomes responsive to the development needs by changing suitably its orientation. Possibility of involvement of local people to be partner in the expanding economic and social opportunities becomes more real.

Sustainability, Development and Co-operation

At present juncture discussion of development issues will be considered incomplete if the impending climate change is not brought under focus. It is necessary to mention that the way modern world economy has been organized since industrial revolution in the

18th century has led to deep ecological changes. Widely used chemicals have destroyed the ozone layer in earth's upper atmosphere with potentials for catastrophic effects on the earth and all life on it. Paul Crutzen the recipient of Nobel Prize in 1995 had argued in his Nobel speech that "his research on ozone had convinced him that the balance of forces on Earth had changed dramatically. It was now 'utterly clear that human activities had grown so much that they could compete and interfere with natural process'....... the earth has entered a new epoch, one that is likely to continue changing in unpredictable and dangerous ways" (Angus, 2015). Impact of such human-environment interactions are becoming more visible in the form climate change reflected in the impending change of 2 degree Celsius rise in mean temperature over the pre-industrial revolution level. This, among other things is leading to, shifting seasons, more frequent and extreme weather conditions, unseasonal rainfalls, flooding and droughts, melting of polar and mountain glaciers, depletion of ground and surface water resources. These changes are going to have enormous effects on the economies world over. The 2010 floods in Pakistan, 2014 flash floods in Uttarakhand and floods in J&K are indicators of this phenomenon. Punjab and Haryana have been bearing the brunt of unseasonal rainfalls during 2014-15 leading to widespread crop loss. It is important to notice that this is going to affect sustainability of development process. In order to make development sustainable it has to be in harmony with nature. The efforts by human beings to harness nature and disrupt natural processes have brought development process in conflict with nature. The attempt to make development in disharmony with nature has led to natural calamities leading to destruction of infrastructure, houses, loss of life and property. It is evident from the flash floods in Uttarakhand and floods in Kashmir in 2014. The depletion of ground water, its pollution and poisoning of soil is becoming a constraint in agriculture development of Punjab and Haryana. IFPRI study (2010) brings out that impact of climate change in the form of 1 degree Celsius rise in temperature will lead to loss of wheat yields by 9 per cent by 2030, 12 per cent by 2050 and 29 per cent by 2080 in developing countries. North-West India and Pakistan are regions which are likely to be affected seriously by climate change and failure of the monsoons. There is greater need that all the states in the region and also Pakistan jointly work on mitigation of harmful effects of climate change. The major variables on which emphasis has to be given in the whole region relate to increase in the area under forests, judicious and efficient use of water resources and shift from the fossil fuel to renewable sources of energy. It is pertinent to note that these measures require a coordinated effort among different states. The increase in the area under forests and their maintenance in J&K and Himachal Pradesh will benefit Punjab, Haryana and Rajasthan and also Pakistan. This will increase the level of precipitation in plains and sustain water flows in the river. Construction of hydro power plants is possible and economical in the hill areas and helps the plain areas to shift more to this renewable source of energy. Improvements in irrigation methods and technologies can lead to improvement in water efficiency use in irrigation leading to saving of water and its conservation. This requires greater cooperation and coordination among the states of North-Western India and also with Pakistan to share the cost and benefits of climate change mitigation efforts. The cooperation on this issue would require joint investment, sharing of information, technology and ideas for a larger issue of sustainable development. At isolated level each state suffers from constraints to meet effectively the challenge of climate change. The joint efforts can help to overcome these constraints and generate several externalities within the country and beyond. This cooperation can go beyond climate change mitigation towards a joint strategy followed by joint efforts to share collective prosperity (Krishan 2008). The states in this region need to move from the competitive mode to mode of cooperation at a larger regional level. The hill states have advantage of setting up hydro power plants at their territories, for which there is fast growing demand within these states and states in the plain areas. Similarly tourist potentials are immense in hill areas which require a lot of investment of financial resources individual and isolated efforts of these states may not be effective in realizing such large investments. The North-Western states can join hands with the neighbouring states for direct investment in power sector, tourism and processing industries. They can also share technical expertise, managerial skills, training facilities in agriculture/horticulture, processing and manufacturing depending on specific resource endowment available at different locations.

Conclusion

The discussion brings out that HDI is the latest and more acceptable measure of development of a country or different states/provinces within a country. It is considered as a better measure compared to per capita income. Generally speaking there is a positive relationship between HDI and per capita income of a country or a state. But sometimes there is disconnect between the two. This is evident in the North-Western States of India. Haryana has the highest per capita income in the region but is third in HDI and Himachal Pradesh is first in HDI but third in per capita income then the latter. Similarly, J&K enjoys a better position in HDI compared to Rajasthan which has higher per capita income. The evidence also brings out that there are losers as well as gainers on both these counts. Punjab lost it lead position both in HDI and per capita income after 2004-05. Himachal Pradesh overtook Punjab in HDI and Haryana overtook Punjab in per capita income. Similarly, J&K was counted as one of the high income states till 1987-88 but became middle income state in 1993-94 and a low income state by 2009-10. However, it continues to enjoy better HDI compared to Rajasthan which is a medium income state of the country. Punjab lost its position of lead both in HDI and per capita income due to a decade of disturbed conditions between 1982-94, is failure to handle agrarian crisis and change the orientation of governance towards development also contributed to this loss of relative positioning. J&K has also lost its advantage of better HDI getting translated into high per capita income due to continued disturbed situation and violence in the state. Kashmir a *'Paradise on the Earth'* could not reap its full potentials of tourism, horticulture and establish processing of fruits. Himachal Pradesh could reap these advantages much better due to tranquility and peace in the state. This state has realized the development dividend of peace. The development for benefit of the people will happen in the environment of peace and will become all inclusive through their active participation and mobilization at grassroots level. The resource endowment provides the potentials for development, which have to be realized through enterprise, initiative and participation of people at local levels. The disturbed conditions act as a barrier to private initiatives, undermine grassroots participation and paralyze development efforts of the administration. Thus conflict resolution becomes inevitable for sustenance of growth& development.

The impending climate change is threatening the Indian sub-continent and specifically the North-Western states in the form of occurrence of extreme weather condition with greater frequency, disturbed monsoons causing droughts and floods, unseasonal rainfalls causing crop loss and disturbed flow of water in the rivers. This is expected to have harmful effects on infrastructure, livelihood of people, yield of crops and sustainability of whole development process. No individual state is capable of arranging full mitigation of harmful impacts of climate change. Jointly, all states in the region can pool their efforts in a coordinated manner to share costs and benefits collectively. It is an opportunity. They need to move out of competitive mode towards cooperative efforts to harness resources and solve problems. In the era of jobless growth, the states in the region should adopt innovative strategy to achieve sustainable development in harmony with nature. In the process, a large amount of employment opportunities can be created to employ the youth facing massive unemployment and frustration. The cooperative efforts will check migration of capital and entrepreneurial skills outside the region and create opportunities for income and employment of youth.

References

1. Augus, Ian (2015), "When Did the Anthropocene Begin..... And Why Does it matter", **Monthly Review**, September pp.1-2.
2. Gill, Sucha Singh (2014), "Development Dividend of Peace: Experience of South Asia", in Ghosh, AmbarNath and KaramkarAsim K. (Eds.), **Analytical Issues in Trade, Development and Finance**, Springer India, New Delhi, pp.171-186.
3. Haq, MahbubUl (1996), **Reflections on Human Development**, OUP, New York, pp.46-57.
4. IFPRI (2010), **Food Security, Farming and Climate Change to 2050: Scenarios, Results, Policy Options,** Washington D.C. pp.76-77.
5. Krishan, Gopal (2008), "Imperative of Cooperation among Indian States", in S.K. Bhaumik (Ed.), **Reforming Indian Agriculture: Towards Employment Generation and Poverty Reduction**, Sage Publications, New Delhi, pp.467-87.

6. Morris, Morris David and McAplin, Michelle B (1982), **Measuring the Condition of India's Poor: The Physical Quality of Life Index**, Pomile & Co. Publishers, New Delhi, pp.1-22.

7. Mukherjee, Sacchidananda; Debashis, Chakraborty; and SikdarSatadhu (2014), **Three Decades of Human Development across Indian States: Inclusive Growth or Perpetual Disparity**, Working Paper No.2014-139, NIPFP, New Delhi, June.

Chapter - 2

Growth and Development in North Western India: An Analysis of Major Issues

— *R.L. Bhat*

Introduction

Any analysis of growth and development in the context of the size and dimensions of Indian economy is a hazardous task. The country is a heterogeneous entity as far as its constituent State and regional economies are concerned. In an attempt of development analysis of any region of the country, one faces the same difficulty as there is not much of homogeneity even within a region in terms of various growth and development parameters. It is with this rider that an attempt has been made in the present paper to analyze various growth and development related issues in context of the North Western region of India. One cannot be sure as to which States/ Union Territories should be logically included in the North Western region as it is not a well defined region. In the context of present analysis, five States viz: Jammu & Kashmir (J&K), Punjab, Haryana, Himachal Pradesh and Rajasthan have been considered. The State of Delhi, being the national capital is a unique entity in itself and as such is not strictly comparable to afore mentioned States. The tiny Union Territory of Chandigarh, which is just a small city and the capital of the two States of Punjab and Haryana, has also been left out for similar reasons. The set of 5 States considered for the present study are in no way a homogenous entity. In terms of topography, J&K and Himachal Pradesh are mainly hilly, the States of Punjab and Haryana are plain and Rajasthan stands somewhere in between these two groups. In case of agricultural and industrial development, poverty, unemployment, vital statistics and social sector parameters each State has its own story. Notwithstanding these limitations, it is worthwhile to make a comparative study of these States as these constitute a region of the national economy which in terms of size is much bigger than many developed countries of the world.

Economic Growth

For any analysis of growth and development of any economy, its income, growths in income are crucial variables which, notwithstanding their limitations, give a peep into the level of development attained. Table 1 provides the data on growth rates of the 5 State economies during the past decade and also for the latest two years, for which data is available. A look at the growth rate in GSDP in 2014-15 shows that the highest growth has been witnessed in Haryana which is already acclaimed as a State with the highest per capita income in the Country. It is followed by Himachal Pradesh, Rajasthan and Punjab in that order and astonishingly State of J&K provides a negative growth rate in this year. In the preceding year of 2013-14, the J&K has a decent growth rate by its standards and Haryana continues to be in the lead. Since growth rate in a particular year or two may be a medium term dynamics and, as such, from a long run perspective a longer period of a decade i.e. 2005-14 has been presented in Table 1. This allows us a better long term trend. Here, Haryana continues to be in lead closely followed by

Table 1: Growth Rate of GSDP of Selected 5 States (2004-05 Prices)

State	*Growth Rate GSDP 2013-14*	*Growth Rate GSDP 2014-15*	*Growth Rate GSDP 2005-14*
J&K	5.63	-1.57	5.93
Himachal Pradesh	6.24	6.50	7.78
Punjab	5.73	5.32	6.74
Haryana	6.97	7.76	8.52
Rajasthan	4.79	5.75	8.14

Source: Economic Survey.

Rajasthan and Himachal Pradesh in that order and J&K continues to be at the bottom. While as the growth rate of Haryana is commendable in the light of its higher per capita income (PCY), the relatively poor growth rate of J&K is a cause of concern. The interesting question is, if Himachal Pradesh could do it, which is comparable in many respects to J&K, why the latter could not do it. Rajasthan's growth rate at a decadal average of 8% plus is satisfying not withstanding its low income base. In that vein, J&K with again a low income base should have returned a higher growth rate. Is the conflict situation being the reason for it? Not really, because the State performed poorly in terms of income growth even during 1970's and 80's, which was a peaceful era and wherein a couple of years negative growth rate in per capita income was reported.

If we analyze the sectoral composition of the GDP and the sectoral growth of the 5 States under consideration, as has been presented in Table 2 and Table 3, we find that in the latest year for which data is available i.e.2014-15 service sector dominates the composition of GSDP

Table 2 Sectoral Composition of GDP (%) of Selected 5 States 2013-14

State	*Agricultural Sector*	*Industrial Sector*	*Service Sector*
Jammu &Kashmir	17.49	24.25	58.26
Himachal Pradesh	19.28	37.87	42.85
Punjab	20.84	28.3	50.86
Rajasthan	20	31.39	48.61
Haryana	14.1	27	58.9
India	17.9	24.2	57.9

Source: Economic Survey, 2013-14.

Table 3: Sectoral Growth Rate of Selected States 2013-14

State	*Agricultural Sector*	*Industrial Sector*	*Service Sector*	*GDP*
Jammu &Kashmir	5.14	7.08	5.7	5.63
Himachal Pradesh	15.3	2.6	5.8	6.2
Punjab	4.7	0.4	6.8	5.25
Haryana	3.1	4.4	9.4	7
India	4.2	5	7.8	6.9

Source: Economic Survey, 2013-14.

in case of Haryana and J&K. However, in case of former the contribution of industrial sector is greater as compared to that of the latter. While as the share of agricultural sector in total GSDP in case of Haryana is the lowest, that for Punjab is highest. While as Haryana's lower share of agricultural sector is due to better performance of industrial sector, the poor performance of the same in sectoral composition of J&K GSDP is not being compensated by industrial sector. While as service sector is the dominant sector in case of both J&K and Haryana at more than 58%, the lower proportion of agriculture and industry contribution in terms of percentage conceals the huge difference in absolute numbers. In Himachal Pradesh, almost 38% GSDP flows from the industrial sector, the highest in the group of States under consideration and J&K is at the bottom. It is intriguing that J&K, which probably has a better historical record of small- scale and cottage industries has shown much poorer contribution of industrial sector in its GSDP particularly in the light of the fact that aforementioned two States have comparable topography and neither has any worthwhile large scale industries. While as Himachal Pradesh has excelled in the processing of horticulture produce and pharmaceutical industry, J&K has not.

The analysis of the sectoral growth in 2013-14 shows that the services sector has grown at a much faster pace in Himachal Pradesh while as J&K State has the lowest growth rate in services. Table 3 shows the sectoral growth rate in 2013-14 for various States under consideration and surprisingly J&K has witnessed much higher growth in industrial sector and Punjab less than half a percent growth in that sector. While as in case of the former it may be the poor base of the previous year, in case of latter it may be the slowing process of industrial development in that State. In case of agricultural sector Himachal Pradesh has witnessed a very high growth of 15% while as Punjab less than 5% growth. In case of latter, it appears that the agriculture sector has reached a plateau and as such cannot be expected to show any high growth rate. The study of GSDP shows that relatively higher growth rate in Haryana has been fuelled by services sector , while as that of Himachal Pradesh has been pushed up significantly by agricultural sector keeping in view the poor growth rate of industrial sector, in the two States.

Poverty

The analysis of incidence of poverty in case of the 5 States under consideration shows that poverty in J&K was very low at 13% compared to 34% in Rajasthan -the incidence in case of other 3 States falling almost midway between the two extremes. The lower incidence of poverty in J&K State is relatively very low in spite of low per capita GSDP because of a fairer distribution of income which is borne out by the lowest value of Gini coefficient in the State. Even otherwise, J&K is a State which has never reported any starvation deaths and that more than 98% households own a house irrespective of its quality. The highest incidence of poverty in Rajasthan is mainly due to low per capita GSDP. A higher poverty incidence in Haryana is mainly because of higher inequality in income distribution. The lowest urban poverty in case of Himachal Pradesh is mainly due to better incomes and better human development indicators in that State. A comparative study of urban and rural poverty shows the lowest gap of 2.4% in case of Haryana, which is seemingly due to better income of rural households in that State. The enormous gap in rural - urban poverty in Himachal Pradesh is a cause of concern. Lower per capita income and its skewed distribution, may be the reason for the same.

Unemployment

The level of income enjoyed by an economy is influenced by the level of employment. Unemployment of labor force not only restricts the generation of income but also poses a challenge to existing socio economic and political fabric. The unemployed for long durations are also an excellent material for those disruptive elements who want to create conflicts. As such, unemployment of labor force is to be viewed from these perspectives. The unemployment may be of various types. However, data on this variable based on Current Usual Status from National Sample Survey in India provides a good insight into its incidence. In the present context, we examine the total unemployment rate in the five States of north western India. One finds from Table 4 that unemployment rate is highest in J&K and lowest in Himachal Pradesh. The distribution of unemployment across rural and urban areas

Table 4: Unemployment Rate as per Current Usual Status of Selected 5 States

State	*Rural*			*Urban*			*Total*		
	Male	*Female*	*Total*	*Male*	*Female*	*Total*	*Male*	*Female*	*Total*
J&K	25	19	22	38	43	40	28	25	27
H P	21	9	15	17	24	21	21	11	16
Punjab	34	7	21	29	8	19	32	8	20
Rajasthan	28	4	16	39	7	24	31	5	18
Haryana	30	9	20	31	9	21	30	9	20
INDIA	29	12	20	32	15	24	30	13	21

Source: NSSO 68th round.

exhibits an almost identical trend. Unemployment rate in urban J&K is very high at 40%. Such a situation supports the argument that the youth of the State want to have wage employment avenues in government sector within the State. It may be pertinent to mention here that the employment in the government sector as a proportion of total population in J&K is highest in the country and this sector has not only reached a plateau but has actually crossed it long back, resulting in visible urban disguised unemployment. The unemployment rate both rural and urban in the comparable State of neighboring Himachal Pradesh is relatively much lower. It indicates that the youth of that State look beyond the government (Himachal Pradesh also has a very high government jobs population ratio) jobs and engage themselves in some wage employment in small scale private sector. The problem of high unemployment in the State of J&K is also partly due to the reluctance of the youth to look for wage employment avenues outside the State and an attitudinal problem towards self employment which has lot of scope within the State. Unemployment rate in the remaining three States of Punjab, Rajasthan and Haryana is almost same with unemployment in urban areas marginally higher in Haryana; 50% more in Rajasthan and marginally lower in Punjab as compared to that in rural areas. Unemployment rate among women in both rural and urban areas is very low in the State of Rajasthan probably because the women in this State engage themselves in physical labor sometimes even at a low wage rate.

Population Growth and Vital Statistics

Lower population growth and better economic development are usually positively correlated variables. Table 5 provides the data on decadal population growth during the latest Census decade and the one prior to that. In both these decades, 1990-2001, J&K tops in terms of population growth percentage which is much higher than the national average. Himachal Pradesh, on the other hand, exhibits the lowest rate of population growth in both decades in the set of 5 States and is significantly lower than the national average. The comparison of these two States shows that their is a huge gap in their population growth both during 1990-2001and 2001-11. The population growth rate in the States of Rajasthan and Haryana during 1991-2001 was almost same as that of J&K but both States witness a much sharper decline during 2001-11 in comparison to J&K. If we compare the birth rate and death rate in the set of five States the birth rate in J&K, Himachal Pradesh and Punjab are much lower in comparison to the other two States of Rajasthan and Haryana. However, except for Rajasthan, birth rate in the remaining four States is below the national average. Death rate data shows that in all the five States it is lower than the national average. Whereas in Punjab, Rajasthan and Haryana it hovers around 6.5, in J&K it is 5.5. However, the difference between the birthrate and death rate does not explain the higher population growth in J&K. Since in migration to the State for a quasi permanent basis does not seem to be significant, it appears that data pertaining to 1991 in the State may have some issues as no Census operations were conducted in J&K in that year due to disturbed conditions. An analysis of the data pertaining to IMR and MMR shows that Punjab has the lowest IMR level and J&K has lowest MMR in the set of 5 States, MMR in case of Himachal Pradesh is not available. That all the three mortality variables in case of J&K are relatively much lower and Total Fertility Rate (TFR) is slightly lesser than 2 suggests that the State is on the verge of crossing the second stage of demographic transition. This is true also in case of Himachal Pradesh and Punjab but the natural growth rate of population in case of Rajasthan and Haryana is still higher. This argument is further strengthened by studying the TFR in the 5 States. The sex ratio which is the broad parameter of the status of women shows that except for

Table 5: Population Growth & Vital Statistics of Selected 5 States

State	*Pop Growth (2001-11)*	*Pop Growth (1991-01)*	*Birth rate*	*Death rate*	*IMR*	*MMR*	*TFR*	*Sex ratio 2011*	*LEB*		
									Male	*Female*	*Total*
Jammu & Kashmir	23.71	29.0	17.5	5.5	37	70	1.9	889	66.5	69.3	68
Himachal Pradesh	12.81	17.5	16	6.7	35	NA	1.7	974	66.5	67.3	67
Punjab	13.73	19.8	15.9	6.3	28	155	1.7	895	69.7	72.8	69.4
Rajasthan	19.9	28.1	25.6	6.5	47	255	2.9	928	63.2	66.4	65.1
Haryana	21.44	28.43	21.3	6.3	41	146	2.3	879	68.9	70.3	69.3
INDIA	17.64	21.54	21.6	7	42	178	2.4	943	67.3	69.6	68.4

Source: (SRS 2013-14)

Himachal Pradesh all the other 4 States have a sex ratio which is lower than the national average. That the sex ratio in case of Punjab and Haryana is lower may be partly because of the child sex ratio as these two States were considered to be notorious for female foeticide. The overall sex ratio in J&K shows a declining trend. In 2001, among the top 10 districts with the highest child sex ratio, four districts were from (the valley of Kashmir) J&K State. However, there is a nose dive down in the sex ratio in last decade.

The Life Expectancy at Birth (LEB) data shows that there is not much variation in expectation of life at birth across the five States and all of them are hovering around the national average with Punjab and Haryana placed above the national average and the other three below it. In tune with the national trend, all the States have a higher life expectancy at birth for females as compared to males, with only Himachal Pradesh nearing the homogenization.

Literacy rate

Table 6 shows the literacy rates in the set of 5 concerned States. Among the set of these 5 States J&K and Rajasthan have the literacy rate lower than the national average. Female literacy, a broader

Table 6: Literacy Rate of Selected 5 States.

State	*Male*	*Female*	*Total*
Jammu &Kashmir	78.26	58.01	68.84
Himachal Pradesh	89.53	75.93	82.8
Punjab	80.4	70.7	75.8
Rajasthan	79.2	52.1	66.1
Haryana	84.06	65.94	75.55
INDIA	80.9	64.6	73

Source: Census, 2011.

parameter of status of women is lowest in the State of Rajasthan. Himachal Pradesh has the highest literacy rate for both males and females whereas J&K has the lowest male literacy rate and Rajasthan has lowest female literacy rate. The female literacy rate in J&K is much lower in comparison to other three States. It is astonishing that the literacy rate in J&K has remained relatively much poorer in spite of the fact that education has been fully subsidized by the State at all levels during the past 65 years. It appears that a problem is not on the supply side but more on the demand side. Education in the State is being demanded by the households mainly for economic reasons i.e. to get a job rather than to simply exist as educated people of a civilized society. The poor literacy rate in the State has resulted in low human development attainments which can hamper its social and economic transformation. In contrast, the adjoining State of Himachal Pradesh has done relatively better in literacy and other human development parameters which has helped in its better development performance. The low female literacy rate in Rajasthan is mainly because of relative backwardness of the State in comparison to say Punjab and Haryana. The main issue which emerges here is that in the two States of Rajasthan and J&K, improvements in female literacy are not picking up faster.

Human Development

A study of Human Development Index (HDI) value and its constituent variables across the 5 States shows that Himachal Pradesh is on top and Rajasthan is at the bottom interns of ranking across various Indian States. The value of HDI in Himachal Pradesh is particularly better because of literacy and per capita income while as Rajasthan's poor performance is due to poor performance of all the three variables. This State lacks behind in all the components of HDI. A relatively better HDI value enjoyed by Punjab is the result of better scores in all the three variables. While as Rajasthan and J&K have below national average HDI value, other three States report HDI values have higher than the national average. The important question is if Himachal Pradesh can have better HDI value what makes economically better off States like Punjab and Haryana to lag behind. It appears that Haryana has not succeeded in transforming its better economic attainments into better human development.

Financial Health

Among the various issues pertaining to growth and development of any economy a study of its financial health is crucially important.

Table 7: Financial Health of the 5 Selected States.

State	*Fiscal Deficit*	*Revenue Deficit*	*C-D Ratio*	*Debt/GDP Ratio*
Jammu &Kashmir	4.1% (2014-15)	2.8 % (2013-14)	47.27%(2014)	NA
Himachal Pradesh	5.7% (2014-15)	2.2%(2013-14)	57.07%(2014)	57.84%(2009)
Punjab	3.2% (2014-15)	1.2%(2013-14)	78.95%(2014)	36.27%(2009)
Rajasthan	3% (2014-15)	1.4%(2013-14)	90% (2011)	41.08%(2009)
Haryana	3% (2014-15)	1% (2013-14)	81% (2014)	17.48%(2009)
INDIA	4 % (2014-15)	2.8% (2015-16)	79%(2014)	23%(2015)

Source: Economic Survey, 2014-15.

Table 7 provides some information on this for the set of 5 selected States. Punjab, Rajasthan and Haryana have less than national average fiscal deficit while as J&K has marginally higher fiscal deficit and Himachal Pradesh has very high fiscal deficit to the tune of 5.7% in 2014-15. The revenue deficit data shows that in 2013-14 Haryana, Punjab and Rajasthan had a low revenue deficit, whereas J&K had a very high at 2.8%. This level of revenue deficit for J&K State shows that capital expenditure is a casualty in the State as major chunk of resources are used to finance revenue expenditure. A study of Credit Deposit ratio shows lowest value for J&K and is high for Rajasthan. The low Cash Deposit CD ratio in case of J&K is mainly due to the reluctance of people to borrow and invest. The high CD ratio in case of Rajasthan is mainly because of lower level of savings and not due to high investment propensity. Debt/GSDP ratio is highest in case of Himachal Pradesh, a poor reflection of its financial health. Since the data on this variable for J&K is not available, it will certainly be a dismal. Whereas the debt GSDP ratio is much lower in case of Haryana due to its better performance, the percentage for adjoining State of Punjab is more than double as compared to Haryana and speaks for a poor State of financial health in case of Punjab a State economy which is certainly performing below its potential.

Concluding Remarks

The analysis of various growth and development variables for five States in the North Western Region (NWR) of the Indian economy shows that the development performance of Himachal Pradesh is the best in the region notwithstanding relatively poor financial health of this State economy While as Haryana shows better performance in economic variables its human development status is not commensurate with its economic attainments. Rajasthan is relatively a poor State (one of the erstwhile BIMARU States) in terms of both economic and human development parameters. J&K State presents a rather dismal picture with low Per Capita Income coupled with low poverty ratio indicating the fairer distribution of income that has not so far helped in human development. The poor performance on the literacy front in the State, pronounced preference for wage employment and that too in the government sector on the part of the youth of the State and total disregard shown to self employment allocations, poor financial health of the State mainly due to poor internal mobilization of resources and disturbed conditions during the last quarter of the century have kept the State in a low performance equilibrium trap. The State of Punjab, in spite of its performance in agriculture and early industrialization has not moved on at a desired pace, both in terms of economic and human development. These conclusions however, are tentative and need to be interpreted in a cautious manner for a more scientific analysis. However, these certainly pin point at least some realities on the ground.

References

1. Babu, S. (2002). “Competition and Competitiveness among States”. *Economic and Political Weekly*, Vol.37, No.13.
2. Brennan, L., McDonald, J., Shlomowitz, R., (2003). Long-Term Change in Indian Health. South Asia. *Journal of South Asian Studies* 26-1, 51-69
3. Chadha, G. K (1986). The State and Rural Economic Transformation: The Case of Punjab 1950-85, New Delhi: Sage Publications India Pvt Ltd.
4. Kumar, N. (2000). Economic reforms and their macro-economic impact. *Economic and Political Weekly*, 35 (10), 803-812.
5. Mitra, A. (1999). Total factor productivity growth and technical efficiency in Indian industries: A study based on panel data for fifteen major states (Working Paper Series No. E/203/99). New Delhi : Institute of Economic Growth.
6. Mittal S., (2008). Development strategy for the hill districts of Uttarakhand (Working Paper No. 217). New Delhi : Indian Council for Research on International Economic Relations.
7. Narta, S.S., &Rashmi C. (2011). An evaluation of industrial promotional agencies in the development of Industries in Himachal Pradesh. Himachal Pradesh University Journal.
8. North, D.C. 1990. Institutions, Institutional Change and Economic Performance. Cambridge University Press, Cambridge, U.K.
9. Patkar, M., &Bhaduri, A. (2011). Industrialization for the people, by the people, of the people. *Economic and Political Weekly*, 10-14.
10. Planning Commission. 2002. India: Vision 2020. Government of India.
11. Rajmal (2010) State Finances and Growth: A Study of Major States of India, Unpublished Ph. D Thesis, Indian Institute of Technology Bombay, Mumbai.
12. Rath, S. (2003). “Grape Cultivation for Export: Impact on Vineyard Workers”, *Economic and Political Weekly*, Vol. 38, No. 5.

13. Sen, Amartya (1999) Development As Freedom, New Delhi: Oxford University Press.
14. Sharda, N.K., Kumar, R., &Chandel, K. (2008). Special economic zones in the emerging economic scenario: Issues and challenges. *Prabandhan: Indian Journal of Management*, 1 (1), 22 - 27.

Chapter - 3

Structural Transformation in Northern States of India

— *Mudasir Afshan*

Introduction

The terms "structure" and "structural change" have been widely used in economic research, although with different meanings and interpretations. Even in earlier economic literature, economic theory has given significant attention to structural change (Quesnay 1758) (Turgot 1766), for Adam Smith (1776) structural features were strongly related to the level of economic development while for Ricardo (1817) changing composition of productive system was requisite for economic growth. While structural transformation was central in the works of classical economists, most neo-classical authors regard this as secondary. In fact if the former stressed the importance of movement of labour from traditional activities, such as agriculture, to modern industry as a driving force of economic development, the faith in allocation efficiency of markets, underlying neo-classical school of thought, leads to consider structural change as an automatic result market development, rather than necessary condition for economic growth. Although the structural change has been defined in different ways, the most common meaning refers to long term and persistent shift in the sectoral composition of economic systems (Chenery& Others 1986, Syrquin 2007). More specifically, the structural change is associated with modifications in the relative importance of different sectors over time, measured by their share of output or employment. Thus, "the structural change analysis assumes that economic dynamics can be studied by focusing on a relatively small number of groups or activities that comprise the economic system and thereby forms economic structure"(Silva Teixeira 2008, 273). Traditionally, in economic literature this analysis has been associated with different growth theories. In Schumpeter's view innovation was essential force leading to structural economic shift (Schumpeter 1939). Kuznets, established the essential link between growth and structural changes. According to UNIDO (2010) diversification and sophistications of productions are identified as the main drivers of middle and low income countries. The productive sectors of the world economy have changed rapidly in the last decade, reinforcing the established trends from past. The services sector was already dominant in 1970 representing 52 percent of world production and 68 percent in 2005, industry 38 per cent in 1970 and 29 percent in 2005 (UNIDO). Even in Europe, the tertiarisation process, shown by rising value added share of services from 47 to 71 percent during 1970-2005, slightly receded in last few years to the advantage of "mining and utilities" and construction industry. The share of agriculture and manufacturing with declining trends during previous decade, stabilized at 2 and 17 percent respectively. This confirms tertiarisation and for Pasinetti (1981) economic growths are linked to continuous structural transformation and change. The structural change implies to investigate the relative sectoral shares in the process of growth and structural shifts as a consequence thereof. It equally implies to study the sectoral linkages and identification of key sectors in the economy as a result of structural shifts. Simon Kuznets (1955, 1971) has established the essential link between growth and structural change and believes that the growth is inconceivable without structural shifts. "High rates of growth are closely associated with, and indeed require, changes in economic structure; the later require shift in production structure and legal and political institutions and in social ideology" (1971 p 348). He further argues that, "it does mean that some structural changes, not only in economic, but also in social institutions and beliefs, are required without which modern economic growth would be impossible". In the analysis of Kuznets the focus is that massive structural changes in the economy and society are necessary and integral part of economic growth process because, according to him, the economy-wide adoption of modern technology brings about common pattern of change. These encompass shift, away from agriculture to manufacturing and industry and services, a replacement of small scale by large scale production units and relate shifts from personal enterprise to impersonal organization of economic firms and from occupation in farming to blue collar jobs to white collar jobs. These changes are inevitably related with income distribution shifts and population& geographical shifts, migration from countryside to urban centres and cities.

In Indian economy there is a marked shift in the relative share of critical sectors and in relation to GDP the percentage share of agriculture in 1950-51 was 73.07, that of industry 14.35 and services 12.58. In terms of Kuznets analysis the sectoral composition of GDP has undergone a perceptible change and the structural shift tends from agriculture to services underlying social, demographic, occupational and institutional shift and changes. The share of services in GDP goes up from 12.58 percent to 57.03 percent (table 1) and agriculture declines from 73.07 percent to 17.90 percent during 1950-51 to 2014-15.

Table 1: Percentage share of principal sectors in Gross Domestic Product at factor cost by industry origin at constant prices in Indian economy

(Rs. in Crores)

Year	*Agriculture*	*Industry*	*Services*
1950-51	73.07	14.35	12.58
1960-61	49.80	17.92	32.28
1970-71	43.85	21.42	34.73
1980-81	38.31	23.04	38.65
1990-91	33.00	24.15	42.85
2000-01	25.27	24.35	50.38
2014-15	17.90	24.20	57.09

Source: Computed from Economic Survey, various issues, Statistical Appendix, Government of India, New Delhi.

Thus, the sectors in Indian economy are broadly identified which have contributing to growth. The northern division of the economy has undergone structural shifts in terms of its sectoral shares in net state domestic product and certain sectors are identified as key economic sectors underlying the present state of economic growth the detailed analysis is given in subsequent chapter.

Pattern and Economic Growth in Northern Region

An attempt has been is made in this section, to examine the relative changes in the structural transformation of selected states of northern region. At the outset an analysis of the relative share of the regional economies under reference in respective NSDP and their relative state of growth has been made in table 2. The data reveals that the sectoral compositions of state economies of northern states have undergone considerable over the period time which is evident from the table below.

The structural changes that have been experienced by the northern states over the five and half decades reveals that relative share of the regional economies under references have shifted from agriculture based economies to other sector based economies. The percentage share of primary sector of these economies towards NSDP has declined between the range 40-60 percent, for instance in Haryana's NSDP, the primary sector share was highest with 64.76 percent in (1970-71) which has sharply reduced to 23.11 percent in 2006-07. Similarly case of HP the relative share of primary sector to its NSDP has declined from 58.56 percent in 1970-71 to 22.38 percent in 2006-07 i.e, more than 60 percent decline. Moreover the share has further declined to 18.76 and 18.64 respectively in 2014-15 in these economies. Almost same trend is followed in U. P. In case of J&K, Haryana and Punjab it has declined by more than 40 percent however these states still seems maintaining their agrarian structure.

The contribution of secondary sector toward NSDP of regional economies has increased considerably. In case of Himachal Pradesh there has been a sharp increase from 16.73 per cent in 1970-71 to 40.47 per cent in 2006-07 slightly declined to 37.91 percent in 2014-15. Similarly in case of Haryana the trend is almost same. In case of Punjab and U.P the percentage contribution of secondary sector towards NSDP in J&K has been almost similar as that of Punjab. In J&K sate the relative share of secondary sector towards NSDP has increased

Table.2: Percentage share of Key sectors in NSDP in the selected northern states (Constant prices)

Year	*Sectors*	*J&K*	*Haryana*	*HP*	*Punjab*	*UP*	*Delhi*
1970-71	Primary sector	56.63	64.76	58.56	58.36	60.26	6.96
	Secondary sectors	14.57	15.22	16.73	15.32	14.93	25.69
	Services sector	28.80	20.01	24.71	26.32	24.81	67.35
1980-81	Primary sector	47.40	54.23	49.91	49.48	52.01	4.37
	Secondary sector	12.90	19.35	19.13	18.49	15.63	24.87
	Services sources	39.70	26.42	30.96	32.02	32.36	70.76
1990- 91	Primary sector	38.49	45.72	40.84	48.33	43.29	3.26
	Secondary sector	16.81	23.47	22.86	22.54	19.79	29.02
	Services sources	44.70	30.81	36.30	29.13	36.92	67.72
2006-07	Primary sector	29.98	23.11	22.38	34.35	31.83	0.85
	Secondary sector	23.48	28.05	40.47	23.61	22.24	20.81
	Services sector	46.54	48.85	37.15	42.04	45.93	78.34
2014-15	Primary sector	15.50	18.76		26.67	21.55	0.63
	Secondary sectors	28.73	26.11		23.55	20.78	9.62
	Services sector	55.77	55.06		49.74	57.64	89.66

Source: Domestic product of states of India, 1960-61 to 2006-07 (second updated edition), April 2009, EPW, research foundation, Mumbai.

Note: Figures for 1970-71 are based on 1970-71 prices, for 1980-81 to 1990-00 are based on1980-81 prices for the period 2001-07, the base period is 1999-00.

from 14.57 percent in 1970-71 to 23.48 percent 2006-07 further to 28.73 percent in 2014-15 which is not encouraging trend.

So far as the contribution of services sector of these economies is concerned, except Delhi, the share was revolving round 30 percent in 1970-71. However, the share in 2006-07 has been around 45 percent. In J&K the services sector contribution to NSDP in 2006-07 was 46.54 percent which has substantially further increased to 55.77 in 2014-15 while as in 2014-15 U.P is showing highest percentage increased in case of service sector (57.64) which is higher than J&K which was higher than Himachal Pradesh (37.15 percent) and Punjab (42.04 percent) and also U.P (45.93 percent), but less than Haryana (48.84 percent). In H.P, it is still less at 43 percent which is less than J&K 55.77 and Punjab 49.14. the analysis of the sectoral composition to NSDP at constant prices therefore reveals that the changes in the relative share of major sectors of various regional economies set a healthy trend as in case of Himachal Pradesh. In these economies, while there has been a decline in primary sector share but at same time an increase in relative share has been found in their secondary sector. However in case of other regional economies including J&K, the trend is somewhat different as their primary sector decline is shifted to increase in tertiary sector(which is not a healthy sign from economic point of view because growth in the tertiary sector is not a sustainable growth).

The decline in the contribution of primary sector in case of J&K, Punjab, and U.P are showing the similar percentage decline. In case of contribution of secondary sector, the percentage increase seems to be similar in case of J&K and Punjab, while as in case of Himachal Pradesh the increase in the contribution of secondary sector has been substantial. It is interesting to note that J&K , Haryana, Punjab exhibit almost similar pattern in respect of contribution of services sector but in case of Himachal Pradesh the increase in the contribution of services sector to NSDP has not been high as is the case in other states.

The declining trend in the contribution of primary sector in the states like Haryana and Delhi has been compensated by the substantial increases in urbanization and developments in infrastructure, transport and communication. Haryana and Punjab have experienced decline inthe contribution of primary sector but have maintained the high growth rate of agriculture where as in J&K the decline in the contribution of primary sector has been accompanied by the decline in the productivity of agriculture.

J&K has also lagged behind the other states in respect of secondary sector because the transformation process has not been sustainable as a result of which the labour absorption capacity of the economy during the last two decades has worsened.

Sectoral Growth and trends- of Northern States – Comparative analysis (based on linear and exponential growth model)

This section of the Chapter examines the NSDP time series data for the selected northern states, at constant prices and estimated the annual growth rates based on simple linear equation and compound growth rates on exponential function. In order to minimize the temporal variation, the time series data has been converted into time series indices to get realistic growth estimates. The decadal as well as annual growth rates of the NSDP show the same pattern and trend at the constant prices.

While estimating the compound growth rates at constant prices the J&K state shows overall deterioration in growth during the decade 1981-90 (table 4). The primary sector has shown its worst performance with (-3.2%) with the level of significance being low at .35 (table 8) as a result of which aggregate NSDP and Per capita NSDP has also come down as compare to previous decade. In case of per capita income the growth has become negative (-0.6%). The secondary sector has improved its position in 2001-07 with 8% of compound growth.

The tertiary sector has registered a higher growth rate of 10.9% in 1971-80 (table 3) with the level of significance being high $R^2 = .90$ (Table 7) as compare to secondary and primary sector. During the period 2001-07 (Table 6), secondary sector shows the increase growth of 8%. The tertiary sector has shown its best performance in 1971-80 at constant prices with 6.41% (at 1993-94 price bases) compound growth rate and lowest performance in 1981-90 with 1.1% compound growth.

Delhi

The data on NSDP constant prices from 1970-71 to 2006-07 also shows the positive trend. From the decadal analysis, it is clear that from 1991 to 2000 the total NSDP of Delhi shows a negative growth of (-3.3%) (Table 5) with R^2= .82 (Table 9).

On the basis of decadal analysis at constant prices the best performance of NSDP was in 2001-07 (table 6) (7.64% compound growth rate) and lowest performance was found in 1981-90 (-3.30% compound growth rate) (table 4). The main factor responsible for decline in the NSDP in the given decade was decline in the growth of primary sector.

From the given analysis of the primary sector of Delhi, it reveals that its performance is lowest in the whole time period. On the basis of decadal growth rates, there was not any significant change in the growth rates of primary sector of Delhi upto 1990. But from 1991-2000, the statistical figures show the considerable decline in primary sector growth rates i.e., (-19.92%). It has improved largely from 2000-01 to 2006-07 and is still negative as the growth rate has reached to -1.72%.

In case of secondary sector there has not been any visible change due to lack of technology and other raw material problem. From decade-wise analysis, contribution of secondary sector shows its best performance for the period 2001-07 with 8.50% compound growth rate in terms of production at constant prices. But in 1991-2000 secondary sector shown its lowest performance of 4.13%.

The whole analysis shows that secondary sector does not contribute much to the NSDP of the state. On an average it contributes only 23% approximately from 1970-71 to 2006-07. The above mentioned figures show some loopholes in the state's industrial sector.

From 1991-2000 the total NSDP of Delhi shows the negative growth of (-3.3%) which may be because of the poor performance of primary sector which shows negative growth of (-19.92%).

From the individual performance of all the three sectors of economy, the tertiary is on upper side and primary sector on the lower side, while as secondary sector is almost stagnant.

On the basis of decadal time period (an constant prices) the tertiary sector shows its best performance in 1981-90 with 7.85% (table 4) with the high level of significance R^2 = .97% (table 8) while as lowest performance in 1991-2000 with 6.09 percent (table 5).

In absolute terms in 1970-71, the tertiary sector contributes 321-44 crore (67.34%) rupees to NSDP while as in 2006-07 it contributes 6453.262 crores as 78.69%. the total change in the contribution of NSDP due to tertiary sector was 11.35% from 1970-71 to 2006-07.

At current prices, tertiary sector has shown its best performance in the decade in 1991-00 and secondary sector with 8.67% growth rate. While during the period 2001-07, it is the secondary sector which is leading with 10.12% and tertiary with 8.58% compound growth rate only.

Haryana

The NSDP of Haryana was increased at an increasing rate from 1970-71 to 2006-07.

Decadal compound growth rate through exponential method (at constant prices) shows that the total NSDP of Haryana state grows more fastly in 2001-07 (8.70%) (table 6) with R^2= .99% while lowest growth was found in 1991-00 (4.18%.) level of significance .95%.

The annual growth rates Haryana shown through given table by the method of linear regression model shows that highest annual growth rates of NSDP at constant prices was found in 1991-2000 (table 13). While the lowest annual growth rate was found in 1971-80 (table 11).

Based on constant prices, the three sectors in Haryana state are showing the same trend in their compound growth rates. Secondary and tertiary sectors are growing parallel showing ups and downs but the primary sector is showing very low growth as well as low level of significance. The whole analysis shows that there is a less contribution of primary sector after green revolution, liberalisation and globalization.

Himachal Pradesh

The total NSDP of H.P at constant prices has shown an increasing trend. The growth trends both linear and exponential given in the (tables) have been calculated. However there were certain slight fluctuations in the mid 90s.

The decadal analysis a constant prices reveals that the contribution of primary sector in all the three decade (i.e., 1970-80, 1980-90, and 91-00) (table 3, 4 and 5) has remained stagnant with less than 2% compound growth. However during the period 2001-07 (table 10), its contribution has increased to 3.11% but the co-efficient of determination is low with (R^2 =.57%) (table 14).

However the secondary sector has shown its good contribution in 1991-00 and tertiary sector in 1981-90 with 6.91% and 7.22% (table 4) compound growth rate respectively. During the period 2001-07 the rate in the two sector has been 8.98% and 6.37% (table 10) and the level of significance is also high with (R^2 = .97%) (table 14).

The linear growth rate of NSDP of HP state have also shown an increase of 4% annually and confirms that it is the secondary sector which is showing its best performance among the three sectors.

At constant prices again it is the secondary and tertiary sector which are taking the leading role in the NSDP of economy while as the primary sector is lagging behind with its high performance in 1991-2000 as 1.87% (table 5) compound growth with very low (R^2 = .22) (table 9) as compared to 1971-80 and 1981-90. While as the contribution of secondary and tertiary sector has been 6.91% and 6.34% (table 5) in the same decade that is showing parallel growth. However during the period 2001-07 the contribution of primary sector has shown increase with 3.11% growth but still it is the secondary sector which is again taking the lead with 8.98% followed by tertiary sector with 6.37% compound growth and 4.65% per capita income (table 6).

The linear equation analysis based on constant prices reveals the same trend of all the sectors of the economy with secondary and tertiary sector at top growing parallel and agriculture showing very low growth with R^2 = .23%.

Punjab

Punjab is the first state of India which has the highest per capita income.The sectoral contribution of the economy of Punjab shows that primary sector has been the main contributor to the NSDP of the state. The relative contribution of primary sector was 58.36% in 1970-71 while in 2006-07 it was only 34.35%.

Decadal compound growth rate at constant prices shows that it has been the secondary and tertiary sector which have contributed more from the very beginning with 6.90%, 7.16%, 6.20% in secondary sector and 7.17%, 4.63% and 4.71% percent in tertiary sector respectively in the decades (1971-80, 1981-90 and 1991-00) (table 3, 4 and 5). The contribution of agricultural sector in the above mentioned decades has been 4.04, 5.25 and 2.41 percent only. During the period 2001-07 (table 6) the contribution of three sectors has been 7.50 (secondary) 4.93 (tertiary) and 2.18 (primary) with 2.61 per capita income. Aggregate NSDP has also come down from 5.40% in 1971-80 (table 3) to 4.44% in 2001-07 (table 6) but still it is higher than the previous decade.

The linear equation based on constant prices depicts, the primary sector is showing ups and downs and is showing upwards moving trend in secondary and tertiary sector upto 1990 but beyond that it is showing downward trend than other two sectors.

Uttar Pradesh

The state of U.P is ranked first in India in terms of population. In UP the sectoral analysis shows that primary sector has remained one of the main contributors to the NSDP of the economy which gives maximum livelihood to its population. The contribution of primary sector to the NSDP at constant prices of the state was 2564.78 crore rupees i.e., 60.25% while in 2006-07 the total contribution in absolute terms has increased to 91632.49 crore but in relative terms the role of primary sector has declined and contributes only 33.66%.

In UP highest contribution of during the decade 1981-90 with 4.7 compound growth rate (table 4) with the level of significance at .95% (table 12). The primary sector has shown its highest performance in 1981-90 (table 4) beyond that it is showing declining trend with the compound growth rate being (1.76%) in 1991-00 and 1.59% in 2001-

07 (table 5 & 6). Secondary sector is showing worst performance in 1991-00 reducing compound growth to 0.01% (table 5) with R^2= .00% (table 9). The highest performance is secondary sector 8.26% is shown in the decade 1981-90 (table 4). Still during the period 2001-07 the performance is good 7.95 compound growth rate (table 6). The services sector in the state has shown good performance in 1971-80 with the compound growth rate being 11.08 (table 3). The performance was lowest in 1991-00 the growth being for 4.13% only (table 5) during the period 2001-07 again the performance is good with the compound growth rate being 5.1% (table 6).

Conclusion

From the above analysis it could be summed up that the overall percentage growth rates of Haryana are lower as compared to other selected northern states under study i.e., J&K, Delhi, Himachal, Punjab and UP there is not any such significant change in the growth rates except in few states.

The sector-wise analysis of NSDP of the northern states depicts that the secondary and tertiary sector have the upward moving trend in all the states of the region with slight changes. But again Punjab and UP does not have the satisfactory result on the given sectors of the economy. The share of agriculture has declined in respect of all the northern states.

It is clear from the analysis, (whether based on percentages, or exponential growth) that it is only the tertiary sector which has grown considerably than primary and secondary sectors, in all the northern states (except Himachal Pradesh where secondary sector has shown more growth) which is not sustainable growth as it does not meet the domestic demand especially basic consumer goods and consumer durables, thus making the economies market - oriented and prone to inflationary pressures. Besides, disproportionate growth of tertiary sector reduces the productive labor absorption capacity of the economies over a period of time making them economically and politically unstable.

Table 3: Compound Growth rate of NSDP at constant prices (absolute basis) for principal sectors for selected northern states for the period 1971-1980

S. No	*State*	*Aggregate*	*Primary*	*Secondary*	*Tertiary*	*Per capita*
1.	J&K	4.30	2.96	4.30	6.41	1.67
2.	Delhi	4.68	4.56	4.92	7.07	1.78
3.	Haryana	4.83	2.58	6.62	8.78	2.16
4.	Himachal Pradesh	3.10	1.42	3.90	5.84	1.02
5.	Punjab	5.40	4.04	6.90	7.17	3.24
6.	UP	2.26	1.24	5.52	11.08	0.37

Table 4: Compound Growth rate of NSDP at constant prices (absolute based) for principal sectors for selected northern states for the period 1981-1990

S. No	*State*	*Aggregate*	*Primary*	*Secondary*	*Tertiary*	*Per capita*
1.	J&K	2.0	-3.2	5.6	10.9	-0.6
2.	Delhi	7.63	4.56	7.52	7.85	3.20
3.	Haryana	6.27	3.85	9.70	7.82	3.72
4.	Himachal Pradesh	4.54	1.58	6.66	7.22	2.67
5.	Punjab	5.44	5.25	7.16	4.63	3.50

Table 5: Compound Growth rate of NSDP at constant prices (absolute based) for principal sectors for selected northern states for the period 1991-00

S. No	*State*	*Aggregate*	*Primary*	*Secondary*	*Tertiary*	*Per capita*
1.	J&K	2.0	3.1	-1.1	4.6	2.00
2.	Delhi	-3.30	-19.92	4.13	6.09	2.01
3.	Haryana	4.18	1.38	5.05	6.98	2.28
4.	Himachal Pradesh	4.90	1.87	6.91	6.34	3.37
5.	Punjab	3.99	2.41	6.20	4.71	2.25
6.	UP	2.92	1.76	0.01	4.13	1.30

Table 6: Compound Growth rate of NSDP at constant prices (absolute based) for principal sectors for selected northern states for the period 2001-2007

S. No	*State*	*Aggregate*	*Primary*	*Secondary*	*Tertiary*	*Per capita*
1.	J&K	5.1	3.4	8.00	4.9	3.5
2.	Delhi	7.64	-1.72	8.50	7.62	4.87
3.	Haryana	8.70	2.75	10.79	11.15	6.60
4.	Himachal Pradesh	6.47	3.11	8.98	6.37	4.65
5.	Punjab	4.44	2.18	7.50	4.93	2.61
6.	UP	4.42	1.59	7.95	5.1	2.40

Source: Growth rates worked out on the data of EPW Research Foundation, Mumbai.

Note: Figures for 1970-71 are based on 1970-71 prices, for 1980-81 to 1990-00 are based on 1980-81 prices and for the 2001-07, the base period is 1999-00

Table 11:Linear growth equations of NSDP at constant prices (based on absolute figures) for principal sectors for selected northern states for the period 1971-1980

S. No	State		Primary	R^2	Secondary	R^2	Tertiary	R^2	Aggregate NSDP	R^2	Per capita	R^2
1.	J&K	Y=	(4467.864) $(1.034)^x$ {70.542}** {.004}**	.95	(2442.760) $(1.080)^x$ {124.451}** {.012}**	.90	(6089.569) $(1.049)^x$ {116.742}** {.004}**	.96	(12974.625) $(1.051)^x$ {144.396}** {.003}**	.99	(13061.430) $(1.035)^x$ {171.830}** {.003}**	.97
2.	Delhi	Y=	(795.516) $(.983)^x$ {22.532}** {.006}**	.60	(9862.598) $(1.085)^x$ {356.211}** {.009}**	.95	(383265.785) $(1.076)^x$ {596.495}** {.004}**	.99	(49048.972) $(1.076)^x$ {878.355}** {.004}**	.99	(36681.999) $(1.049)^x$ {806.738}** {.005}**	.95
3.	Haryana	Y=	(15597.021) $(1.028)^x$ {413.166}** {.006}**	.81	(11451.104) $(1.108)^x$ {134.677}** {.003}**	.99	(19346.583) $(1.111)^x$ {235.437}** {.003}**	.99	(46078.403) $(1.087)^x$ {639.018}** {.003}**	.99	(2286.584) $(1.066)^x$ {331.238}** {.004}**	.99
4.	Himachal Pradesh	Y=	(3759.500) $(1.031)^x$ {196.948}** {.0120}**	.58	(4048.305) $(1.089)^x$ {122.195}** {.007}**	.97	(4556.027) $(1.064)^x$ {94.919}** {.005}**	.97	(12304.752) $(1.065)^x$ {137.856}** {137.856}**	.99	(20601.656) $(1.046)^x$ {233.541}** {.003}**	.98
5.	Punjab	Y=	(23716.637) $(1.0218)^x$ {367.363}** {.004}**	.89	(10911.852) $(1.075)^x$ {626.722}** {.014}**	.86	(24308.152) $(1.049)^x$ {82.193}** {.001}**	.99	(58783.541) $(1.044)^x$ {1039.121}** {.004}**	.96	(24687.317) $(1.026)^x$ {404.7261}** {.001}**	.91
6.	UP	Y=	(57863.146) $(1.016)^x$ {763.024}**	.86	(26015.242) $(1.079)^x$ {961.683}**	.94	(66172.430) $(1.051)^x$ {388081.761}***	.02	(149527.311) $(1.044)^x$ {2278.201}**	.97	(9246.522) $(1.024)^x$ {147.563}**	.89

** Significant at 0.99 probability level * Not Significant

Note: Figures with {} shows the standard error.

Table 12: Linear growth equations of NSDP at constant prices (based on absolute figures) for principal sectors for selected northern states for the period 1981-1990

S. No	State		Primary	R^2	Secondary	R^2	Tertiary	R^2	Aggregate NSDP	R^2	Per Capita	R^2
1	J&K	Y=	640.569 + -19.183x (58.212)** (9.382)*	.34	126.419 + 9.220x (9.512)** (1.533)**	.81	289.988 + 28.699x (88.881)** (14.324)**	.33	1045.935 + 22.764x (34154)** (5.504)**	.68	1820.067 + .10194x (50.762)** (8.181)**	.16
2	Delhi	Y=	103.490 + 5.959x (7.666675)** (1.236)**	.74	540.412 + 65.825x (42.526)** (6.854)**	.92	1413.953 + 184.480x (90.817)** (14.636)**	.95	2057.855 + 256.412x (117.948)** (19.009)**	.95	3803.267 + 147.242x (122.791)** (19.789)**	.87
3	Haryana	Y=	1482.921 + 74.850x (125.357)** (20.203)*	.93	427.893 + 78.508x (38.779)** (6.249)**	.95	684.175 + 88.273x (40.842)** (6.582)**	.96	2594.989 + 241.631x (167.301)** (26.963)**	.91	2164.667 + 101.297x (103.652)** (16.705)**	.82
4	Himachal Pradesh	Y=	344.601 + 6.474x (25.654)** (4.135)*	.23	109.909 + 11.576x (12.671)** (2.042)**	.80	178.525 + 21.172x (14.333)** (2.309)**	.91	633.035 + 39.223x (41.535)** (6.694)**	.81	1551.067 + 50.424x (85.282)** (13.745)*	.63
5	Punjab	Y=	2059.177 + 146.157x (68.858)** (110.097)**	.96	719.545 + 80.119x (28.708)** (4.627)**	.97	1303.421 + 78.894x (25.463)** (4.104)**	.98	4082.143 + 305.170x (94.816)** (15.281)**	.98	2566.533 + 108.794x (40.243)** (6.486)**	.97
6	UP	Y=	7117.193 + 201.243x (149.267)** (24.056)**	.89	1721.856 + 242.473x (119.578)** (19.272)**	.95	3874.134 + 369.996x (206.022)** (33.203)**	.94	12713.183 + 812.817x (428.585)** (69.073)**	.95	1214.600 + 33.764x (30.148)** (4.859)**	.86

*** Significant at 0.99 probability level * Not Significant

Note: Figures with ( ) shows the standard error.

Table 13: Linear growth equations of NSDP at constant prices (based on absolute figures) for principal sectors for selected northern states for the period 1991-2000

S. No	State		Primary	R^2	Secondary	R^2	Tertiary	R^2	Aggregate NSDP	R^2	Per Capita NSDP	R^2
1.	J&K	Y=	485.858 + 18.202x (10.042)** (1.618)**	.94	223.562 + 3.447x (58.383) (9.409)**	.02	591.909 + 1.046x (9.758)** (.003)**	.97	1515.839 + 31.037x (123.870)** (19.963)**	.23	1728.200 + 35.509x (15.394)** (2.481)**	.96
2.	Delhi	Y=	200.131 + -19.446x (21.672)** (3.492)**	.79	1485.221 + 73.364x (80.071)** (12.904)**	.80	3379.632 + 280.247x (123.430)** (19.892)**	.96	132434.424 + -11244.874x (143700.245)** (23159.39139)**	.03	5690.533 + 123.376x (137.824)** (22.212)**	.79
3.	Haryana	Y=	2589.322 + 38.098x (80.608)** (12.991)*	.52	1166.018 + 78.503x (45.831)** (7.386)**	.93	1458.484 + 159.186x (92.962)** (14.982)**	.93	5213.825 + 275.787x (141.112)** (22.742)**	.95	3281.667 + 85.224x (73.837)** (11.899)**	.87
4.	Himachal Pradesh	Y=	442.135 + 9.055x (11.413)** (1.839)**	.75	232.106 + 23.911x (7.039)** (1.134)**	.98	342.385 + 34.320x (34.950)** (5.632)**	.82	1016.627 + 67.287x (35.4300)** (5.710)**	.95	2031.133 + 84.376x (61.789)** (9.958)**	.89
5.	Punjab	Y=	3658.773 + 99.354x (82.869)** (13.355)	.87	1555.937 + 132.696x (75.303)** (12.136**	.94	1960.461 + 121.367x (47.944)** (7.726)**	.97	7175.172 + 353.419x (97.219)** (15.668)**	.98	3654.733 + 91.921x (34.639)** (5.583)**	.97
6.	UP	Y=	9583.584 + 184.324x (173.697)** (27.994)	.84	64673.490 + -2167.580x (103918.906)* (16748.048)*	.003	7563.489 + 399.547x (211.374)** (34.066)**	.94	21221.578 + 732.209x (402.385)** (64.850)**	.94	1569.333 + 22.194x (26.421)** (4.258)**	.77

** Significant at 0.99 probability level * Not Significant

Note: Figures with ( ) shows the standard error

TTable 14:Linear growth equations of NSDP at constant prices (based on absolute figures) for principal sectors for selected northern states for the period 2001-07

S. No	State		Primary	R^2	Secondary	R^2	Tertiary	R^2	Aggregate NSDP	R^2	Per Capita NSDP	R^2
1.	J&K	Y=	4442.866 + 167.952x (73.525)**(16.441)**	.95	2302.634 + 265.893x (190.534)** (42.605)**	.89	5983.219 + 357.408x (150.994)** (33.763)**	.96	12728.579 + 791.305x (230.757)** (51.599)**	.98	12942.571 + 519.679x (215.535)** (48.195)**	.96
2.	Delhi	Y=	793.626 + -12.645x (20.536)** (4.592)*	.60	9318.959 + 1135.865x (556.111)** (124.350)**	.94	36679.003 + 3837.874x (1152.505)** (257.708)**	.98	46893.556 + 4921.989x (1564.664)** (349.869)**	.97	35976.143 + 2153.107x (1112.747)** (248.818)**	.94
3.	Haryana	Y=	15500.170 + 479.674x (475.244)** (106.268)*	.80	10405.860 + 1802.955x (490.296)** (109.634)**	.98	17449.221 + 3187.098x (917.233)** (205.099)**	.98	43355.251 + 5469.726x (1688.168)** (377.486)**	.98	21632.714 + 1877.393x (638.230)** (142.713)**	.97
4.	Himachal Pradesh	Y=	3756.2000 + 126.599x (222.506)** (49.754)**	.56	3770.433 + 507.395x (246.502)** (55.119)**	.94	4414.078 + 365.989x (145.798)** (32.601)**	.96	11940.711 + 999.983x (229.978)** (51.426)**	.99	20295.143 + 1130.643x (314.194)** (70.256)**	.98
5.	Punjab	Y=	2361.674 + 562.086x (404.185)** (90.378)**	.89	10326.329 + 1106.829x (940.408)* (210.282)*	.86	23906.211 + 1425.564x (200.268)** (44.781)**	.99	57863.931 + 3094.609x (1430.316)** (319.828)**	.95	24548.429 + 715.929x (473.497)** (105.877)**	.90
6.	UP	Y=	57745.257 + 979.261x (849.173)** (189.881)**	.84	24584.311 + 2798.737x (1597.726)** (357.262)**	.92	2214079.697 + -264609.985x (2576334.395)* (576085.884)*	.04	147237.500 + 7814.484x (3325.212)** (743.539)**	.96	9201.429 + 244.464x (173.405)* (6.305)**	.88

*** Significant at 0.99 probability level * Not Significant

Note: Figures with ( ) shows the standard error.

References

1. Quesnay F.1758. Table EconomiqueThe Economics of Structural Change, Vol. III, International Library of Critical Writings.
2. Turgot, ARJ. 1766. "Reflections on Formation and Distribution of Wealth" in R.L. Meek ed Turgot on Progress Sociology and Economics
3. Adam Smith 1776 "An Inquiry in to Nature and Causes of Wealth of Nations" (in Campbell R.H Skinner, A.S. Todd) World Bank.Ox Univ Press.
4. David Ricardo, 1817, Principles of Political Economy and Taxation (in Hageman, H.M. Landesman and R. Scazzieri)ed Vol. I, Critical Writings 2003
5. Chenery H, S. Robinson & M. Syrquin 1986 "Industrialization and Growth, A Comparative Study". World Bank, Oxford Univ Press
6. Silva E.G & A.C Teixeira 2008, "Surveying Structural Change: Seminal Contributions and Bibliometric Account of Structural Change in Economic Dynamics.
7. Schumpeter J.A 1939, Business Cycles: A Theoretical, Historical and Structural Analysis of Capitalist Process McGraw Hill, N Y London.
8. Simon Kuznets 1971, Economic Growth of Nations: Total Output and Production Structure. Camb Mass, Harvard Univ Press[1] Simon Kuznet 1955,"Towards Theory of Economic Growth Ed in R. Lakachman, National Policy for Economic Welfare at Home and Abroad, Garden City, N.Y.
9. Simon Kuznet, 1979, Modern Economic Growth: Rate Structure and Spread (N.D: Oxford and IBH publication, Co.
10. UNIDO 2010, Structural Change in the World Economy: Main Features and Trends, Vianna.
11. Pasinetti, L.L 1973, "The Notion of Vertical Integration of Economic Analysis" Microeconomica, Vol 25.
12. M. Afshan, 1991, An Economic Appraisal of HMT Watch Factory, Srinagar Unpublished Work.
13. Digests of statistics from 1960-61 onwards issued by Directorate of Economics and Statistics, J&K government.
14. Domestic product of States of india,1960-61 to 2006-07 April 2009. EPW, research foundation, Mumbai.

Chapter - 4

An Empirical Study of Disparities within North Western Region

Aijaz Ahmad Bhat
Javaid Iqbal khan

Abstract

Since Independence Indian states have experienced differences in degree and pace of economic growth. Some states have been forerunners in terms of growth and others have languished. Regional disparity has been one of the major concerns before Indian policy makers and planners. After independence decrease in inter-state disparity has been emphasized during successive five year plans but the problem continued unabated. As per the World Bank report (2006) "India-inclusive growth and success delivery: building of India's success" sharp diffrensation across states since the early 1990s exists. Acceleration of growth in some states and deceleration in others has been a hall mark of Indian development experience in post independepence period. The report further adds that more worryingly growth failed to pick up in states such as Bihar, Orissa and Uttar Pradesh. Gap in performance between India's rich and poor states has widened dramatically during 1990s. The Eleventh Five Year plan (2007-2012) also highlighted that regional disparities have continued to grow and the inter-state disparity has accentuated. The benefits of economic growth have largely confined to better developed states and regions.

It is in this back drop that present chapter is conceptualized. An analysis of interstate- disparity has been carried out. Variation in celebrated development indicators like per capita income, Human development index, Poverty and Unemployment are reported. Data for the present analysis is drawn from various secondary sources various reports of NSSO; planning commission data series from the CSO have been also used. Keeping in view the expanse of the theme the present paper is confined to the north western region only.

Key Words: *Disparity, Inclusive development, Human development index.*

Introduction

Regional disparities in the levels of development have ignited a debate on the existing inequalities between the developed and underdeveloped countries in general and between different regions within countries in particular. Regional imbalances may be natural due to unequal resource endowments or man-made due to neglect of some regions and preferences for others in terms of investment and developmental effort. Regional imbalances may be inter-state or intrastate; they may be total or sectoral. In case of a developing country like India it becomes more important to study these disparities. It is generally believed that the new policy intervention in the post reform period has widened the gap between rich and poor states. India presents a picture of wide regional variations in terms of indicators of economic growth and development. Among all the indicators which highlight the disparity between states per capita income (a proxy variable for economic growth) is a major source of worry. This regional disparity creates social unrest. Generally, certain Indian states have exhibited acceleration in economic growth and other indicators while others have been left far behind. Apart from income disparity, disparities in human development are striking across states. The backward regions/states are not only economically backward but are also facing huge disparities in literacy, Infant child mortality and other social indicators. Regional disparity is multidimensional. As such to account for all its dimension is beyond the scope of any single study. It is in this backdrop present paper will investigate with inter-state disparities for north western states in terms of

(1) Per capita income

(2) Human Development Index

(3) Poverty

(4) Unemployment

Inter-state differences in per capita income in north Indian states

Historically, the emergence of backward regions coincides with the British rule in India. The British were concerned with development of only those states or regions which possessed facilities of prosperous manufacturing and trading activities. Rest of the states were neglected and remained backward. Indian planning process was initiated to reduce the regional imbalances and to achieve regional economic development. But, the measures taken under various plans were half hearted and hence failed to gain momentum. Economic reforms of 1980 and liberalization process in 1990s widened the regional differences (Himanshu). In the process of liberalization the role of Government was reduced. Private and foreign investment became more important for economic development. In last two and half decades, it has been witnessed that flow of private investment was directed to such states where investors earned more returns on their projects. States that had better infrastructure facilities, conducive environment and better approach attracted large share of private investment, This further added to the increase in income disparities. Consequently per caipta income differentials have been further widening. Private investment in destination regions increased employment. Such employment opportunities in the better off states create pressures of outmigration in the backward states. This eventually led to brain drain on one hand and myriad of socio-economic issues in the better off states. On the other hand this internal migration depletes skill in the backward regions and further leads to economic backwardness of that particular region. It also puts pressure on the developed regions to provide more employment and generate income. These developments further accentuate the income differentials. This is evident from the table below.

Table 1: (State wise per capita income at constant prices of northern Indian states)

Year	*Haryana*	*H. Pradesh*	*J&K*	*Punjab*	*Rajasthan*
1993-94	-	-	-	-	-
1994-95	4.465727	7.766249	1.42836	1.018003	14.3717
1995-96	-0.0206	4.35145	1.830719	2.202892	1.540239
1996-97	8.894842	5.120626	3.795899	5.348741	8.545064
1997-98	-1.05967	4.533019	2.549848	1.073892	8.571096
1998-99	2.958052	5.376031	2.253483	3.613088	1.431943
1999-00	4.98452	4.784408	1.883982	3.656433	-0.44943
2000-01	4.17281	5.21118	0.073106	1.558009	-4.65796
2001-02	2.77707	3.110138	2.49667	1.971999	6.590162
2002-03	3.319011	3.004188	2.06272	1.320402	-8.62339
2003-04	6.723361	6.310394	2.731679	4.362242	23.42713
2004-05	6.587066	5.752924	2.786997	5.392712	-1.31603
2005-06	7.133818	7.177297	4.197464	4.506016	4.676935
2006-07	9.163495	7.875113	4.420385	8.763921	9.626772
2007-08	6.486584	7.370473	4.891129	7.677229	3.265406
2008-09	6.253293	6.294592	4.963016	4.538348	7.180219
2009-10	9.78694	7.004131	3.065632	5.011268	4.88391
2010-11	5.592928	7.727855	4.237956	5.269627	12.52423
2011-12	6.0132	6.281117	4.836467	5.096651	3.499154
2012-13	4.808912	5.161039	4.198143	3.569224	2.905657
2013-14	5.56	7.09	7.33	6.32	6.07
2014-15	7.98	7.48	-0.96	4.92	6.11
Coefficient of variation	0.514142	0.24873	0.593929	0.507013	1.294211

Source: Central Statistical Organization, GOI.

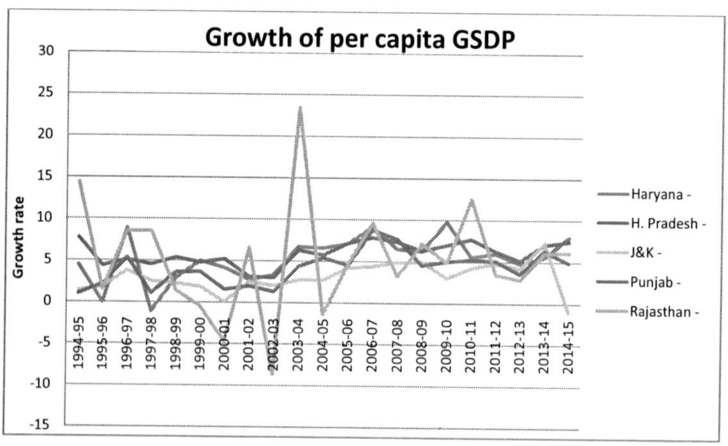

Per capita income growth rates in the northern states have been fluctuating over the reference period. Growth rates of per capita income of Himachal Pradesh and Haryana have income above national average over the reference period. As per Economic survey of Rajasthan (2007-2008) flow of FDI and other remittances has been higher in year (2003-04) due to which growth rate increases in the said year. Punjab and Jammu & Kashmir in comparison with other states report lower per capita income growth rate. Contribution of industrial and service sector has helped in improving the growth rates of Himachal Pradesh and Haryana and Rajasthan. At the same time contribution of these two sectors has been lower in Jammu and Kashmir, and Punjab. Contribution of Agriculture and allied activities has been lower in Jammu and Kashmir as compared with other northern states. Setting up of more industrial ventures and inflow of FDI and FII has been highest in Himachal Pradesh which helps its growth rate to improve. Also Tourism and Hospitality sector of Himachal Pradesh and J &K has contributed to their GSDP but because of conducive environment and political stability in Himachal Pradesh contribution of tourism in GSDP has been relatively higher as compared to Jammu and Kashmir in backdrop of political and security related issues in J&K. Development of ICT industries in states like Himachal Pradesh, Haryana Punjab have actively contributed in their growth rates. Larger contribution of industrial and service sector to GSDP in case of Himachal Pradesh, Haryana can be partially explained by higher inflows of FDI and FII to these states. However, all states except Himachal Pradesh have shown higher coefficient of variation over the reference period

Human development disparities

The composite index of human development for northern states is presented in the above table 2. HDI level has been consistently high for states like Punjab and Himachal Pradesh whereas other three states are improving but lagging far behind. Inter- state comparison of socio-economic development of selected northern states of India on HDI indicators shows some stark differences. Human capabilities and abilities are in any case not independent of income growth. Accordingly variations in HDI for northern Indian states as reported in case of per capita income are re-imposed in the relative positioning of these states in the Human development index. A case in point is the comparison of Jammu and Kashmir and Himachal Pradesh. Within the determinants of Human development index Jammu & Kashmir has a relatively low position as compared to Himachal Pradesh. Jammu and Kashmir lags behind Himachal and Punjab in literacy rate. Further higher infant mortality rate is another major concern for J & K. This indicates that some states are forerunners in some indicators of Human development index while other are languishing back in terms of other indicators.

TABLE 2: Human development disparities

S. No.	*State*	*HDI value and rank (1993)*	*HDI value and rank (1990-2000)*	*HDI value and rank (2004-05)*	*HDI value and rank (2009-10)*	*HDI value and rank (2011-12)*	*HDI value (2015)*
1.	Haryana	0.367(10)	0.490(7)	0.544(7)	0.516(7)	0.493(7)	0.6701
2.	Himachal Pradesh	0.430(7)	0.550(5)	0.605(4)	0.655(3)	0.647(3)	0.6614
3.	J & K	0.316(13)	0.406(10)	0.439(9)	0.443(11)	0.479(9)	0.6613
4.	Punjab	0.562(4)	0.578(3)	0.640(3)	o.584(6)	0.538(6)	0.6489
5.	Rajasthan	0.155(20)	0.265(17)	0.278(18)	0.240(20)	0.324(16)	0.5768

Source: Sacchidananda Mukherjee, Debashis Chakraborty2 and Satadru Sikdar3 Working Paper No.139

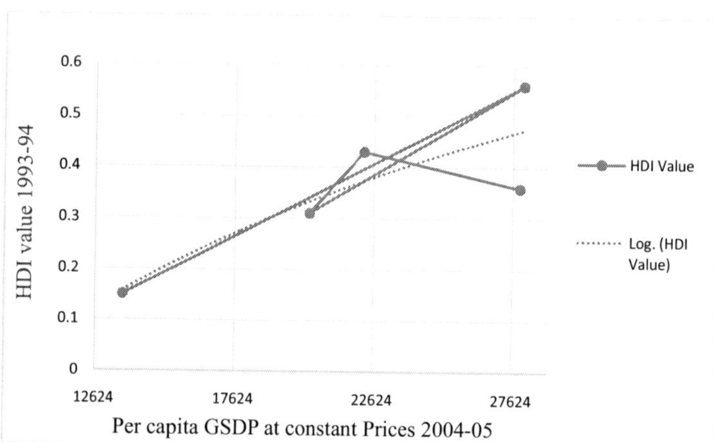

Figure 1: Relationship between HDI Value and Per capita.

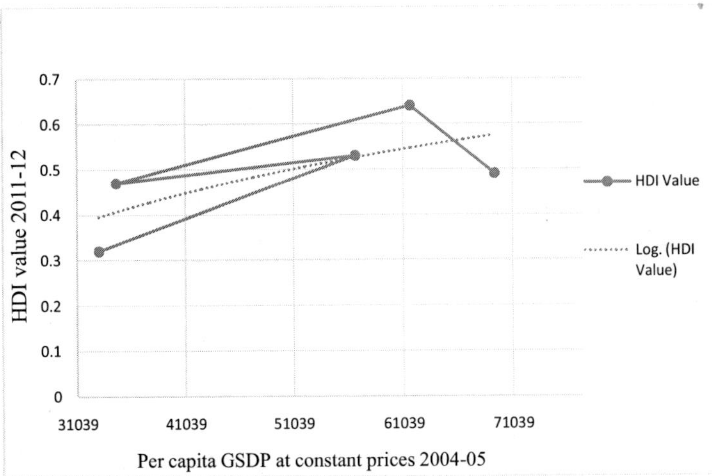

Figure 2: Relationship between HDI Value and Per capita.

A positive relationship between HD and economic growth exists in both directions implying that while higher growth path augments HD formation in a country the latter also contributes positively in propelling the former (Srinivansan 1994, Mukherjee and chakraborty 2011). As is exhibited by Jammu and Kashmir and Himachal Pradesh here.

The above two figures shows that per capita GSDP is a significant determinant of Human development. Two conclusions emerges from the figures

Firstly income elasticity of human development is higher across all income groups. In other words, impact of per capita income in achievement of HDI is significant for most of the states. Secondly income elasticity of human development is higher for lower income states as compared to higher income states.

POVERTY

In India, the generally accepted definition of poverty lays emphasis on minimum level of living rather than reasonable levels of living. This attitude seems to be borne out of a realization that it has not been possible to provide even a minimum quantum of basic needs to the population for decades and therefore, to talk about a reasonable level of living or good life would appear to be wishful thinking. Several programmes have been initiated since the development of planning to alleviate the poverty for the good of people but for more than six decades on such identified parameters poverty is still prelevant in the country. The trickledown theory of per capita income getting correlated with reduction in poverty seems not to have borne much fruit. As regards northern Indian states the trend is quite stark

Table Poverty in north Indian state (2011-12) prices

States	*Rural*	*Urban*	*Total*
Haryana	18.6	23.0	20.1
Himachal Pradesh	9.1	12.6	9.5
J & K	8.1	12.8	9.4
Punjab	0.2	1.6	1.2
Rajasthan	14.6	15.9	15.9
Poverty rates during 2015			
Haryana	11.64	10.28	11.16
Himachal Pradesh	8.48	4.33	8.06
J & K	11.54	7.20	10.35
Punjab	7.66	9.24	8.26
Rajasthan	16.05	10.69	14.72

Source: Planning Commission.

The table indicates that poverty is lower in states of Punjab, J & K, Himachal Pradesh and higher in states of Haryana and Rajasthan. In these states poverty largely emanates from semi-feudal relations of production in Agriculture. Often rural poverty is attributed to rapid population growth. It is asserted that rapid population growth puts pressure on land base and as a consequence real per capita income of labor falls. Besides this, poverty in state of Rajasthan and Haryana can be partially attributed to the non- realization of Green revolution and other poverty programmes. Linking of poverty to per capita income reveals that the states where per capita income has shown increase, poverty has reduced and in states where per capita income has followed fluctuating trend poverty has not reduced much.

UNEMPLOYMENT

Unemployment in a broader sense is defined a situation when a labor does not find employment opportunity despite its willingness to work on existing rate. India is a developing economy the nature of unemployment therefore, sharply differs from the one that prevails in industrially advanced economies. The unemployment in India can be defined as, prevalence of chronic under-employment or disguised unemployment in the rural sector and the existence of involuntary urban unemployment among the educated class. The data pertaining to northern states of India reveals that unemployment rate is highest in states of Jammu and Kashmir and Himachal Pradesh as can be seen from table.

Table 4: Unemployment rate in North Indian states

S. No.	*States*	*Unemployment rate*
1.	Haryana	2.1
2.	Himachal Pradesh	4.5
3.	J&K	4.7
4.	Punjab	2.5
5.	Rajasthan	3.2
	All India level	2.6

Source: National sample survey organization Report based on (usual principal status) 2013- 14.

Table no 4 presents a clear picture of comparative position of unemployment rates in the northern states and shows that unemployment rate is higher in Himachal Pradesh and Jammu & Kashmir compared to other states. This can be explained in terms of steady decline in employment elasticity in all major sectors of economic activity. The lower unemployment rate in Rajasthan, Haryana and Punjab may partly be attributed to high absorption of (MGNREGA) funds in these states. Himachal Pradesh which has performed well in terms of others indicators lags behind in terms of employment generation. This may be due to higher levels of education in the state resulting in people less attracted towards and high aspiration for manual jobs as observed by some studies (Dutta & Sunndram). Positive interventions by way of policies/schemes/entrepreneur skill development programmes etc. are needed to generate employment for educated youth.

CONCLUSION

Inter-state analysis of disparities in the North western regions reveals differentials in PCY, HDI as well as poverty. States that had better infrastructural facilities, conducive environment and better approach attracted large share of private investment this further added to the increase in income disparities. Within the determinants of HDI Jammu and Kashmir state has relatively low position as compared to other north-western states. The trickledown theory of PCY correlated with reduction in poverty seems not to have borne much fruits in Jammu and Kashmir as compared to Punjab and Haryana.

For a developing country with an aspiration of becoming a super power by 2020, it is all the more necessary to reduce the inter-state disparities. Various measures supposedly undertaken by the government have made little impact on these disparities. A more positive approach is needed from the part of government to reduce such disparities which would include changes in distribution of assets, redistributive transfers, increased spending on health and education and creation of quality jobs and social safety net for those states which are left behind otherwise, the dream of faster inclusive dream will remain dream. Similarly the criteria used for devolution of funds under finance commission need to be revisited.

References

1. Adabar K. (2004),"Economic Growth and Convergence in India ", Working Paper: Institute *for social and Economic Change*, Nagarbhavi, India.
2. Bandyopadhyay, S, S. (2011), "Rich States, Poor States: Convergence and Polarization in India", *Scottish Journal of Political Economy,* 58(3), pp. 414-436.
3. Chikte, R.P. (2011), "Income Convergence and Regional Growth in India: Before and After Liberalization", *South Asia Economic Journal*, 12(2), pp. 239-269.
4. Dasgupta, D, P. Maiti, R. Mukherjee, S.Sarkarand S. Chakrabartiy (2000), "Growth and Inter-state Disparities in India", *Economic and Political Weekly*, 35(27), pp. 2413-2422.

5. Dreze, J. and A. K. Sen (2013), "*An Uncertain Glory: India and Its Contradictions" (London: Allen Lane).*
6. Gosh, B., S. Marjit and C. Neogi (1998), "Economic Growth and Regional Divergence in India, 1960 to 1995, *Economic and Political Weekly,* 33(26), pp. 1623-1630.
7. Gosh, M. (2010), "Regional Economic Growth and Inequality in India during Pre and Post- Reform Periods", *The Journal of Income and Wealth,* 32(2), pp. 71-88.
8. Kaldor, N. (1970), "The Case for Regional Policies, *Scottish Journal of Political Economy,17*(3),pp.337-348.Reprinted in *Scottish Journal of Political Economy,*November,2013 with Commentary by A.P. Thirlwall
9. Kumar, U. and A, Subramanian (2012), "Growth in India's States in the First Decade of the Twentieth Century: Four Facts, *Economic and Political Weekly,* 47(3), pp. 48-58
10. Lucas, R. (1988), "On the Mechanics of Economic Development, *Journal of Monetary Economics,* 22, pp. 3-42.
11. Myrdal, G. (1957), "*Economic Theory and Underdeveloped Regions* (London: Duckworth).
12. Nayyar, G. (2008). "Economic Growth and Regional Inequality in India", *Economic and Political Weekly,* 43(6), pp. 58-76.
13. Sachs, J., N. Bajpai and A. Ramiah (2002), "Understanding Regional Economic Growth in India", *Asian Economic Papers,* 1(3), pp. 32-62.
14. Solow, R. (1956), "A Contribution to the Theory of Economic Growth, *Quarterly Journal of Economics,* 70(1), pp. 65-94.
15. Thirlwall, A.P. (1980), "Regional Problems are Balance of Payments Problems", *Regional Studies,* 4. pp. 419-425. Reprinted in *Regional Studies,* 41(S1), pp. S89-S96.
16. Thirlwall, A.P. (2013), "*Economic Growth in an Open Developing Economy: The Role of Structure and Demand* (Cheltenham: Edward Elgar).
17. Toner, P. (1999), *Main Currents in Cumulative Causation,*(London: Macmillan).

Chapter - 5

A Comparative Study of Income Inequality of North-Western States of India

— *Fayaz Ahmad Bhat & Effat Yasmin*

Abstract

This paper attempts to estimate income inequality across North-Western states of India. Punjab, Himachal Pradesh and Jammu & Kashmir have been selected to estimate the same. This study is based on 68th NSSO consumption expenditure round data of Type 1 and Type 2. The monthly per capita consumption expenditure (MPCE) is used as a proxy for monthly per capita income. As such income inequality, has been calculate by employing three different measures —Gini Coefficient, Generalised Entropy measures and Atkinson's measure of inequality. The study finds highest value Gini coefficient and Theil's entropy for Himachal Pradesh as compared to Punjab and J&K. Inspite of various measures taken by government of India from time to time the inequality has increased since reforms. India is second most unequal country globally, with millionaires controlling 54 percent of its wealth (Indian Economic Summit 2015). The level of inequality and disparity has grown dramatically over the period of time. To examine the magnitude of inequality at all India level is beyond the scope of this paper, hence the focus of the present paper is on North Western Region only.

Key Words: *Income Inequality, North-Western Region, Consumption Expenditure, Entropy Index, Atkinson's Index, etc.*

Introduction

The primary focus of world economic attention from the second half of the 20th century has been on the ways to accelerate the growth rate of national income. Economists and politicians irrespective of time and space as well as ideology held the quest for growth (of GSDP) in highest esteem and priority. Governments can rise or fall if their economic growth performance ranks high or low on the global score-card (Todaro, 2000). However, growth seems to be growth *per se* if it does not lead to visible positive transformation in the lives of people. Globally, growth has served mainly to benefit the few- the richest 20 per cent of the population (Thirlwal, 1986).

How inequality is generated and how it reproduces over time has engaged a great deal of scholarship over last half a century. The patterns and determinants of changes in inequality are subject of perennial interest to economists and policy makers alike (Prasad,2002).As argued by Atkinson (1973), that 'Inequality is what economics should be all about'. By almost every standard and measure global inequality has grown substantially over last three decades. Concurrently national inequality has grown in most countries over the same time period.There is a case today for more outspokenness about the ills and causes of inequality (Jolly,2006). Otherwise there will come a time when looking back at today's world human beings will wonder about how primitive we were that we tolerated all this (Basu, 2005).It is often argued that the mechanisms, which promote economic growth, also promote economic concentration and a worsening of the relative and perhaps the absolute position of the lower income groups (Tendulkar, *et al,* 1995).

Kumar, B. (1984) finds that in 1965-66, 60 percent of India's population was receiving income below Rs. 27 per month while as 110 million people receive income less than Rs. 13 per month (in 1965-66). An increasing trend in inequality between the different strata of population over the period is reported. In 1972-73, number of people receiving income less than the subsistence level at Rs. 40 per capita per month has increased to 80 percent.Ezekiel, H. (1984) estimates from India show that the consumption expenditure of the bottom decile has increased during the period 1979-80 to 1984-85. The increase has been reported to be from Rs 34.12 to Rs 61.17 per month at 1979-80 prices. The study shows prevalence of inequality in the bottom decile of population across the rural and urban sectors but is reported to be statistically insignificant.Ali, N. (1985) using tax data for individuals and Hindu undivided families (HUF) calculated Gini co-efficient, Pareto income distribution and Kuznets' index. This study reported that inequality has decreased in India from 1953-54 to 1975-76. Gini co-efficient decreased from 0.4085 to 0.3040 between 1953-54and 197576, on the other hand Pareto coefficient (á) increased from 1.7239 to 2.1450. In another study, Ali Nasir (1985) while analysing agricultural development and income distribution in J&K found that for farm land the Lorenz curve has been far away from the line of equal distribution. Inequality, however,is found greater among apple cultivating households. His study reveals that bottom 20 percent of paddy farms share 4.83 percent of the total income and the bottom 20 percent of apple farms share only 3.41 percent of the total income; the top 20 percent of paddy growing households share 48.50 percent of the total income and the top 20 percent of apple farms share 56.7 percent of the total income. This indicates greater income concentration among the apple calculating households. The share of the top 10 percent has been calculated to be 40 percent of the total income (apple farms), while the same has been about 32 percent in case of the paddy cultivating households. The Gini's concentration coefficient worked out to be 0.6566 for apple farms and 0.4100 for the paddy farms.

Misri and Bhat (1994) while using NSS consumption expenditure data for J &K concluded that monthly per capita total consumption expenditure, both nominal and real, has displayed an increasing trend across the fractile classes during different NSS rounds. But the improvement is not much appreciable. The increase is sharper at current prices compared to constant prices. This is in line with the impact of price inflation on the purchasing power of money incomes (Friedman). They further found out that all the indices of inequality turned out to be very low and exhibited a fair degree of stability across different NSS rounds. Basole, A. and Basu, D. (2015) have used NSSO data of different consumption expenditure rounds to calculate consumption inequality in 2004-05 and 2011-12. The study reports an increase in consumption inequality mainly because the share of non-food spending has increased in the household budget. The relative Gini-coefficient of food and non-food spending, has not increased much but since non-food spending by its very nature, is likely to be more unequal at any point in time overall inequality increases. It was also found that the absolute and intermediate Gini-coefficient of non-food expenditure has increased several folds between 1987-88 to 2011-12.

The review of above studies enriched the background knowledge of concepts and methodology to be used in the present study. Various conceptual and methodological issues have been discussed by different researchers by using various sources of data like NCEAR, RBI, NSSO, CSO, etc. The main tools and techniques to study the growth and inequalities have been Lorenz Curve, Gini Coefficient, Range, Standard Deviation, and Size Distribution. The latest consumption expenditure round of NSSO data has not been used by any study so far as North-Western states of India are concerned.Maximum studies on the problems under reference have used only the conventional 'Gini Coefficient' for estimating the inequality. But 'Gini Coefficient' has its own limitations. It is against this backdrop that an attempt has been made in study to calculate consumption inequality. Thepresent study along with 'Gini Coefficient' has made use of other measures of inequality belonging to Generalized entropy class and normative measure of inequality (Atkinson Index) to make a comparative analysis of income (consumption) inequality among the three sample states.

Data and Methodology

The comparison in the average living standards between countries, between regions, and between social or occupational groups should ideally be analysed with the help of size distribution of income. Since the data on size distribution of income for the selected states are not available we are constrained to press into service consumption data as a proxy for income data. Even at national level, the data on distribution of income is not available. The major studies on distribution of income and living standard have used consumption data collected by National Sample Survey Organisation (NSSO).However, study conducted by

NCAER (NCAER, 1962, 1964, 1966), have used individual income data for nationwide representative sampled population. These surveys were then discontinued and as such income related data ceases to be available thereafter.

Could consumption expenditure be used as a surrogate for income distribution? The answer is yes and no. The use of consumption expenditure data as a proxy for income is justified on the ground that the two are significantly correlated in developing countries like India. Consumption is considered as a better proxy for permanent income distribution than income (Bardhan, 1974). As against this, some economists argue that the income groups and shape of their consumption function will determines the use of consumption as a proxy for income. It is just possible that a decrease in consumption inequality may accompany an increase in income inequality. (Dev. *et.al.* 1992).

Be that as it may, the present study, in the absence of any alternative has used consumption as a surrogate for income. As such levels of living are defined in terms of monthly per capita expenditure (MPCE). The NSS concept of MPCE, is defined first at the household level (household monthly consumer expenditure ÷ household size). This measure serves as the indicator of the household's level of living.Next, each individual's MPCE is defined as the MPCE of the household to which the person (man, woman or child) belongs. This assigns to each person a number representing his or her level of living. The distribution of persons by their MPCE (i.e., their household MPCE) can then be built up, giving a picture of the population classified by economic level.

Schedule Type 1 of NSSO employ Uniform Reference Period (URP) and Mixed Reference Period (MRP) for capturing MPCE while schedule Type II uses the Modified Mixed Reference Period (MMRP).The present study uses MPCE (MRP from type I schedule and MMRP from type II schedule) to capture increased inequality in the income across states. Rationale for using these measures emanates from the fact that MMRP captures consumption baskets on the all the three measures of recall period. The MRP capture consumption basket upon which expenditure is reported for 30 days and 365 days only. It is as such logical to evaluate income inequality on both these measures so as to draw a clear picture with respect to consumption patterns both in the short as well as the long run.URP capture consumption expenditure in a segregated manner only for 30 days and 365 days. This measures as such lead huge scope for misrepresentation of income inequalities for, it neglects the immediate consumptions expenditures of the household made on daily basis. The variations/differentials across the selected states are evaluated as such celebrated measures of inequality as the a. Gini coefficient; b. Generalised Entropy measure; and c. Atkinson's Inequality Measure. In next section, we broadly review the conceptual framework of these indices.

Monthly Per Capita Expenditure (MPCE) gives summary measure of the central tendency of the size distribution of consumption expenditure. Gini Coefficient, Theil's Index (00) and Atkinson's Inequality Index used in the present study to capture the extent of relative inequality in MPCE are based on three different models. These indices have been widely used due to their unique properties (Coulterr, 1998).

1. Gini Coefficient

Formally

$$GC = \frac{1}{2\,n^2\,\overline{y}} \sum_{i=1}^{n} \sum_{j=1}^{n} |y_i - y_j|$$

Where GC = GiniCoefficient; n is different pairs of income; $\overline{y}$ is the mean income. $|y_i - y_j|$ is the absolute difference between incomes of individuals i and j. The Gini coefficient considers differences over all pairs of incomes and one-half of the mean of absolute values of differences between all income pairs.

Gini Coefficient is defined as a ratio with values between 0 and 1. A low Gini coefficient indicates more equal income or wealth distribution, while a higher coefficient indicates more unequal distribution. Zero corresponds to perfect equality (everyone having exactly the same income) and 1 corresponds to perfect inequality (where one person has all the income, while everyone else has zero income). The Gini coefficient requires that no one has a negative net income or wealth.

2. Theil Index

Theil Index belongs to such measures I(y) that satisfies all axioms inequality, is a member of the '*Generalized Entropy (GE) class of inequality measures*'. Within the family of GE indices, we use: the mean log deviation GE_0 and the Theil Index GE_1.

GE_0 (Theil's L) is given by

$$GE_0 = \frac{1}{N}\sum_{i=1}^{N} ln\left(\frac{\bar{y}}{y_i}\right)$$

GE_1 (Theil's T index), which may be written as:

$$GE_1 = \frac{1}{N}\sum_{i=1}^{N} \frac{y_i}{\bar{y}} ln\left(\frac{y_i}{\bar{y}}\right)$$

where N is the number of individuals,

yi is the income of individual i, i =1,2,...,n,

and(1/n) Óy$_i$, the arithmetic mean income.

For resource distributions described by only two quintiles, the Theil index is 0 for 50:50 distributions and reaches 1 at 82:18, which is very close to a distribution often referred to as "Pareto Principle". Higher inequities yield Theil indices above 1. The Theil index:

- is 0 for an inequality represented by a 50:50 distribution (the distribution is completely equal),
- is 0.5 for an inequality represented by a 74:26 distribution,
- is 1 for an inequality represented by a 82:18 distribution (which is slightly above the equivalent to the frequently cited 80:20 distribution),
- is 2 for an inequality represented by a 92:8 distribution and
- is 4 for an inequality represented by a 98:2 distributions.

---

1. $_{\varepsilon}$is an inequality aversion parameter ($0<\varepsilon<\infty$). It measures a societal concern about inequality and put a normative measure on it.

3. Atkinson's Inequality Measures

Atkinson (1970) proposed another class of inequality measures. Novelty of this class of measures lies in its introduction of the weighting parameter ε (which measures aversion to inequality)[1].

Where y_i is the average consumption expenditure in i^{th} size class.

$\bar{y}$ is the overall mean consumption expenditure; N is the number of individuals.

The Atkinson coefficient lies between 1 and 0. When $A_\varepsilon = 0$ there is perfect equality and when A_ε attains a value of one perfect inequality exists in a given society. The more unequal is the income distribution, the more adverse society is to inequality. Greater will be the value of the index.

Results and Discussion

In a variety of ways economic inequalities generate significant economic costs for a society, which could be curtailed – if not eliminated – by a more equal distribution of economic resources. Greater economic equality can promote greater economic efficiency by contributing to the achievement of the following goals: (i) To improve the allocation and development of human resources, (ii) to reduce social tensions and political instability etc., (iii) to reduce popular opposition to needed economic reforms and (4) To foster cooperation as a basis for low-cost solutions to "coordination failures".The results obtained from the empirical analysis of measurement of income inequality in the sample North-Western states of India are presented in following tables.

Table 1:Income Inequality in North-Western States

S. No	*State/region*	*GE(0)*	*GE(1)*	*Gini*	*A(0.5)*	*A(1)*	*A(2)*
1.	Jammu & Kashmir	0.14	0.16	0.29	0.07	0.13	0.22
2.	Himachal Pradesh	0.19	0.22	0.34	0.09	0.17	0.28
3.	Punjab	0.17	0.20	0.32	0.08	0.15	0.25

Source: Author's Calculation based on Micro-Level Unit Data NSSO (68th Consumption Expenditure Round)

Among the North-Western states, Himachal Pradesh exhibits higher income inequality followed by Punjab and J&K. The results hold true for all the indices used in this study.

An attempt has been made to account for the income inequalities among the sample states by using Consumption Expenditure Data Type II. This measure is expected to provide a broad-based understanding of the underlying inequalities across all measures of consumption expenditure. Schedule II, it is reiterated, captures consumption expenditure on MMRP status. However, the results of this analysis as is reported in Table 2 do not seem to be any different from the results reported in table 1.

Table 2: Income Inequality in North-Western States

S. No.	*State/Region*	*GE(0)*	*GE(1)*	*Gini*	*A(0.5)*	*A(1)*	*A(2)*
1.	Jammu & Kashmir	0.13	0.15	0.28	0.07	0.12	0.21
2.	Himachal Pradesh	0.18	0.20	0.33	0.09	0.16	0.27
3.	Punjab	0.16	0.19	0.32	0.08	0.15	0.25

Source: Author's Calculation based on Micro-Level Unit Data NSSO (68th Consumption Expenditure Round)

In light of the results drawn above, and also w.r.t to the indices used as well as the type of recall period employed, the relative position of each North-Western states of India does not exhibit any change. Thus, it is inferred that the relative position of the concerned states is neutral to approach as well as measurement.

Empirical evidence by means of this paper indicates that income inequality among the North-Western states is the highest in case of Himachal Pradesh and lowest in J&K. The state of Punjab falls in the middle of the two states. Explanation for such a relative positioning of the North-Western states on inequality indices, estimates from a variety of social-cultural, economic and political features that uniquely identifies with each of them. For instance, the state of J&K has the distinction of being one of the earliest in the sub-continent to initiate redistribution in land to the tiller, as early as 1931 (Malviya, 1955). This was accompanied by one of the earliest liquidations of rural debt that the state witness in early 1950s(AfazlMirza, 1976).These simple redistribution and affirmative action measures were responsible for eradicating huge asset and income inequality among the population.Nothing of such sort is reported in case of Himachal Pradesh and Punjab in around the same period of time.On contrary Punjab, has seen an appropriation of land in the immediate aftermath of partition. Green revolution and mechanization of agriculture that followed it, has bread huge income inequality within Punjab. The state of Punjab apart from exhibiting huge asset inequalities partly due to limited penetration of green revolution technologies which were readily adopted by big land lords has an overwhelming share of disadvantaged and deprived populations' viz. the SCs. As a proportion of its own population SCs account about 88.6 lakh, which comprises of 31.9 percent of the total population of state (Census, 2011).As reported by SukhadeoThorat (2010) as also various other studies relative deprivation of SCs and STs across India is well established phenomena? Their larger share in Punjab's population accentuates the inequality paradigm within this state. The same gets re-imposed more strikingly in inter-state comparisons. Similarly, the state of Himachal Pradesh has a 25.2% population SCs which is a valid reason of higher income inequality along with the geographical location.

Conclusion

The income inequality has been estimated by using NSS unit level consumption expenditure data sets of type 1 and type 2. While estimating income inequality across the North-Western States it has been found that all measures calculated shows highest values income inequality for Himachal Pradesh and followed by J&K and Punjab. This implies there is more unequal distribution of income in Himachal Pradesh followed by Punjab. As these states has a significant number of scheduled castes populations and in J&K the level of inequality is lowest. In case of SCs the problems are of low growth MPCE and high intensity of poverty and had experienced lowest decline in poverty. The simple story of India is that the rich is getting richer, the richest of the rich are getting still richer, the poor are becoming poorer and more numerous, and the middle class is hollowed out.

References

1. Ali, N. (1985): *Changing Pattern of Size Distribution of income in India,* Paper presented in Gokhale Institute Pune in staff Seminar March 1985.
2. Atkinson, A. B. (1970): *On the measurement of inequality,* Journal of Economic Theory, Vol. 2, P. 244-263.
3. Atkinson, A.B. (1973): *Wealth, Income and Inequality,* Penguin Education: Australia.
4. Bardhan, P.K. (1974): "The Pattern of Income Distribution in India: An overview", in Srinivasan, T.N and Bardhan, P.K., Poverty and Income Distribution in India, Statistical Society, Calcutta.
5. Basu, K. (2005): *Globalization, Poverty and Inequality: What is the Relationship? What can be done?* Research paper No. 2005/32, *World Institute for Development Economic Research,* United Nations University, Helsinki.
6. Bhattacharya, N. (1992): "Some Observation on the Database for Poverty Studies" in Poverty in India - Database Issues, Kedekodi, G.K. and G.V.S.N. Murthy(eds), Vikas Publishing House, New Delhi.
7. Dev, M.K. *et al* (1991): "Rural Poverty in India: Incidence, Issues and Policies", Discussion Paper No. 55, Indra Gandhi Institute for Development Research. Bombay.
8. Ezekiel, H. (1984): *The Economic Times Statistical Survey of Indian Economy,* Vikas Publishing House Pvt. Ltd. New Delhi.
9. Gupta, S.K. and Ramaratnam, D.S., (1975): "Consumption Expenditure Surveys and Family Budget Enquires", in Database of Indian Economy: The Role of Sample Survey, Vol. II, Dandekar V.M. and Venkataramia (Eds).
10. Jolly, R. (2006): *Inequality in Historical Perspective,* Research Paper No. 2006/32, *World Institute for Development Economic Research,* United Nations University, Helsinki.
11. Kumar, B. (1984): *Planning, Poverty and Economic Development,* Deep and Deep Publications New Delhi.
12. Mahalanobis, P.C. and Sen, S.B. (1954): "Some Aspects of Indian National Sample Surveys", Bulletin of international Statistical Institute, 394, pp. 53-54.
13. Minhas, *et al.* (1974): "Rural Poverty, Land Distribution and Development Strategy", reprinted in Poverty and Income Distribution in India, T.N. Srinavasan and P.K. Bardhan (eds), Calcutta Statistical Publishing Society.
14. Misri M. L. and Bhat M. S. (1994): *Poverty, Planning and Economic Change in Jammu &Kashmir,* Vikas Publishing House Pvt. Ltd.
15. Mukerjee, M. and Chatterjee, (1974): "On The Validity of NSS Estimates of Consumption Expenditure", in Poverty and Income Distribution in India,

T.N. Srinavasan and P.K. Bardhan (eds), Calcutta Statistical Publishing Society.

16. Prasad, E.S. (2002): *Wage Inequality in the United Kingdom,* 1975-1999, *IMF Staff Papers,* Vol. 49, No. 3, pp. 339-363.
17. Radhakrishnan P.N. *et. al.*, (1974): "Data on Distribution of Consumption Expenditure: An Evaluation", Sankhya, Series C, Vol. 36, parts 2-4.
18. Rudra, A. (1974): "Minimum Level of Living -A Statistical Examination", in Poverty and Income Distribution in India, T.N. Srinavasan and P.K. Bardhan (eds), Calcutta Statistical Publishing Society.
19. Sundram, R.M. (1987): "Growth and Income Distribution in India -Policy and Performance Since Independence", Sage Publications.
20. Tendulkar, B.D. and L.R. Jain (1995): *Economic Growth, Relative Inequality, and Equity: The Case of India, Asian Development Review,* Vol. 13, No. 2, P. 138-168.
21. Thirlwal, A.P. (1986): *Growth and Development,* London: Macmillan Education ltd.
22. Throat Sukhadeo (2010: "Growth, Inequality and Poverty during 1983/ 2005 – Implications for Inclusive Policy" , presidential address at 93rd Annual Conference of The Indian Economic Association, organised by University of Chandigrah, December 27-29, 2010.
23. Todaro, M.P. (2000): *Economic Development,* 7th Edition, Longman: Pearson Education Ltd.
24. Vaidyanathan, A. (1986): "On the Validity of NSS Consumption Data", Economic and Political Weekly, Vol. XXI, No. 6.

Chapter - 6

Inequality of opportunity in employment in North Indian States

— *Javaid Iqbal Khan*

Abstract

Issues related to employment of an individual are multi-dimensional. Many of them are externalities. Inability of an individual cannot always be the only reason for sub-optimal employment outcomes. Circumstances and the socio-cultural aspects of an individual are as important as human capital in determining the labor market outcomes especially employment. It is in this direction that the present paper investigates employment scenarios in North Indian states within the frame work of coverage of employment opportunities and access to available employment avenues. The main argument put forth in the present paper is that "availability of employment opportunities at a given point of time are a strong determinant of workforce participation". To determine laws/policies with regard to distribution of these opportunities across different sections of the society is one of the fundamental equity related issues in the present day Indian economy. Detailed analysis based on unit level data of NSSO for 2004-05 and 2011-12 for the selected states in the present paper suggests that within the North Indian States variation in coverage and opportunity of access to available employment avenues is significant. The state of Jammu and Kashmir has recorded an increase in the coverage rate as well as the opportunity index and a decline in the D-Index. This phenomena is not exhibited by any other North Indian State. Similarly, Himachal Pradesh continues to rank higher in both coverage and opportunity and lowest on D-Index. Haryana has slipped to the fourth spot in coverage as well as the opportunity index and tops the dissimilarity index in 2011-12. Punjab position on the opportunity index has more or less remained the same during the reference period.

Introduction

Employment of resources is the most important plank of economic development. It assumes significance of proportions in case of employment of human resource. There are various approaches addressing the reasons for employability of an individual. These include the quantum of human capital acquired by an individual during the course of his lifetime as well as the macro economic situation at a point of time among others. However, scant attention has been paid towards availability of employment opportunities to individuals. Coverage of employment and access to the prevalent opportunities in the labor market remains largely unattended.

The concept of opportunity and access to a particular good or service is the corner stone of egalitarianism in the Rawlsian scheme of things (see Rawls, 1971). The philosophical tradition of equal opportunities (E.oP) is rich, diverse and long. (see; Sen 1980: Dworkin 1981 Robert Nozick 1974 and Roemer 1993, 1998). However, the present study is an informed extension of the same ideology with an attempt to evaluate the extent of opportunities in and access to employment across the North Indian States. This political-philosophy lineage as, such determines the motivation as well as explains the scope of this study.

It is against this backdrop that an attempt has been made to look into the prevalence of opportunities of employment across the North Indian States and find out changes if any, between the last two quinquennial rounds of the NSSO (NSSO, 2004-05 and NSSO 2011-12). The main objective of the present paper is to look into the inter-state disparities in opportunity of employment across the North Indian States of Jammu and Kashmir, Himachal Pradesh, Haryana and Punjab. Population has been disaggregated into different age groups to bring forth the disparities in access to employment at different life stages across all the states. This is important in light of the various dynamics associated with age and its relationship to labor market participation. The World Bank proposed Human Opportunity Index, (HOI, 2009) is invoked to achieve this objective. More specifically the present paper pursues the following objectives:

1. To calculate the Human Opportunity Index (HOI) for the selected North Indian States for 2004-05 and 2011 -2012;
2. to account for the availability of employment opportunities across the selected states for the age groups of 25- 39 40 – 64 and 40 – 64 years;
3. to rank the selected states in accordance with their respective HOI; and
4. to understand the changes in the respective positioning of the selected states on the calculated Index.

Human Opportunity Index HOI framework, (Barros et al., 2008, 2009) as modified by Ana Abros, et.al, (2013) is used in the present study. HOI brings together the total number of employment opportunities available to the population and the fairness in distribution of these opportunities across the sub sections of the society. HOI *(H)* for a particular opportunity is the average coverage rate[1] of access $(\bar{c})$ multiplied by a factor [2] *(1-D)*.

$$H = \bar{c}\ (1 - D) \tag{1}$$

D is the dissimilarity index[3] (henceforth, D-index). With disjoint types[4], one can compute *D* as follows:

$$D = \frac{1}{2\bar{C}} \sum_{k=1}^{m} a_k \ |\bar{C} - C_k \tag{2}$$

Here *k* denotes a type (group of individuals with a specific set of circumstances); C_k the specific coverage rate of group *k*; a_k the share of group *k* in total population; and *m* the numbers of disjoint groups defined by circumstances. *D* equates to zero when C = $\bar{C}$ for all *k* types, in which case HOI equals the coverage rate. It can be shown that *D* is equal to the *share* of total opportunities that are — misallocated in favor of (against) types that have coverage rates higher (lower) than $\bar{C}$.

This also implies that any reallocation of opportunities to — vulnerable groups (those with coverage less than $\bar{C}$) from — non-vulnerable groups (with coverage more than $\bar{C}$) will reduce D and increase HOI. Thus, HOI improves when inequality between types decreases with a fixed number of opportunities in a society, or when the number of opportunities increases and inequality among types stays constant.

In the labor market participants are characterized by both circumstances as well as characteristics. As such inequality of opportunity between groups is to be measured. For the same, we estimate the dissimilarity index (D - Index), by running a logistic regression model to estimate the relationship between circumstances as well as characteristics of the participants in the labor market. Inequality of opportunity is estimated by decomposing the contribution of the circumstance effect to the D – Index. Decomposition proposed by Shorrocks (2012) as adopted by World Bank (2009, 2013) has also been adopted for the present study.

Data and its analysis

The present study uses the 61st (2004-05) and 68th (2011-12) quinquennial rounds[5] of the Employment/Unemployment survey data sets of NSSO, India. Access to employment on the '*Usual principal activity status*' is the outcome variable. It captures the employment status of a person in the year preceding to survey, and hence is the most comprehensive of all the available measures. Religion, Social status, Location, Gender of the ith individual and Education of House hold head are all established and agreed upon circumstances, affecting the ability of a person to enrich his/her capabilities and realize from and contribute to human capital. Among the characteristics, education and age are again well established in the literature on human capital. An attempt has been made to calculate the Human Opportunity Index (HOI) for the national level as well as for the selected states after controlling for the socio-religious category status of the population, age and education.

Table 1. Model for estimation of Human Opportunity for the Indian Labor market

Opportunity: Access to employment (UPSS)			
Nature of Variable	***Broad Category***		***Operational Explanation***
Independent	Circumstance Variable	Location	Rural/urban
		Sex	Male/Female
		Socio-religious Status	SC/ST
			Hindu - OBC
			Muslim -OBC
			Muslim General
			Other Minorities
		Economic status of household	Ownership of Land
		Education of Household head	Primary Education
			Secondary Education
			Higher secondary/Diploma
			Graduate & above
	Characteristic variable	Age in years (15-64)	Group I (15-24 years),
			Group II (25-39 years) and
			Group III, (40-64 years)
		Education	Primary Education
			Secondary Education
			Higher secondary/Diploma
			Graduate & above

Source: Own Calculations based on NSSO 61st and 68th quinquennial rounds.

In India, employment opportunities are being outpaced by the growing labour force since mid-1980's. During the reference period of the present study, 2004-05 to 2011-12 major changes have taken place in the Indian labor market. Overall employment in the country rose markedly by 59.4 million between 1999-2000 and 2004-05. But during the next five years, 2004-05 to 2009-10, net employment generated fell severely to only 4.7 million (Mehrotra et al 2013). Employment growth recovered subsequently, with 10 million new jobs registered between 2009-10 and 2011-12. Net increase to jobs created over 2004-05 & 2011-12 was as such 14.7 million as against 59.4 million between 1999-2000 & 2004-05. These developments are reflected by a decline in coverage rate (5.59) as well as in the opportunity Index (6.70) at the national level (see table 2). This has been corresponded by an increase in the dissimilarity index by a magnitude of 3.79. State level analysis (for the North-Western States) of the above variables reveal that except for the state of Jammu and Kashmir there has been a conformity with respect to the national level behavior of coverage rate, both in case of the dissimilarity index as well as the opportunity index. The state of

Jammu and Kashmir has recorded an increase in the coverage rate as well as the opportunity index and a decline in the D-Index. This phenomenon has not been exhibited by any other North Indian state. It has as such changed its place from being ranked at 4 to 2nd within the group of 04 states located in the northern part of the country. Its rank in the dissimilarity index has appreciated from being at rank 1st in 2004-05 to be at 3rd spot in 2011-12. Himachal Pradesh though, continues to rank higher in both coverage and opportunity and the least on D-Index. Haryana has slipped to the fourth spot in coverage as well as the opportunity index and tops the dissimilarity index in 2011-12. Earlier in 2004-05 it ranked 2nd in coverage as well as opportunity and 3rd on the D-index. Punjab has continued to be at the 3rd spot in terms of coverage, both in case of D-index as well as opportunity index. Thus, in the relative sense Jammu and Kashmir and Haryana have shown some dynamism on the identified variables. Jammu and Kashmir has shown positive changes on all the indices, while as Haryana has exhibited negative changes. Himachal Pradesh and Punjab have maintained their relative rankings.

Table 2: Variation in Opportunity of Employment (2004-12 to 2011-12)

State \ *All India*	*Variable*	*Year*		*Ranking*		*Change over time*	
		2004-05	*2011 - 12*	*2004-05*	*2011 - 12*		
All India	*Variable*	*Values*	*Values*	*Not Applicable*			
	Coverage (C)	62.2046	56.6127			Negative	*In the variable*
	Dissemilarity (D)	18.4382	22.2298			Negative	
	(HOI)	**50.7352**	**44.0278**			Negative	
Jammu and Kashmir	Coverage (C)	57.0088	61.7942	4	2	Positive	In the relative position of the state w.r.t the variable sunder study
	Dissemilarity (D)	*21.1236*	*16.2386*	*1*	*3*	Positive	
	(HOI)	**44.9665**	**51.7597**	**4**	**2**	**Positive**	
Himachal Pradesh	Coverage (C)	76.0757	71.6460	1	1	Constant	
	Dissemilarity (D)	*9.4951*	*13.5420*	*4*	*4*	Constant	
	HOI	**68.8522**	**61.9437**	**1**	**1**	**Constant**	
Punjab	Coverage (C)	61.8727	54.7701	3	3	Constant	
	Dissemilarity (D)	*19.1204*	*23.9027*	*2*	*2*	Constant	
	(HOI)	**50.0424**	**41.6786**	**3**	3	Constant	
Haryana	Coverage (C)	62.3705	49.1341	2	4	Negative	
	Dissemilarity (D)	16.8871	*28.3193*	*3*	*1*	Negative	
	(HOI)	**51.8380**	**35.2197**	**2**	4	Negative	

Source: Own Calculations based on NSSO 61st and 68th quinquennial rounds.

Disaggregating the opportunity index for employment across age groups reveals certain interesting features. For the prime age group of 25-39 years there has been a decline in employment opportunities at the national level, at least over the reference period (Table 3). This has been compounded by higher retraction rates in the agricultural sector, coupled with a decline in employment elasticity in all major industries as well as the public sector. However, across the states, Jammu and Kashmir has shown a marginal decline in the coverage rate and has exhibited a stagnant opportunity index for the 25-39 years' age group. There has been 2 points decline in the D-index over the reference period in case of Jammu and Kashmir. With these developments and consequent upon higher declines in coverage rate and opportunity index in the states of Haryana and Punjab, Jammu and Kashmir has moved to second slot in 2011-12 from the fourth in 2004-05. Himachal Pradesh continues to top the North Indian States in coverage as well as the opportunity of employment. It exhibits the least D-index as such is close to the egalitarian perspective of distribution of available employment opportunities.

Table 3: Variation in Opportunity of Employment for age group of 25 – 39 years (2004-12 to

All India / ***State***	***Variable***	***Year***		***Ranking***		***Change over time***	
		2004-05	***2011 - 12***	***2004-05***	***2011 - 12***		
	Variable	*Values*	*Values*				
All India	Coverage (C)	72.9868	65.7732	*Not Applicable*		Negative	*In the variable*
	Dissemilarity (D)	16.1515	22.5929			Negative	
	(HOI)	**61.1983**	**50.9131**			Negative	
Jammu and Kashmir	Coverage (C)	66.5279	65.5983	4	2	Positive	In the relative position of the state w.r.t the variables under study
	Dissemilarity (D)	21.7452	19.8974	1	3	Positive	
	(HOI)	**52.0612**	**52.5459**	**4**	**2**	**Positive**	
Himachal Pradesh	Coverage (C)	87.9444	87.5504	1	1	Constant	
	Dissemilarity (D)	5.0386	4.9505	4	4	Constant	
	HOI	**83.5132**	**83.2162**	**1**	**1**	**Constant**	
Punjab	Coverage (C)	71.7115	65.4462	3	3	Constant	
	Dissemilarity (D)	17.1973	24.1732	2	2	Constant	
	(HOI)	**59.3791**	**49.6257**	**3**	**3**	**Constant**	
Haryana	Coverage (C)	74.0346	59.9709	2	4	Negative	
	Dissemilarity (D)	16.2978	28.9425	3	1	Negative	
	(HOI)	**61.9686**	**42.6138**	**2**	**4**	**Negative**	

Source: Own calculations based on unit level data of NSSO 61st and 68th quinquennial rounds.

Punjab has not changed places on any of the variables over the reference period and continues to occupy the 3rd rank on both coverage as well as opportunity. It ranks 3rd on the D-index. Haryana is ranked lowest on all the parameters. Thus, in the crucial age group of 25-39 years coverage of employment opportunities and access to them is the least for Haryana and Jammu Kashmir in 2011-12 and 2004-05 respectively. Thus, Jammu and Kashmir, compered to other northern states has done well at least in extending coverage of employment and access to them across the populace over the reference period.

Analyzing the same variables for the age group of 40 – 64 years in table 4 some interesting trends and patterns are found. There is a general decline in coverage rate as well as opportunity Index for this age group both at the national level as well as across the selected states. This is understandable, given the changes that have occurred in the Indian labour market over the reference period. Given the socio-economic context of India, the reference age group is the most active participant in the labor market among all age groups. By the age of 40 years each and every able – bodied individual is supposed to be out there offering his labor. Hence coverage rates have got to be higher. However, over the reference period this has not happened. More disheartening is the fact that the access to available opportunities have witnessed a continuous fall throughout the reference period. The dissimilarity which captures the inequity in access to available opportunity has also risen over the period of time. Inter-state comparisons reveal a great deal of variation in magnitude of the changes in all the variables over the reference period. Himachal Pradesh continues to be best placed in terms of coverage, access as well as in dissimilarity. The net decline in coverage and access has been minimal. Punjab and Haryana on the contrary have shown appreciable declines in both coverage as well as the human opportunity index in employment. Jammu and Kashmir has exhibited lower declines in all ratios. However, the D-index has increased for all states. Increase in D-index for Himachal is negligible. Thus, on a general basis, Himachal Pradesh has retained the top slot in the present age group w.r.t coverage and the opportunity index. It has also continued to exhibit the lowest D-index. Jammu and Kashmir has retained the 2nd slot in terms of coverage and HOI. It occupies the 3rd slot on D-index. Punjab continues to occupy the 3rd rank on coverage. However, it has moved to the 3rd slot in terms of HOI in 2011-12, which is an improvement over 2004-05 were in it ranked 4th. Haryana continues to occupy the 4th position on coverage and has slipped to the 4th slot from the 3rd in 2004-05 making way for Punjab, in 2011-12.

D-index has been reported the highest in case of Haryana followed by Punjab, Jammu and Kashmir and Himachal Pradesh.

Table 4: Variation in Opportunity of Employment for age group of 40 – 64 years (2004-05 to 2011-12)

All India *State*	*Variable*	*Year*		*Ranking*		*Change over time*	
		2004-05	*2011 - 12*	*2004-05*	*2011 - 12*		
	Variable	*Values*	*Values*				
All India	Coverage (C)	71.2173	66.2741	*Not Applicable*		*Negative*	*In the variable*
	Dissemilarity (D)	16.0110	21.2645			*Negative*	
	(HOI)	**59.8147**	**52.1812**			*Negative*	
Jammu and Kashmir	Coverage (C)	78.2426	70.1138	2	2	Constant	In the relative position of the state w.r.t the variables under study
	Dissemilarity (D)	13.3762	20.1265	*3*	*3*	Constant	
	(HOI)	**67.7767**	**56.0024**	**2**	**2**	**Constant**	
Himachal Pradesh	Coverage (C)	86.9543	86.3962	1	1	Constant	
	Dissemilarity (D)	5.0944	5.2038	*4*	*4*	Constant	
	HOI	**82.5245**	**81.9003**	**1**	**1**	**Constant**	
Punjab	Coverage (C)	69.5510	61.8937	3	3	Constant	
	Dissemilarity (D)	17.5465	23.8992	*1*	*2*	Positive	
	(HOI)	**57.3473**	**47.1016**	**4**	**3**	**Positive**	
Haryana	Coverage (C)	69.3710	59.4731	4	4	Constant	
	Dissemilarity (D)	16.5248	27.3896	*2*	*1*	*Negative*	
	(HOI)	**57.9076**	**43.1837**	**3**	**4**	***Negative***	

Source: Own calculations based on unit level data of NSSO 61st and 68th quinquennial rounds.

Conclusion

This paper attempts to account for interstate differentials in employment in a scientific manner. Employment opportunities across states and access of individuals to them are explicated. The distributional aspects of coverage as well as access are delineated upon. Disaggregation of employment opportunities across three age groups on the identified parameters reveals interesting interstate differentials and dynamics over time. Across all age groups Himachal Pradesh is placed better among the sampled states for all parameters. There has occurred a change in relative positioning of the other three states between 2004-05 and 2011-12. The state of Jammu and Kashmir has appreciated its relative position while as the state of Haryana has slipped to the fourth spot. Punjab's relative position has more or less remained unchanged. Precisely put, Himachal Pradesh though, continues to rank higher in both coverage and opportunity has figured lowest in terms of D-Index. The state of Jammu and Kashmir has recorded an increase in the coverage rate as well as the opportunity index but has witnessed a decline in the D-Index.

References

1. Ana Abras, Alejandro Hoyos, Ambar Narayan and Sailesh Tiwari (2013) ,attempted to quantify inequality of opportunity in labor market outcomes in Europe and Central Asia using the Human Opportunity Index (HOI) methodology.
2. Dworkin, R.(1981a.), “What is equality? Part 1: Equality of welfare,” Philosophy & Public Affairs 10, 185-246.
3. Dworkin, R.(1981b), “What is equality? Part 2: Equality of resources,” Philosophy & Public Affairs 10, 283-345.
4. Nozick R, Anarchy, State and Utopia (1974) ,Basic Books, New York. p. 1974.
5. Rawls, J. (1971), Theory of justice, Harvard University Press.
6. Roemer, J. (1993),”A pragmatic theory of responsibility for the egalitarian planner,” Philosophy & Public Affairs 22, 146-166.
7. .... Roemer, J. 1998. Equality of opportunity, Harvard University Press’
8. Santosh Mehrotra, Sharmistha Sinha, Jajati K. Parida, Ankita Gandhi (2014); *Why a Jobs Turnaround Despite Slowing Growth?* Institute of Applied Manpower Research, Planning Commission, Government of India IAMR Occasional Paper No:1/2014.
9. Sen, A.(1980), “Equality of what?” in S. McMurrin (ed.), The Tanner Lectures on Human Values, Vol.1, Salt Lake City: University of Utah Press. Delivered at Stanford, May 22, 1979. Available at: http://www.ophi.org.uk/wp-content/uploads/Sen-1979_Equality-of-What.pdf

Notes

1. Refers to the total number of opportunities available to the members of a society for attaining a certain outcome.
2. *(1-D)* is the equality factor that is equal to one if access to the opportunity is independent of the circumstances, in which case HOI is equal to the average coverage rate. *D* can be interpreted as *the share of the total number of opportunities that needs to be reallocated between types to ensure equality of opportunities*, (Ana Abros, et.al, 2013)
3. measures the extent of equitable distribution of the opportunities across different groups in a given society.
4. Disjoint types refers to different groups within a society that are segregated on the basis of difference in circumstances, like religion, location, gender or social group.
5. The quinquennial survey on employment and unemployment is one of the most comprehensive surveys conducted regularly by the National Sample Survey Organization in India.

Chapter - 7

Health Micro Insurance and Healthcare Utilisation in North India

— ***Sheikh Aftaab-ul-Maroof and Mohi-ud-Din Sangmi***

Abstract

Health Micro insurance while being committed to provide financial protection to the poor against different perils and their adverse consequences is also contributing in improving healthcare utilization by the poor. Poor households with lower resource base are often not in a position to bear the rising health expenditure following a health shock. A health coverage program by reducing the financial barriers for access to healthcare, improves its utilization by the poor. The present study is an impact assessment of Rashtriya Swasthya Bima Yojana, a Government of India sponsored health coverage scheme. The study has been conducted in three north-Indian states Haryana, Punjab and Himachal Pradesh. The scheme has been assessed in terms of its impact on healthcare utilization by the poor. The study has also provided a comparative view of the results from the three states on different variables under study. Overall, the program has been successful in improving the healthcare utilization and reducing the delay in availing treatment. People have been found using better sources of treatment.

Key words: Micro insurance, Healthcare Utilization, Rashtriya Swasthya Bima Yojana and Fund mobilization,

Introduction

Microinsurance is the insurance for low income people, who

generally because of poverty, unawareness and lower affordability do not have an access to insurance facilities. Micro-insurance is envisioned to assist the poor people to cope up with shocks, such as health shocks, death, crop loss and natural hazards (Dercon, 2005; Dror and Jacquier, 1999; Barnet Barrett and Skees, 2008; Gine Townsend and Vickery, 2008). Risks which are uninsured have welfare implications which go beyond consequences for short term consumptions and is a cause of persistent poverty (Dercon, 2004; Townsend, 1994).

The word 'Micro' should be clearly understood first. 'Micro' in insurance industry shows the target towards low income segment of the market. In developing countries like India, microinsurance targets the people at below poverty line. In developed countries, microinsurance is for the people who are below the poverty line or marginally above it. In general, microinsurance, is for people ignored by mainstream commercial insurance schemes, persons who have not had access to appropriate products because of their lesser affordability.

As in case of conventional insurance, microinsurance also has two broad dimensions; one is Life and other General. Health falls within the general insurance side of microinsurance and has been considered as a critical and vital area. It provides relief to the poor by making them able to utilize healthcare facilities, which are otherwise unaffordable. In the same lines crop insurance is encouraging the marginal farmers for growing cash crops by reducing their threat related to natural hazards like adverse weather.

In terms of research, microinsurance is considered as an emerging field. Initially lots of studies were conducted on the concept and its main aspects. Demand and supply areas have been critically discussed. Microinsurance is expected to produce positive effects for the poor households which are generally deprived. For evaluating this commitment in terms of its achievement, lots of impact studies have been conducted.

Health risks being critical in terms of exposure, have been given due attention while developing products for the people under poverty. Universal health coverage programmes is a centrally sponsored mechanism of providing financial protection to the people in times of adverse health conditions. Poor people under a health program feel less constrained to access the healthcare due to their improving affordability which ultimately shows positive health outcomes (Giedion et al., 2013).

Under a health coverage program, people are expected to show improvement in the utilization of healthcare due to reduction in their affordability and access to healthcare constraints. Number of studies have used absolute measures of utilization like, *number of doctor visits / number of hospitalizations*. Another way of measuring utilization is to assess *need-based* healthcare utilization, which is a relative measurement and a better way of assessment.

Like other countries, India too has been committed to develop a protective mechanism for the poor, and to provide them a financial shield against adverse consequences of risk exposures. A Universal Health Coverage Program (Rashtriya Swasthya Bima Yojana) was started by the Government of India in 2008, to cover in-patient healthcare expenditures of below poverty line households. It aimed at reducing the financial constraints for and improving healthcare utilization by the poor. The objective of RSBY is to protect below poverty line (BPL) households from major health shocks that require hospitalization. This protection aims at making treatment more affordable so as to increase the amount of health care that a household can consume and also to limit the disastrous financial impact that households often experience due to out of pocket spending. RSBY is a classic demand side intervention using a sophisticated version of a voucher combined with targeting. Benefits covered under RSBY involve cost of hospitalization for 725+ procedures at empanelled hospitals up to 30,000 rupees per annum per household plus 100 rupees transport cost per visit up to 1000 rupees. In order to avail the benefits, a household must be on the official state BPL list. Benefit is limited to five members of the household including household head, spouse and three dependents. In order to get enrolled a household has to pay Rs 30 per annum as registration fee. The scheme is financed to the tune of 75% by Government of India and 25% by respective state governments. The present study is an attempt to assess the working of *Rashtriya Swasthya Bima Yojana,* in terms of improving healthcare utilization by the people under poverty The study also reveals results of inter-state analysis for the North Indian states of Punjab, H.P and Haryana.

Review of Literature

According to Radermacher et al. (2012), by increasing people's access to services, microinsurance is attempting to provide lot of benefits. People are able to quickly and cost effectively access the covered benefits. The reason being an improvement in affordability and sometimes other dimensions. It is possible to improve access (a common feature of majority of the schemes is some form of coverage for the direct costs of health care) (Maroof and Sangmi, 2016; Giedion, 2013). Increase in healthcare utilization rate is believed to increase better health outcomes. Micro health insurance encourages policy holders to use modern medical providers (Wagstaff and lindelow, 2008), which can further improve health outcomes by bypassing traditional healers. Micro Health Insurance can improve the quality of care as the insurance company can negotiate the terms with the health care provider in advance, place customer advocates in hospitals, build new facilities and employ skilled personnel for their clients' use. By improving low-income people's access to these services, MHI is also thought to increase equality both spatially and between economic and gender groups. Impact evaluation of MHI has of late emeged as growing field of study.Impact can be evaluated on such variables as utilization rate, quality of care, waiting time, health status, equity etc (Radermacher et al., 2012).

Micro health insurance by reducing the financial and other barriers to acess is encouraging the healthcare utilization (Giedion et al., 2007, Radermacher et al. 2012). Number of studies have been conducted which showed that MHI has been able to increase utilization of healthcare. Various studies have showed that women covered under MHI scheme are more likely to give birth in a health center under examination of qualified professionals (Sosa et al. 2009, Naguyen et al. 2012, Giedion et al. 2007, Harris and Rubi 2009).Naguyen et al. (2012) found that because of the voucher program, pregnant women were significantly more likely to seek care from qualified providers for Antenatal care, delivery and postnatal care. Wagstaff and Yu (2007) Yip et al. (2009) also found that RMHC scheme has increased the probability of an outpatient visit by 70 percent and reduced the probability of self medication by a similar percentage. Trujillo (2003) found a positive but small effect on the use of out-patient medical care and a positive impact on preventive care and hospital utilization. Giedion et al. (2007) revealed that the Colombian subsidized health insurance scheme has not only dramatically increased health insurance coverage among the poor, but also has improved access to and use of key health services.

The impact of MHI on utilization of healthcare has not been uniform for different socio-economic variables. Wagstaff et al. (2009) observed that poor have seen a large increase in out-patient care and the rich a large increase in the in-patient care. It is further found that NCMS has apparently large input among the poor in the use of out-patient care at village and township levels, and the smaller impact in the use of out-patient facilities at country hospital level. The impact of NCMS on the use of out-patient care has been found lower among the poor in terms of use of services at higher level facilities but higher in terms of lower level facilities. Partly because of this, the upward pressure on household out-of-pocket spending is much less pronounced among the poor.

Studies have found a mixed impact of MHI on utilization because of health condition of the people. As Trujillo (2003), observed that "less healthy individuals are less likely to participate in the Social Health Insurance with an Equalization Fund (SHIEF) and individuals with a chronic health conditions are more likely to be enrolled in the SHIEF." Delaying the health treatment is one of the major causes of severe health problems. Delaying the treatment can increase the severity of the problem. Kraft et al. (2009) have done a study to evaluate the impact of care delay, and the experimental impact of insurance on reducing delays. The Authors find a positive impact of the insurance in the Philippines, on the increase in the number of children whose hospital care is not delayed.

The studies like Wagstaff (2010), Thornton et al. (2010), King et al. (2009), Bauhoff et al. (2010), have found a negative impact of MHI on utilization. The reasons being OOP expenses not covered, short implementation time, the perceived quality of care, or access restriction imposed by insurance companies (Bauhoff et al. 2010, King et al. 2009).

Taking the above discussion into consideration, it is clear that in majority of the cases MHI has been successful in increasing the utilization of healthcare by improving affordability of the people under the program. Health care utilization being one of the important dimensions of impact has also been considered for analysis for the present study to find out whether MHI has increased health care utilization in the areas under study. If not, what might be the reasons for that?

Objectives

The study has been undertaken to achieve the following objectives:

1. To study the impact of health microinsurance on healthcare Utilization;
2. To study the spillover effect of health microinsurance on Out-patient healthcare Utilization;
3. To evaluate the delay in healthcare utilization by the households
4. To assess the source of healthcare availed by the people.
5. To make a comparatively analysis of the states under study on different considered variables.

Hypothesis

1. There is no significant difference between policy holders and non-policy holders in terms of in-patient healthcare utilization.
2. There is no significant difference between policy holders and non-policy holders in terms of delaying the in-patient treatment.
3. There is no significant difference between policy holders and non-policy holders in terms of out-patient healthcare utilization.
4. There is no significant difference between policy holders and non-policy holders in terms of delaying the out-patient treatment.

Data collection

The study is mainly based on primary data and the data collection was done by using a pre-tested and well structured interview schedule for beneficiaries of Rashtriya Swasthya Bima Yojana (RSBY). A total of 450 respondents from three North-Indian states (Himachal Pradesh, Punjab and Haryana) have been contacted during the survey. Out of them 150 were RSBY enrolled (treatment group) and 300 not-covered under RSBY households (control group). From each state, data has been collected from one district performing better in terms of enrolling poor under RSBY (See table 1.1) for the sample composition. The selection of sample is described below.

Sampling Design

The impact of microinsurance is assessed by a comparison of 'treatment' group, consisting of programme participants, to a 'control' group of non-participants. Participant group of respondents were selected after receiving list of insured households from the Ministry of Labor and Employment, Government of India. They included such households were in at least one hospitalization had occurred and where the household has received the treatment. Participant group of respondents were selected through a multi-stage sampling method. Each non participant household for comparison was selected from the same locality where a participant household was located after taking due care that all socio economic characteristics of participant and non-participant should be similar.

Table 1.1: Sample composition

Sl. No.	*State (District)*	*No. of Insured HH*	*No. of Uninsured HH*	*Total*
1	Himachal Pradesh (Kangra)	50	100	150
2	Punjab (Amritsar)	50	100	150
3	Haryana (Rohtak)	50	100	150
	Total Households			**450**

Results and Discussion

Health microinsurance by reducing financial hurdles to healthcare is expected to improve its utilization by the poor. People from poor households generally because of lower affordability are unable to avail quality healthcare, and end up with delaying the treatment and often avoid it. For assessing the utilization of in-patient treatment, *Number of hospitalizations per illness (when doctor has advised for hospitalization)* has been used for analysis. This is an established need based measure. Table 1.2 shows that households in the treatment group at average have made 95% need-based in-patient healthcare utilization, and the households within control group at average have made 71% in-patient healthcare utilization. For outpatient treatment the utilization rate is 91% for the treatment group and 89% for the control group (table 1.3).

Table 1.2: In-patient healthcare utilization

Status of Sampled Households	*No. of Hospitalizations per Illness Episode*		
	Mean	*Std. Dev.*	*Freq.*
Control	0.71	0.29	300
Treatment	0.95	0.15	150

Source: Field Survey by the Scholar.

Table 1.3: Out-patient healthcare utilization

Status of Sampled Households	*No. of Out-patient treatment visits per illness*		
	Mean	*Std. Dev.*	*Freq.*
Control	0.89	0.12	300
Treatment	0.91	0.11	150

Source: Field Survey.

Delay in treatment

A two-way approach has been used for assessing the *delay in treatment*. One is *number of times treatment delayed during a particular period* and other is *average number of days delayed for treatment in each case (Extent of Delay)*.

First approach for in-patient treatment shows that at an average 0.10 times treatment has been delayed by the households under intervention group and the households under control at average have made 0.79 times treatment delay (table 1.4).

Table 1.4 Number of times in-patient treatment delayed

Status of Sampled Households	*No. of times hospitalization delayed in last 12 months*		
	Mean	*Std. Dev.*	*Freq.*
Control	0.79	0.91	300
Treatment	0.10	0.30	150

Source: Field Survey.

For out-patient treatment this approach shows at average 1.23 times treatment delay by control group and 0.83 times by treatment group (table 1.5).

Table 1.5: Number of times out-patient treatment delayed

Status of Sampled Households	*No. of times treatment delayed in last 3 months*		
	Mean	*Std. Dev.*	*Freq.*
Control	1.23	1.08	300
Treatment	0.83	0.90	150

Source: Field Survey.

The second approach has been able to highlight an important aspect of delay, i.e. *average no. of days symptoms persisted before treatment was sought.* Table 1.6 shows that at average HHs from control group have made delay of 0.49 days before getting hospitalized, but the HHs from treatment group shows an average delay of 0.16, which is lower and a positive sign.

Table 1.6: Average number of days symptoms persisted before treatment was availed (In-patient treatment)

Status of Sampled Households	*Average no. of days delayed for hospitalization in each case*		
	Mean	*Std. Dev.*	*Freq.*
Control	0.49	0.73	300
Treatment	0.16	0.45	150

Source: Field Survey.

For out-patient treatment, the delay is same for treatment and control group, which at average is of one day (table 1.7).

Table 1.7 Average number of days symptoms persisted before treatment was availed (Out-patient treatment)

Status of Sampled Households	*Average no. of days delayed for Out-patient treatment in each case*		
	Mean	*Std. Dev.*	*Freq.*
Control	0.99	0.40	300
Treatment	0.91	0.47	150

Source: Field Survey

Source of Healthcare

Poor households often, because of affordability constraints and unawareness, do not avail quality healthcare. RSBY has empanelled number of private and public hospitals within a state to provide quality in-patient healthcare. In the present study, respondents were asked to reveal their sources of treatment. Table 1.8 shows that HHs (98%) from the treatment group as expected have availed treatment from RSBY empanelled hospitals; whereas 3 HHs from the treatment group got the treatment from the hospitals not covered under RSBY citing the reasons oftime consumption in paper work under RSBY. At the same time, most of the HHs (93%) from the control group received in-patient treatment from the public hospitals and 6.33% from the private. The results reveal that poor households rely on public hospitals for in-patient treatment and few HHs only are able to receive treatment from private

Table 1.8: Source of In-patient treatment

Source of in-patient treatment	*Status of Sampled Household*		*Total*
	Control	*Treatment*	
Nothing (not happened)	2 (0.67%)	0 (0%)	2 (0.44%)
RSBY Hospital	0 (0%)	147 (98%)	147 (32.67%)
Public Hospital (Not covered)	279 (93%)	2 (1.33%)	281 (62.44%)
Private Hospital (Not covered)	19 (6.33%)	1 (0.67%)	20 (4.44%)
Total	300 (100%)	150 (100%)	450 (100%)

Source: Field Survey.

hospitals. Most of the HHs from the control group have cited reasons of lower affordability for selecting the hospital with best infrastructure and adequate treatment facilities. Against this, as mentioned above, RSBY has empanelled number of hospitals both public and private in a state to provide in-patient healthcare facilities to the poor, which means people, can choose any of the hospital for free treatment.

RSBY while providing financial protection and improving healthcare utilization have lot of spillover effects. It improves standard of healthcare utilization by the poor in "out-patient treatment" as well. The evidence of which is clearly provided in the tables 1.9and 1.10. Table 1.9 provides data regarding the source of out-patient treatment during the last 12 months and table 1.10highlights the out-patient treatment source before one year. Informal means as a source of treatment has prevailed for the 63.33% of the respondents. The same has from the last 12 months fallen to 42%, which in other words means that 21% of the HHs have expressed a change in the source of treatment and are using public and private provisions.

Table 1.9 Source of Out-patient treatment

Source of Out-patient treatment	*Status of Sampled Household*		*Total*
	Control	*treatment*	
Informal	126 (42%)	33 (22%)	159 (35.33%)
Public Provisions	154 (51.33%)	104 (69.33%)	258 (57.33%)
Private Provisions	20 (6.67%)	13 (8.67%)	33 (7.33%)
Total	300 (100%)	150 (100%)	450 (100%)

Source: Field Survey.

76.6% of the HHs from the treatment group have revealed the informal means as a source of treatment before one year and it has reduced to 22% during the last 12 months, which means 54% of the HHs have shown an improvement in their standard of out-patient healthcare treatment during the last 12 months.

The above figures reveal that RSBY households have shown more improvement in availing formal out-patient healthcare than their counterpart households in the control group.

Table 1.10: Source of Out-patient treatment before one year

Source of Out-patient treatment	*Status of Sampled Household*		*Total*
	Control	*treatment*	
Informal	190 (63.33%)	115 (76.67%)	305 (67.78%)
Public Provisions	106 (35.33%)	32 (21.33%)	138 (30.67%)
Private Provisions	4 (1.33%)	3 (2%)	7 (1.55%)
Total	300 (100%)	150 (100%)	450 (100%)

Source: Field Survey.

Results from the table 1.11 shows that all the variables show a significant difference between treatment and control group hence providing the base to reject the null hypotheses in case of all the variables.

Table 1.11 Showing the results of T test.

Variable	*Treated*	*Control*	*Mean Difference*	*T-Stat*	*P value*
No. of Hospitalization per Illness	0.95	0.7158	0.2341	9.148	0.000
No. of times Hospitalization delayed	0.10	0.793	-0.6933	-9.02	0.000
Average No. of days delayed for each hospitalization	0.16	0.49	-0.333	-5.13	0.000
No. of Out-patient Healthcare visits per illness	0.91056	0.8869	0.0236	2.0698	0.039
No. of times out-patient treatment delayed	0.833	1.23	-0.3966	-3.86	0.000
No. of days delayed for out-patient treatment	0.906	0.99	-0.083	-1.97	0.048

Source: Field Survey

Inter-state comparison

An attempt has been made to compare the states under study on different study variables. Table 1.12 reveals that in all the three states people under RSBY have been found more utilizing the healthcare facility in comparison to the people not covered by the program. After analyzing the results, it is found that RSBY has been more successful in Himachal Pradesh followed by Haryana and Punjab in improving the healthcare utilization..

Table 1.12: Comparative Inpatient healthcare utilization.

Status of Sampled Households	*No. of Hospitalizations per Illness Episode*								
	Haryana			*Punjab*			*Himachal Pradesh*		
	Mean	*Std. Dev.*	*Freq.*	*Mean*	*Std. Dev.*	*Freq.*	*Mean*	*Std. Dev.*	*Freq.*
Control	0.78	0.28	100	0.69	0.29	100	0.67	0.29	100
Treatment	0.94	0.16	50	0.93	0.17	50	0.98	0.10	50

Source: Field Survey.

Similarly, RSBY seems to be contributing in reducing delay in treatment. Here also Himachal Pradesh reveals more positive results with mean score of 0.04 for treatment group in comparison to 0.12 and 0.14 for Haryana and Punjab respectively.

Table 1.13: Number of times hospitalization delayed

Status of Sampled Households	*No. of times hospitalization delayed in last 12 months*								
	Haryana			*Punjab*			*Himachal Pradesh*		
	Mean	*Std. Dev.*	*Freq.*	*Mean*	*Std. Dev.*	*Freq.*	*Mean*	*Std. Dev.*	*Freq.*
Control	0.58	0.84	100	0.88	0.97	100	0.92	0.89	100
Treatment	0.12	0.32	50	0.14	0.35	50	0.04	0.19	50

Source: Field Survey.

Table 1.14 put forth contradictory results in comparison to table 1.13 where RSBY seems to be reducing the treatment delay more in Himachal Pradesh. At average people under programme in Himachal

Pradesh have almost at average never avoided the treatment, but among the states within the sample people in Himachal Pradesh have delayed more number of days before availing the healthcare facility in comparison to other states. In other words Extent of delaying the treatment is found less in Punjab than Haryana and Himachal Pradesh. One of the reasons may be the transportation facility to hospital, which is found to be efficient in Punjab than in Haryana and Himachal.

Table 1.14: Extent of Delay

Status of Sampled Households	*Average no. of days delayed for hospitalization in each case*								
	Haryana			*Punjab*			*Himachal Pradesh*		
	Mean	*Std. Dev.*	*Freq.*	*Mean*	*Std. Dev.*	*Freq.*	*Mean*	*Std. Dev.*	*Freq.*
Control	0.34	0.51	100	0.06	0.31	100	1.08	0.82	100
Treatment	0.14	0.45	50	0.08	0.34	50	0.26	0.53	50

Source: Field Survey.

There has not been much difference found in terms of source of healthcare availed by the people in different states under study. People under RSBY have mostly availed the treatment from empanelled hospitals, whereas not people covered by the program are found dependent mostly on Public hospitals (table 1.15 a & b)

Table 1.15 a: Source of Inpatient treatment for Control Group

State	*Source of in-patient treatment (Control group)*				
	Nothing (not happened)	*RSBY Hospital*	*Public Hospital (Not covered)*	*Private Hospital (Not covered)*	*Total*
Haryana, Rohtak	0	0	93 (93%)	7 (7%)	100
Punjab, Amritsar	0	0	90 (90%)	10 (10%)	100
Himachal Pradesh, Kan	2 (2%)	0	96 (96%)	2 (2%)	100
Total	2	0	279 (93%)	19 (6.33%)	300

Source: Field Survey.

Table 1.15 b: Source of Inpatient treatment for Treatment Group

State (District)	*Source of in-patient treatment (Treatment Group)*				
	Nothing (not happened)	*RSBY Hospital*	*Public Hospital (Not covered)*	*Private Hospital (Not covered)*	*Total*
Haryana (Rohtak)	0	48 (96%)	2 (4%)	0	50
Punjab (Amritsar)	0	50 (100%)	0	0	50
Himachal Pradesh (Kangra)	0	49 (98%)	0	1 (2%)	50
Total	0	147 (98%)	2 (1.33%)	1 (0.67%)	150

Source: Field Survey.

Conclusion

Microinsurance by reducing barriers to access the healthcare, improves utilization by poor. Rashtriya Swasthya Bima Yojana being a Government of India sponsored health coverage program for the poor, has been successful in improving the healthcare utilization significantly. People, under the program have been found to exhibit lesser delay in treatment. Most of the households under coverage are utilizing the healthcare from the empanelled hospitals. Indirectly the program seems to be setting a positive impact on the out-patient treatment domain as well, as people are found avoiding the informal means of treatment. Thus Health micro insurance by way of centrally sponsored scheme is an efficient way of improving healthcare utilization by the poor. The programme has been found more successful in the state of Himachal Pradesh in comparison to Punjab and Haryana. Affordability is a very critical determinant of healthcare utilization, and many of health coverage programmes; focusing the poor throughout the globe, have given due consideration to this factor while designing the programs. Consumer awareness about the facility has to be sufficiently improved, which would further improve the utilization of healthcare. The present study has not been able to reduce the bias due to the observable characteristics between the two groups of respondents. There is scope for further research on the subject using the rigorous impact assessment tools like propensity score matching, Difference-in-differences etc.

References

- Barnett, Barry J., Christopher B. Barrett, and Jerry R. Skees. "Poverty traps and index-based risk transfer products." *World Development* 36, no. 10 (2008): 1766-1785.
- Bauhoff, Sebastian, David R. Hotchkiss, and Owen Smith. "The impact of medical insurance for the poor in Georgia: a regression discontinuity approach." *Health Economics* 20, no. 11 (2011): 1362-1378.
- Dercon, Stefan. "Growth and shocks: evidence from rural Ethiopia." *Journal of Development Economics* 74, no. 2 (2004): 309-329.
- Dercon, Stefan. *Insurance against poverty*. Oxford University Press, 2005.
- Dror, David M., and Christian Jacquier. "Microinsurance: Extending Health Insurance to the Excluded." *International social security review* 52, no. 1 (1999): 71-97.
- Giedion, Ursula, Alfonso Sierra, Eduardo Andrés, Yadira Beatrice Diaz, and William D. Savedoff. "The Impact of Subsidized Health Insurance on Access, Utilization and Health Status in Colombia." In *Yadira Beatrice and Savedoff, William D., The Impact of Subsidized Health Insurance on Access, Utilization and Health Status in Colombia (May 2007). iHEA 2007 6th World Congress: Explorations in Health Economics Paper*. 2007.
- Giedion, Ursula, Eduardo Andrés Alfonso, and Yadira Díaz. "The impact of universal coverage schemes in the developing world: a review of the existing evidence." (2013).
- Giné, Xavier, Robert Townsend, and James Vickery. "Patterns of rainfall insurance participation in rural India." *The World Bank Economic Review*22, no. 3 (2008): 539-566.
- Harris, Jeffrey E., and Sandra G. Sosa-Rubi. *Impact of" Seguro Popular" on Prenatal Visits in Mexico, 2002-2005: Latent Class Model of Count Data with a Discrete Endogenous Variable*. No. w14995. National Bureau of Economic Research, 2009.
- King, Gary, EmmanuelaGakidou, Kosuke Imai, Jason Lakin, Ryan T. Moore, Clayton Nall, Nirmala Ravishankar et al. "Public policy for the poor? A randomised assessment of the Mexican universal health insurance programme." *The lancet* 373, no. 9673 (2009): 1447-1454.
- Kraft, Aleli D., Stella A. Quimbo, Orville Solon, RitiShimkhada, Jhiedon Florentino, and John W. Peabody. "The health and cost impact of care delay and the experimental impact of insurance on reducing delays." *The Journal of pediatrics* 155, no. 2 (2009): 281-285.
- Maroof, S. A., & Sangmi, M. (2016). Microinsurance as a risk mitigating mechanism for the poor. *International Journal of Research in Economics and Social Sciences, 6(1), 338-347.*

- Nguyen, Ha TH, Laurel Hatt, Mursaleena Islam, Nancy L. Sloan, Jamil Chowdhury, Jean-Olivier Schmidt, Atia Hossain, and Hong Wang. "Encouraging maternal health service utilization: an evaluation of the Bangladesh voucher program." *Social science & medicine* 74, no. 7 (2012): 989-996.
- Radermacher, Ralf, Heidi McGowan, and Stefan Dercon. "The impact of microinsurance." *Microinsurance compendium* 2 (2012).
- Thornton, Rebecca L., Laurel E. Hatt, Erica M. Field, Mursaleena Islam, Freddy Solís Diaz, and Martha Azucena González. "Social security health insurance for the informal sector in Nicaragua: a randomized evaluation."*Health economics* 19, no. S1 (2010): 181-206.
- Trujillo, Antonio J. "Medical care use and selection in a social health insurance with an equalization fund: evidence from Colombia." *Health economics* 12, no. 3 (2003): 231-246.
- Wagstaff, Adam, and Magnus Lindelow. "Can insurance increase financial risk?: The curious case of health insurance in China." *Journal of health economics* 27, no. 4 (2008): 990-1005.
- Wagstaff, Adam, and Shengchao Yu. "Do health sector reforms have their intended impacts?: The World Bank's Health VIII project in Gansu province, China." *Journal of health economics* 26, no. 3 (2007): 505-535.
- Wagstaff, Adam, Magnus Lindelow, Gao Jun, Xu Ling, and Qian Juncheng. "Extending health insurance to the rural population: An impact evaluation of China's new cooperative medical scheme." *Journal of health economics* 28, no. 1 (2009): 1-19.
- Wagstaff, Adam. "Estimating health insurance impacts under unobserved heterogeneity: the case of Vietnam's health care fund for the poor." *Health economics* 19, no. 2 (2010): 189-208.
- Yip, Winnie, Hong Wang, and William Hsiao. "The impact of Rural Mutual Health Care on access to care: Evaluation of a social experiment in rural China." (2009).

Chapter - 8

Economic and Ecological Implications of Climatic Variability in North Western Himalayas

— ***Dr Mohammad Shafi Bhat***

Abstract

North Western Himalayan (NWH) region is a fragile ecosystem which has got considerably affected by climatic variability during the 20th century. In this region and beyond over the past century both mean maximum and mean minimumtemperature has considerably increased and precipitation witnessed a significant decline. The discharge data of the major rivers in the region, namely Ravi, Beas and Satluj have registered a study decline which has a negative impact on the irrigation facilities for agricultural operations in this fertile region of the country. Water table in Punjab and adjoining areas is going down with every passing year. The multi-faceted impacts of climatic variability have been observed in the agricultural productivity which is either showing signs of stagnation or marginal decline across the region. On account of erratic weather conditions horticulture production in J &K and Himachal Pradesh is observed to be adversely affected. Extensive land-use changes and shifts in cropping pattern in the last fifty years are putting extra pressure on water resources in this region. Moreover the frequency and intensity of extreme weather events such as floods, droughts and other hydro-meteorological hazards increased; thereby putting life, property and long-term developments goals in the region at risk. To combat the negative effects of climate change proper long-term adaptation and mitigation measures ought to be be initiated to protect the environment and livelihoods across the region. In this backdrop present paper attempts to account for climatic variability in North-Western Himalayas. This emergent variability is then correlated with economic and ecological aspects of the sustenance in this region and beyond.

***Key words**: Fragile ecosystem, climatic variability, hydro-power, agricultural productivity, marginal decline, hydro-meteorological hazards, adaptation and mitigation.*

Introduction

North Western Himalaya (NWH) stretches between 72°–80°E longitude and 30°–37°N latitude covering Jammu & Kashmir, Himachal Pradesh and parts of Uttarakhand, India. The Great Himalayan and the Pirpanjal ranges surrounding the Kashmir Valley, the Zanskar, Ladakh and Karakoram ranges in the north and the Siwalik range in the south, confer the region with a unique physiographic setting of perennially snow-capped peaks interspersed with valleys and lakes.North western Himalayan region has been marked by pronounced climatic variability in the 2oth century. Generally a decrease in annual rainfall and increase in temperature has been registered in various parts of Jammu and Kashmir, Himachal Pradesh and Punjab. Volume of the major rivers has been affected and water table is receding across the region. Productivity of agriculture and horticulture has also got affected on account of climatic variability, which has been validated by various researches carried out at national and international level. The fragile landscapes of the Himalayan region are highly susceptible to natural hazards, leading to ongoing concern about current and future climate change impacts in the region (Cruz et al., 2007). Climate change concerns in the Himalayas are multifaceted encompassing floods, droughts, landslides, human health, biodiversity, agriculture livelihood, and food security (Barnett, Adam, and Lettenmaier, 2005).

A study carried out by (Kumar & Joshi. 2008) indicates that the mean annual temperature in the Alaknanda valley (western Himalaya) has increased by 0.15 °C between 1960 and 2000. Satellite imagery suggests almost 67 % of the glaciers in the Himalaya have retreated. For example, in Nepal this process is as fast as 10 m/ year (Ageta &

Kadota 1992). The average temperature of Kashmir valley has gone up by 1.05 °C over the last two decades (Sinha, 2007).

Impact of changing climate is also perceptible on vegetation. In some parts of the high altitude, the biodiversity is being lost or endangered because of land degradation and the over use of resources; in 1995, about 10 % of the known species in the Himalaya were listed as 'threatened' (IPCC, 2002). However, impact of Climate Change on biodiversity and vegetation in the region is yet to be carefully studied to establish such a relationship.

Climate change can influence the socio-economic setting in the Himalaya in a number of ways. It can influence the economy (e.g. agriculture, livestock, forestry, tourism, fishery, etc.) as well as human health. Specific knowledge and data on human wellbeing in the Himalaya is limited, but it is clear that the effects of Climate Change will be felt by people in their livelihoods, health, and natural resource security, among other things (Sharma et al., 2009). The consequences of bio-diversity loss from Climate change are likely to be the worst for the poor and marginalized people who depend almost exclusively on natural resources. Poverty, poor infrastructure (roads, electricity, water supply, education and health care services, communication, and irrigation), reliance on subsistence farming and forest products for livelihoods, sub-standard health indicators (high infant mortality rate and low life expectancy), and other indicators of development make the Himalaya more vulnerable to Climate change as the capacity to adapt is inadequate among the inhabitants.

Climate change has a powerful impact on human health directly (e.g., impacts of thermal stress, death/injury in floods and storms) and indirectly through changes in the ranges of disease vectors, water-borne pathogens, water quality, air quality, food availability and quality, cardiovascular mortality and respiratory illnesses, and malnutrition from crop failures (Patz et al., 2005).

Climate change and variability are likely to influence current vector-borne diseases epidemiology as it is estimated that by the year 2100, average global temperatures will have increased by 1.0 - 3.5 °C (Watson et al., 1997), increasing the likelihood of many vector-borne diseases.

With a rise in surface temperature and changes in rainfall patterns, the distribution of vector mosquito species may change (Reiter, 1998).

Some of the documented impacts on mountain agriculture that are linked with Climate Change in the Himalayan region are: (i) Reduced availability of water for irrigation; (ii) Extreme drought events and shifts in the rainfall regime resulting into failure of crop germination and fruit set; (iii) Invasion of weeds in the croplands and those are regularly weeded out by the farmers; (iv) Increased frequency of insect-pest attacks; (v) Decline in crop yield (Negi&Palni, 2010).

Many of the crop species in the Himalaya vary in their response to CO_2. C3 crops such as wheat, rice, and soyabeans respond readily to increased CO_2 levels. Corn, sorghum, sugar-cane, and millet are C4 plants that follow a different pathway. The initial short term studies indicated that photosynthesis is stimulated more in C3 species as compared to C4 species in response to CO_2 enrichment (Uprety& Reddy, 2008).

Dash et al., (2007) reported that the western Indian Himalayas saw a 0.9°C rise over 102 years (1901-2003). They report that much of this observed trend is related to increases after 1972. Using winter (Dec-Feb) monthly temperature data from 1975-2006, Dimri and Dash (2011) also found a warming trend over the western Indian Himalayas, (1.1-2.5°C) with the greatest observed increase in (T max).

Bhutiyani, Kale, and Pawar, (2007) in their study over the Northwest Indian Himalayan region, found 1.6°C warming (0.16°C / decade) in the last century. Singh et al., (2008) observed increasing trends in (T.max) and seasonal average of daily maximum temperature for all seasons except Monsoon over the lower Indus basin in the Northwest Indian Himalaya.

In a recent study, Bhutiyani et al., (2010) observe a statistically significant downward trend (at 5% significance level) in Monsoon and average annual rainfall in the Northwest Indian Himalaya during 1866-2006. A similar trend was noted for 1960-2006 over the western Indian Himalaya region (Sontakke et al., 2009) but without any mention of statistical significance. The literature shows intra-regional differences in winter rainfall trends over Western Indian Himalaya. Dimri and Dash

(2011) noted, significantly decreasing winter precipitation (Dec-Feb) in the region for 1975-2006 amid lack of spatially coherent phases among stations.

Several studies involving field based observations and satellite imagery have shown that a majority of Himalayan glaciers are retreating. A notable exception is the Karakorum region where some glaciers have shown advancement (Hewitt, 2005). Important climatic conditions that make Karakoram glaciers different from the rest of the Himalayas include, orographic conditions that enhance precipitation in the source area, an all-year accumulation regime, concentration and role of avalanche, and ablation buffering due to thick debris cover (Hewitt, 2011).

Precipitation analysis on all India level reveals that long term weighted average mean annual precipitation in India during 1901-2010 has been 1180mm. Trend analysis reveals that there is a marginal increase of 3 mm in the mean annual rainfall during the study period. However, the analysis of south-west Monsoon confirms the prevalence of slight declining trend with an overall decline of 17mm of rainfall during the period from 1901-2010 on all India level. The regional analysis of the south-west Monsoon indicates that rainfall has declined by 60 mm on annual basis in North-Western Region and 53 mm in North-Eastern Region (IMD Pune 2012).

Database and methodology: The present study is based on secondary sources of data which have been obtained from Department of agriculture Govt. of Punjab, Directorate of Horticulture Himachal Pradesh, Directorate of Horticulture J&K. Meteorological data has been obtained from (IMD) Indian meteorological Department Pune. To draw the inferences and conclusions, regression analysis and Mann-Kendall test and time series analysis have been used to identify trends in climate and productivity in the region.

Impact of climatic variability in Punjab

After independence in 1947, Punjab was divided between India and Pakistan, with the eastern part retained in India. In 1966, the state was further subdivided into the states of Punjab and Haryana, while some hilly tracts formed state of Himachal Pradesh. The present Indian Punjab has 20 districts. On the basis of agro-climatic conditions, we divide the state into three regions: Zone I, the sub-mountainous region; Zone II, the central belt; and Zone III, the south-western cotton belt.

Declining Rainfall: Punjab state normally (on long term basis) receives more than 600 mm of annual rainfall, most of which is received in the months of July, August and September, brought by southwest monsoon originating from Bay of Bengal. However, during the decade of 2000, average annual rainfall has declined less than 450 mm during 1998-2005. Not only has the precipitation fallen, it has also become irregular with uneven spread over space and time. The frequency of drought has gone up; we had drought years in 1987, 1997, 2002, 2007 and 2009, which clearly demonstrates that the frequency of droughts has gone up lately. It has however been observed that the droughts do not have any major direct impact on crop production and productivity in the state. It is usual while the production in the rest of the country declines during the drought years, the production in Punjab increases owing to assured access to the ground water. Record production of 8.8 million tons of paddy during 2002 and 9.1 million tons in the last year strengthens this argument. The respective production of wheat during these years was also 15.5 and 15.6 million tones. However, the droughts have significant adverse social and economic impacts on the Punjab economy. The drought conditions necessitate increased use of diesel to pump out the ground water which pushes up the cost of cultivation of paddy. Consequently, the expenditure on irrigation increases. Due to deficient rainfall during the months of July, August and September 2009, additional power estimated to be worth Rs 450 crore and additional diesel oil amounting to Rs 300 crore were used to lift groundwater for saving paddy crops. Deficient rainfall further engenders the sustainability of ground water resources which is already being over-exploited to maintain the current levels of rice production for the food security of the nation. In the drought of 2009, the water table went down more than one metre in central districts of the state (compared to around 70 cms in the previous year during the same months). The droughts, therefore, necessitate the increased investments in irrigation. Farmers are increasingly opting for the submersible pumps than the centrifugal pumps due to drought conditions and falling ground water. It is estimated that during drought yearsthe water level recedes more depending upon the deficiency in rainfall and the investments on deepening of tube-wells and submersible pumps go higher. The increased diversion of electricity from industrial to agriculture sector to save the farm production severely harms the industrial output, profits and hence the industrial employment. This has its own socio-economic implications.

Variability in Temperature: Similarly, the variability in temperature especially in winter months of January to March has increased and the minimum and maximum temperatures have gone up. The following figure also gives a rising trend in the growing degree days during these three months, which seem very crucial for wheat

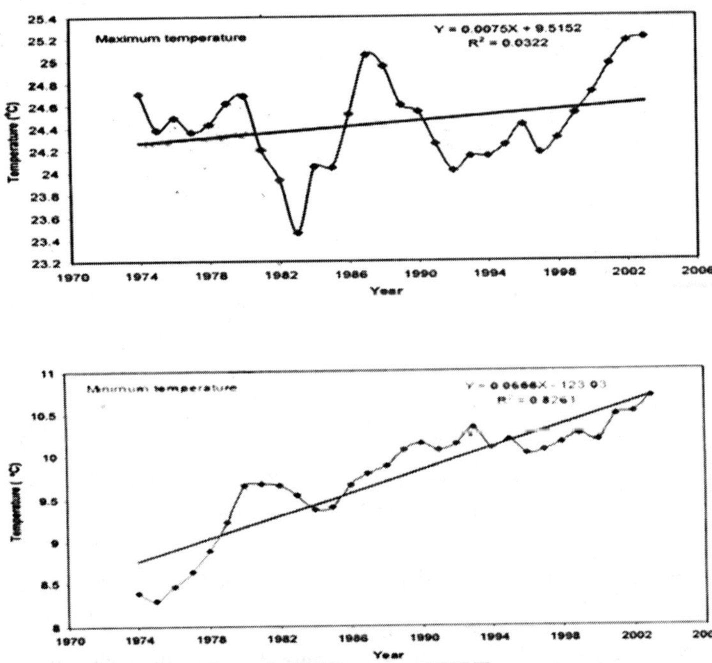

Source: IMD (Indian Meteorological Department) PUNE.

Fig.1.1 Rabi season maximum and minimum temperature (Five yearly moving average) at Ludhiana

cultivation. It implies that the amount of heat accumulating in the environment during these months has steadily gone up over the period of time. Figure 1.1 gives a clear idea about the increase in mean maximum and mean minimum temperature during Rabi season in Punjab region. Its impact on productivity of wheat, the most important Rabi crop can be inferred from figure (1.2) which depicts the productivity trends in Punjab plains from 1960-2014.

These changes have seriously impacted the agricultural production system in terms of economic and physical impacts. The impact of rise in temperature has started appearing in wheat productivity, which fell from 2001 to 2005 continuously. Simple regression analysis has not established any impact of change in the temperature on wheat yield during these crucial months. It calls for some more sophisticated techniques which can dig deeper in any such relation which is being hypothesised during recent times. The increase in winter temperature has shortened the Rabi season and has also effected productivity of other crops such as mustard in the region.

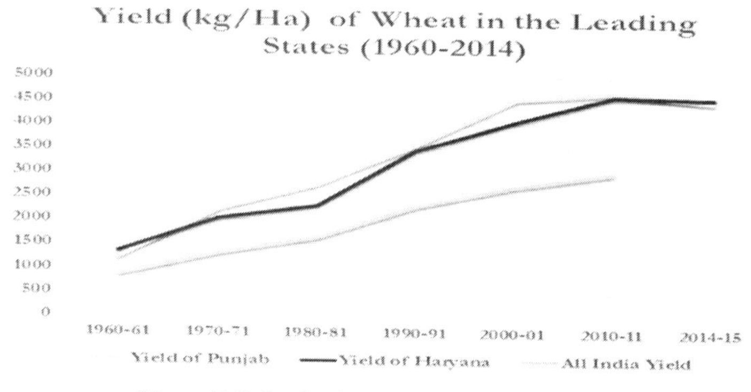

Figure (1.2) Productivity trends of Wheat (Rabi crop) in Punjab Plains from 1960-2014.

Impact of climatic variability on the volume and discharge of rivers

To analyse the impact of climatic variability on the flow of measure Rivers in the north western Himalayas seasonal and annual trends have been worked out. The results of trend analyses of discharge in the winter,

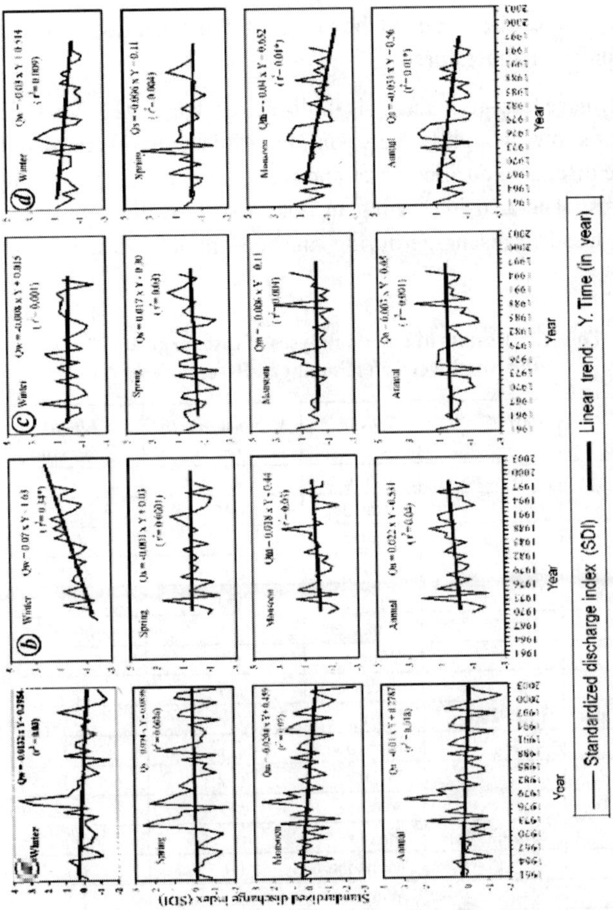

Figure 1.3: Temporal variation and linear trends in average discharge in winter (Qw), spring (Qs), monsoon (Qm) and annual (Qa) in the rivers of theNWH. a,***Satluj(1961–2004);*** b,***Chenab(1970–98);*** c,***Ravi (1961–95)and*** d,***Beas(1961 95).*Significantat95% confidencelevel.***

spring and monsoon seasons along with average annual discharge from (1961–2004) are depicted in figure 1.3. The data indicates that in the last four decades, monsoon discharge in the Beas River has shown a statistically significant decrease and winter discharge in the Chenab River has shown a statistically significant increase. Barring these, statistically insignificant variation in discharge is observed in other basins during all the three seasons, indicating episodic fluctuations. These may have been caused because of the variations in the precipitation and temperature.

Furthermore long-term analysis of discharge data (1922–2004) of Sutlej River shows a slightly increasing but statistically insignificant trend in the discharge during winter and spring months, despite rising temperatures. It is also interesting to note a statistically significant decreasing trend in discharge during monsoon months in the Sutlej River.

Tble 1.1: Results of trend analyses of discharge in the Northwestern Himalayan Rivers

Station/site	***Period***	***Season***	***Mann-Kendall test***	***Linear Regression***
Beas/Thalot	1961-2000	Spring	(-)	(-)
		Monsoon	(-)*	(-)*
		Winter	(-)	(-)
		Average	(-)*	(-)*
Ravi/Madhopur	1962-200	Spring	(+)	(+)
		Monsoon	(-)	(-)
		Winter	(-)	(-)
		Average	(+)	(+)
Chenab/Akhnoor	1961-2000	Spring	(-)	(-)
		Monsoon	(+)	(+)
		Winter	(+)	(+)
		Average	(+)	(+)
Satluj/Barra	1962-2000	Spring	(+)	(+)
		Monsoon	(-)	(-)
		Winter	(-)	(-)
		Average	(-)	(-)

*Significant at 95% confidence level. (+), Increasing; (–), Decreasing Trend

By and large it has been observed that that there is a steady decline in the discharge of rivers in Punjab which is evident from table 1.1. Moreover Mann Kendall test and linear regression confirms a statistically significant declining trend in the annual discharge of Beas River. The decline in the flow of rivers may be attributed to the rising temperature, glacial recession and significant decline in precipitation in the NWH region.

Over-exploitation of Ground Water Resources: Despite the positive benefits created from the rice-wheat system, the Punjab presently faces a number of problems that threaten its sustainability. The most important is the over-exploitation of its ground water resources, due in large part to the growth in GCA under paddy. Table 1.2 shows the water table depth in central Punjab over time and highlights that the share of area in which the water table is greater than 10 meters rose from just 3 percent in 1973 to almost 93 per cent in 2007. The exploitation of groundwater resources has gone up to such an extent that water demand (more than 39.75 MAF) has exceeded the ground water availability (29.64 MAF). Compounding this has been a reduction in state rainfall by nearly 35 percent from 1980 to2000.

Table 1.2: Per cent area under critical water-table depth in Central Punjab, 1973 to2004

Year	*Percentage area>10m*	*Percentage area>15 m*	*Percentage area> 20 m*
1973	3.7	0.56	0.39
1980	5.7	0.57	0.38
1990	26.7	2.95	0.38
2000	53.2	14.11	0.12
2001	65.7	21.73	1.22
2002	72.7	26.15	4.26
2003	79.9	32.73	5.73
2004	84.6	36.57	12.47
2010	94.0	48.0	21.0

Source: Punjab Statistical Abstract, Various Years.

The declining ground water has major economic implications for Punjab farming. The fall in the water table necessitates larger amounts of power required to lift the same amount of power. It has resulted into a steady increase in the expenditure on irrigation (at 1981-82 prices) from Rs 446 per ha in 1989-90 to Rs 819 per ha in 2004-05. In the drought year of 2002-03, this expenditure scaled the peak of Rs 1379 per ha. Such expenditure is expected to further jump in the drought year of 2009 for which the cost estimates are not yet available.

A striking feature of cropping patterns in the Punjab over the past two decades is the rapid growth in the area under paddy. Between 1980/81 and 2008/09, the gross cropped area (GCA) under paddy jumped from 17.5 percent to about 35 percent (Table 1.3). Much of these gains in rice came at the expense of cotton, maize, and othercrops.

Table 1.3: Area and production of wheat and rice in the Punjab, selected years (1970/71-2008/09)

Crop	*Unit*	*1970-71*	*1980-81*	*1990-91*	*2000-01*	*2008-09*
Wheat	**'000 ha**	2,299	2,812	3,273	3,408	3490
	% GCA	40.49	41.58	43.63	42.95	44.40
	Mill. Tons	4.9	7.7	12.2	15.6	15.4
Rice	**'000 ha**	390	1,183	2,015	2,612	2735
	% GCA	6.87	17.49	26.86	32.92	34.79
	Mill. tons	0.7	3.2	6.5	9.2	11.0

Source: Punjab Statistical Abstract, Various Years.

One of the major contrasts of Punjab agriculture from that in rest of the country is that it is almost entirely under assured irrigation. Currently, 98 per cent of the cultivated area in Punjab is under assured irrigation. It becomes very difficult to define or measure the extent of production risk prevalent in Punjab agriculture in such asituation. The yield levels are seldom affected by even a significant fall in rainfall due to larger dependence on ground water which mitigates the negative impacts of any such fall. The variability in the productivity of grain crops especially the most important crops of wheat and rice is very less.

In recent years, the climatic changes have become more frequent impacting production system. The changes are in terms of decline in rainfall, rise in temperature during the periods of critical growth especially that of wheat. Furthermore rise in humidity levels are causing more frequent and severe incidences of pest attacks and disease.

Impact of climatic variability in Himachal Pradesh

Himachal is situated in the western Himalayas. Covering an area of 55,673 kilometers (34,594 miles), Himachal Pradesh is a mountainous state with elevation ranging from about 350 meters (1,148 ft.) to 6,000 meters (19,685 ft.) above the Mean Sea Level. Area-wise, Hamirpur is the smallest district of the Pradesh which covers an area of 1,118 sq. kilometers (2.01%) and Lahaul & Spiti has the largest area of 13,835 sq. kilometers (24.85%).

Comprehensivestudiesof meteorological data in Shimla district of Himachal Pradesh on long term trends in maximum, minimum and mean annual air temperate indicates a significant increase in air temperature (1.6^{0}C) in the NWH region, with winter warming at a faster pace than other seasons. In last century North Western Himalayan region warmed significantly higher than the global average. There is a significant increase in winter temperature in Himachal and across North West Himalayan region in the 20th century which is evident from (Table 1.4).

Table 1.4:ObservedIncrease inWinterAirTemperature

Observation Stn.(Period)	*Mean Max (°C)*	*MeanMin (°C)*	*Average Winter (°C)*
Shimla	2.6	1.00	1.800
(1901-2010)			
(1991-2010)	1.83	0.14	0.898
(2001-2010)	3.42	0.74	2.800
Solang	0.99	-0.08	0.45
(1991-2010)			
(2001-2010)	2.84	-1.12	1.98
Northwest Himalaya(1901-2010)	1.7	1.7	1.7

Analysis of data reveals that the temperature rose at a lower rate till1 930, thereafter grew at a modest rate during the decade of 1961-1970.Warming rate was higher during the period from 1991-2002 as compared to the earlier periods. Furthermore it has also been observed that the rate of increase in maximum temperature is more pronounced at higher altitudes than the lower altitude regions in the state. As per trend analysis carried on different altitudes in Himachal Pradesh decreasing trend of snowfall has been observed which can be inferred from(1.5).

Table 1.5:AltitudinalVariationinSnowFallTrends.

Observatory Stn	*TimePeriod*	*TimePeriod*
	Observationsbasedondepthofsnowfall	
Bhang	(-)1974-2010	(-)1991-2010*
Solang	(-)1982-2010	(-)1991-2010*
Dhundi	(-)1989-2010	(-)1991-2010
Patseo	(-)1983-2010	(-)1991-2010

(+) Increasing, (-) Decreasingtrend
(=95%confidencelevel)*

An analysis of data from 1866-2010 with respect to precipitation variation in the north western Himalayas has revealed that change in winter precipitation is minimum but there is significant decrease in monsoon precipitation. Results of Mann- Kedall test of annual, winter and monsoon precipitation in Shimla & North Western Himalaya confirms a decreasing trend (Table-1.6).

Table 1.6: TrendAnalysis of Annual, Winter & MonsoonPrecipitation

Observatory Stn.	*DataPeriod*	*TrendAnalysis*	
		Mann-Kendall's Test	*Linear Regression*
Annual Precipitation	1866-2010	(-)*	(-)*
Shimla			
North West Himalaya	1866-2010	(-)*	(-)*
Winter Precipitation	1866-2010	(-)*	(-)*
Shimla			
North West Himalaya	1866-2010	(-)*	(-)*
Monsoon Precipitation	1866-2010	(-)*	(-)*
Shimla			
North West Himalaya	1866-2010	(-)*	(-)*

(+) Increasing, (-) Decreasingtrend

(=95%confidencelevel)*

Short term analysis of meteorological data from 1985-2010 reveals that the minimum temperature of March varied from 11.4 to 1.9°C leading to frost incidences, which adversely affected the lowering and fruit setting. Similarly, Blanke and Kunz (2009a) also concluded in their study that the more advanced flowering, brought about by warmer January to March temperatures coincided with late spring frosts, thereby enhancing the risk of yield loss due to spring frost in April. An overall decreasing trend over the years with erratic rainfall pattern in the Bajaura region of Kullu valley was obtained for the period of 1973-2009. The annual rainfall was found to be decreasing at the rate of 0.8mm per year and an overall decrease of 27 mm in the 37 years. Rains and snowfall during November, December and January are more beneficial in fulfilling chilling requirement of apple crop. Decreased rainfall in these months results in moisture stress. A decreasing trend in rainfall was observed in all three months with maximum decrease in January (45.9mm), which is detrimental month for good chill accumulation, followed by December and November with (11.7mm) and (10.4mm) respectively. The impact of climate change on temperature and precipitation in Himachal Pradesh is clearly evident from figure number 1.4 and 1.5.

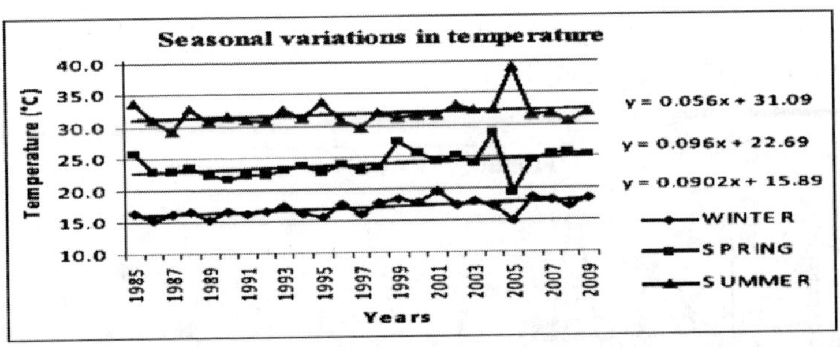

Figure 1.4: Seasonal Variations in Temperature in Himachal Pradesh.

Increase in winter temperature (1.2°C/1985-2009)has considerably reduced the chilling period-which is an important requirement for the apple cultivation. As chilling hours for the period from November to February are important for bud-breaking in apple, the cumulative chill unit' requirement of apple for Kullu (Bajaura) region were determined

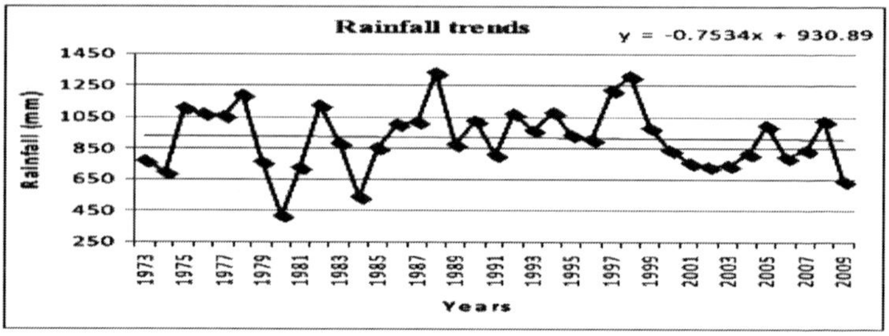

Figure 1.5: Seasonal Variations in Temperature in Himachal Pradesh.

and analysed. The cumulative chill units showed an overall decreasing trend with an averagede crease of 9.52 chill units peryear with total decrease of 238.0 chill units over a period under reference in the Kullu region. The negative impacts of reduced chilling hours due increased winter temperature are visible on the productivity of apple in the region. The apple productivity in the study area decreased at the rate of 0.02 tonnes/ha per year which is evident from (Fig. 1.6). The rise in average temperature, long spells of drought during summers, less snowfall during winters over the period, might have resulted in low production and poor quality of apple crop. Gautam *et.al.,* (2005) also indicated inadequate winter chilling, occurrence of spring frosts, hail sand droughts as key factors of climate change leading to poor fruit set thereby affecting productivity.

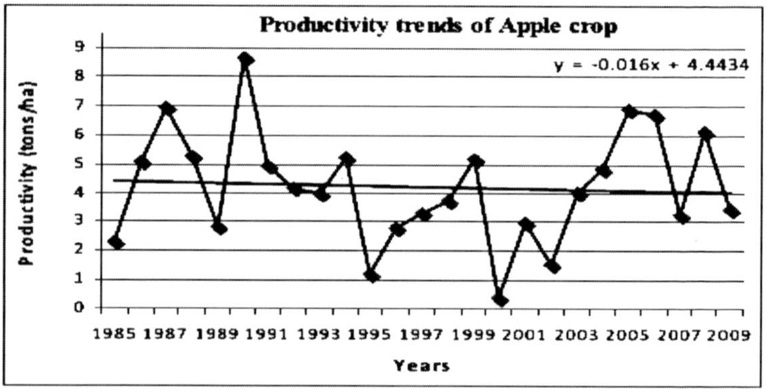

Figure 1.6 Trends in apple productivity in Himachal Pradesh

The implications of climate change on the agriculture of Himachal Pradesh are evident in the declining productivity of horticulture sector. Apple production is negatively affected on account of both yield as well as quality. Apple is the leading cash crop in Himachal Pradesh occupying about 47% of the total area under fruits and 72% of total area under temperate fruits, contributing about 75% of total fruit production in the state and more than Rs. 1000 crores towards the Gross State Domestic Product (GSDP). The production level has gradually touched to 892.1 metric tonnes with8.79 tonnes/hectare productivity in 2010-11(Anon,2013). In Himachal Pradesh, evidences of climate change could be clearly deciphered by changes like receding snowfall in the Himalayas and shifting of temperate fruit belt to upper reaches. The trends in apple production in Himachal Pradesh from 1985-2010 are given in figure 1.6.

The State of Jammu and Kashmir lies between 32.17" and 36.58" North altitude and East to West, the State lies between 73.26" and 80.30" longitude. (Raina, 2002). The state experiences varied climatic conditions on account of diverse topography and altitudinal aspects. More than 2/3 of its population is engaged in agriculture and allied activities and their livelihoods are influenced by fluctuations in the climatic pulse of the region.

Analysis of temperature record at Srinagar reveals that mean maximum temperature has increased 0.6°C and mean minimum

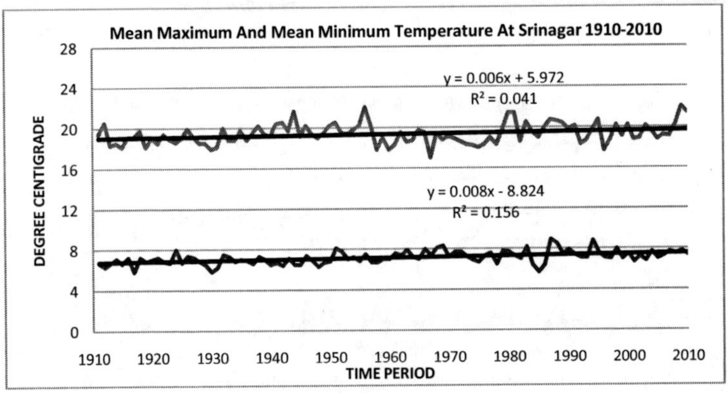

1.7 Trends in the mean maximum and mean minimum temperature at Srinagar from 19010 to 2010.

temperature registered a net increase of 0.8°C in the last century. Winter season was the worst affect by the warming trend as it witnessed 1.2°C in mean maximum temperature during the corresponding period. Figure 1.7 gives a clear idea of the trends prevailing in the mean maxi and mean minimum temperature at Srinagar from (1910 to 2010).

The long Trend Analysis of the climatic data of the Kashmir valley confirms a significant increasing trend in mean maximum and mean minimum temperatures. However Mann-Kendall test (Table 1.7) does not confirm any statistically significant trend in precipitation.

Table 1.7 Mann-Kendall test and linear Regression Analysis of climatic variables at Srinagar 1900-2010.

VARIABLE	*TEST*	*Test stat.*	*a=0.1*	*a=0.05*	*a=0.01*	*RESULT*
Mean max.	Mann-Kendall	1.969	1.645	1.96	2.576	S (0.05)
Temp.	Linear regression	2.05	1.663	1.987	2.633	S (0.05)
	Student's T	-0.28	1.663	1.987	2.632	NS
Mean min.	Mann-Kendall	4.131	1.645	1.96	2.576	S(0.01)
Temp.	Linear regression	4.35	1.663	1.987	2.633	S (0.01)
	Student's T	-2.63	1.663	1.987	2.632	S (0.05)
RAINFALL	Mann-Kendall	1.325	1.645	1.96	2.576	NS
	Linear regression	1.189	1.663	1.987	2.633	NS
	Student's T	**-1.815**	**1.663**	**1.987**	**2.632**	**S (0.1)**

On the contrary precipitation has registered a 10 % increase during the course of 2oth century, which is an exception in the North West Himalayan region. Despite the fact that annual rainfall increased in

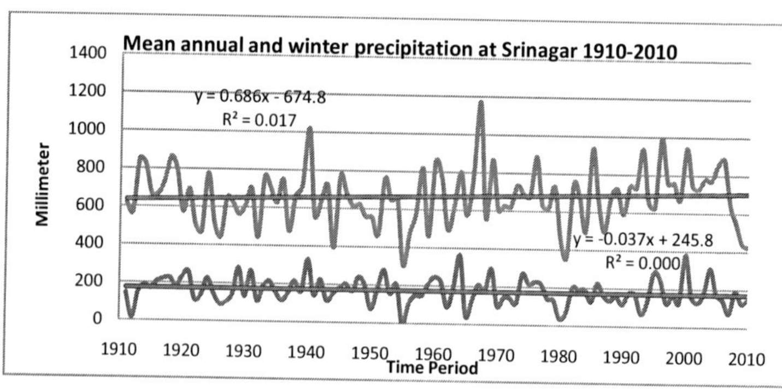

Figure 1.9 Trends in annual and winter precipitation at Srinagar.

Kashmir valley in the period under reference; winter rainfall witnessed a significant decline which can be inferred from (figure 1.9).

Increase in temperature in has accelerated glacial recession in Kashmir Himalayas. A study carried by (Jeelani and Hassnain, 2010) has revealed that significant glacial recession has taken place in the Lidder catchments in the Pahalgam valley which sustains 48 glaciers with an ice covered area of about 39 km2. Kolahoi glacier has receded 1 km from 1962 -2008 which translates into a decrease of 15% in almost 50 years. The inventory data published by geological society of India shows that the total area under glacial cover in Sind and Lidder basins was 78.8 km2 in 1962 while as the glacial cover was 66.81 km2 in the same area as calculated from the satellite imagery in 2001. The loss of glacial cover was 11.99 km2 which translates into a decrease of 18% from 1962-2001. Increasing temperature, declining winter precipitation, and glacial recession will have severe ecological and socio-economic ramifications for valley of Kashmir and adjacent lowlands which depend upon the water resources originating from this region.

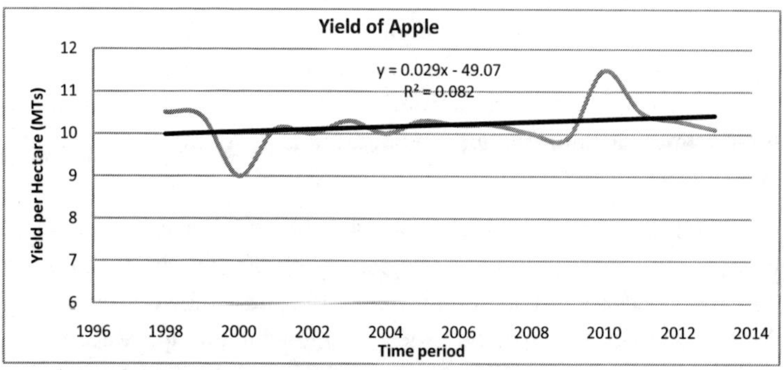

Figure 1.10: Yield of Apple per hectare in Jammu & Kashmir

The increasing temperature has multifaceted implications on the ecology and agriculture of Jammu and Kashmir. Rabi crops and horticulture production gets negatively affected and the yields either show signs of stagnation or marginal decline. The reduced chilling hours due to aggressive warming of winter season has affected the fruit setting and consequently the yields of apple in the state. More over it has also pre-poned the flowering pheonology of apple and thus made it susceptible to the spring frost thereby impacted the fruit set. Winter snowfall has decreased and spring rainfall has increased over the period of time. Moreover incessant rainfall in spring and summer month has also impacted the quality of apple in the state. Thus it can be assumed that climatic variability is negatively affecting the livelihood patterns, water resources, agricultural productivity and natural resources across North western Himalayan region and beyond.

Conclusion

The present study acknowledges the prevalence of significant warming trend across North Western Himalayan region. There is significant increase in mean maximum and mean minimum temperatures especially in the mountainous belt. Despite the fact, that average temperature in the low lands of Punjab remained stable, even though the winter temperatures are steadily rising across the region. Along with the increase in average temperature annual rainfall and snowfall has witnessed a significant decline in Himachal Pradesh which is reflected in the steady decline in the discharge of most of rivers in the region. The water table in Punjab has significantly receded during the last forty years. Mean maximum and mean minimum temperature in Jammu and Kashmir is also sharply rising thereby enhancing glacial recession. Although precipitation has shown a marginal increase in Jammu and Kashmir; winter precipitation is declining at an alarming rate.

The implications of climatic variability are felt across the region. Productivity of Rabi crops is stagnating or marginally declining in Punjab. On account of declining water table and erratic rainfall cost of production has gone up in the region. Rising winter temperature, which reduces the required chilling hours during December and January has adversely affected the apple productivity in Himachal Pradesh. Furthermore extreme fluctuation in temperature in spring season and consequent spring frost has affected the fruit set and ultimately the productivity of apple in the region. Erratic rainfall is also affecting the quality of temperate fruits. Therefore proper adaptation and mitigation strategies should be put in place to combat the fallout of climate change

Chapter - 9

Institutional Aspects of Groundwater Management in North Indian States*

— **_Dr Falendra K. Sudan_**

Abstract

The groundwater has traditionally been dealt in north Indian states with in a laissez-faire mode without attention to the sustainability of the resource. Groundwater institutions are in an evolutionary phase and no simple blueprints for management success are appropriate. Groundwater overexploitation is a major concern. In Punjab, the level of exploitation is already at the level of around 98 per cent and Haryana follows with 80 per cent. The situation is also precarious in state of Rajasthan where the level of exploitation is about 62 per cent. Several parts of north Indian states have seen a steep decline in water tables. The implications of this trend are serious. Artificial recharge has augmented groundwater supply and delayed the crisis. Significant policy efforts by respective state governments have occurred in recent past and have shown significant localized progress in key areas of groundwater governance, however, the major performance challenges and institutional issues

* This paper has been presented in the Summer Symposium on Sustainable System (4S) 2010 during 15-17 June, 2010 at Aalto University, School of Science and Engineering, Finland. Thanks are due to Prof. Jennifer McKay, Director, Centre for Water Policy and Law, University of South Australia, Adelaide, Australia for suggesting to work on the paper. The critical suggestions offered by the participants of the 4S especially Prof. Kari Heiskanen, Aalto University, Prof. Janne Hukkinen and Prof. Ari Ekroos, University of Helsinki are deeply acknowledged.

continue to persist. Therefore, the correction of institutional and governance bottlenecks in the development of groundwater is very vital. The development of groundwater resources should be so regulated as not to exceed the recharging possibilities, as also to ensure social equity. The detrimental environmental consequences of over-exploitation of groundwater need to be effectively prevented by legislation and its enforcement by local government bodies. Groundwater recharge projects should be developed and implemented with community participation for augmenting the available supplies.

I. Introduction

Following Commons (1934), North (1990) and Ostrom (1990), groundwater institutions can be defined as rules that define action situations, delineate action sets, provide incentives, and determine outcomes both in individual and collective decision setting in the context of groundwater governance, which can be broadly categorized as legal rules, policy rules, and organizational rules (Saleth and Dinar, 2004). Groundwater institutions also share the same features characterizing all other institutions such as subjective in origin and operation but objective in manifestation and impact (Hodgson, 1998), path-dependent in the sense that their present status and future direction are dependent on their earlier course and past history (North, 1990), stable and durable (Adelman, et al., 1992; Hodgson, 1998), hierarchic and nested both structurally (North, 1990; Ostrom, 1990) and spatially (Boyer and Hollingsworth, 1997) and embedded and complementary not only with each other but also with their environment defined by the cultural, social, economic and, political milieu (North, 1990). Institutional arrangements for groundwater governance play an important role in allocating, managing and sustaining scarce groundwater resources, which have long been a vital legal, constitutional, and social issue (Marothia, 2003). Undoubtedly, institutional arrangements for groundwater governance largely influence the welfare outcomes; however, groundwater governance in India is confronted by several institutional challenges and grappling with poor performance, deterioration of infrastructure, high levels of extraction and related economic and environmental problems (Shah, Giordano and Wang, 2004). At the same time, there is little agreement about appropriate institutional arrangements for groundwater governance and criteria for successful institutional design (Olson, 1965; Hardin, 1968; Uphoff, 1986; Wade, 1987; Ostrom, 1990, 1992, 1993; Ostrom, Gardiner and Walker, 1994; Hanna et al., 1995; Balland and Platteau, 1996; Hussain and Bhattacharya, 2004; McCay and Acheson, 1987; Mollinga, 2001; McCay, 2002). Thus, redefining groundwater institutions remains the top priority in the water policy arena.

In India, the spread of green revolution and development of drilling technology allowed the spreading of intensive groundwater abstraction in agriculture since mid 1960s, however, this was not accompanied simultaneously by the evolution of institutional arrangements. Therefore, the groundwater has traditionally been dealt in north Indian states with in a laissez-faire mode. The groundwater has been used to irrigate crops typically without attention to the sustainability of the resource, which has twofold effects: (a) the unregulated groundwater use has permitted spectacular expansion of agricultural growth and lifted millions of people out of poverty, and (b) many aquifers are now under severe stress and groundwater cannot wholly sustain the production. Introducing aquifer management is a time-consuming and politically challenging endeavour in overexploited areas. The north Indian states of India have started to proactively manage their groundwater resources; however, it is still in infancy stage and there are as yet few well-established examples of good practices and effective groundwater management. As compared to surface water management, groundwater institutions in north Indian states are in an evolutionary phase and no simple blueprints for management success are appropriate. With the above backdrop, the main objectives of the paper are to examine the groundwater scenario and the institutional arrangements and instruments available for groundwater governance in selected north Indian states and to highlight some key policy options regarding the way forward in groundwater management for the future.

II. Groundwater Scenario

Groundwater is being used in India since the Vedic times, for over 6,000 years. Today, India has 16 per cent of world's population and only 6 per cent of world's water resources and 2.5 per cent of world's land. The annual precipitation in India is estimated to be 4000Bm^3, the southwest monsoon being the major contributor (3000Bm^3). The major and medium river basins contribute over 90 per cent of the total runoff in the country. The Indo-Gangetic planes have enormous amount of water, but the current method of utilization is not appropriate (Serageldin, 1998). Of the total water potential of 1869Bm^3, only 1122Bm^3 can be put to beneficial use. Out of this, 690Bm^3 is surface water and 432Bm^3 is replenishable groundwater (Ministry of Water Resources, 1998). Currently, total water use (including ground water) is 634 Bm^3, of which 83 per cent is for irrigation. The demand for water is projected to grow to 813 Bm^3 by 2010, 1093 Bm^3 by 2025 and 1447 Bm^3 by 2050, against utilizable quantum of 1123 Bm^3. Clearly, there will be a considerable gap between the water need and availability in next few decades.

What really needs to be addressed is the demand-supply imbalance at the local level, which has already acquired serious proportion in north Indian states, as manifested by declining water tables. The increased use of and access to groundwater is often considered as instrumental behind the spread of the new agricultural technology in Punjab and Haryana. The pattern of development of groundwater in north Indian states has created a number of sustainability, equity and efficiency concerns. At national level, groundwater overexploitation may not be considered to be a major problem as India exploits only about 30 per cent of annual utilizable potential. However, groundwater overexploitation is a major concern in north Indian states. For example, in Punjab, the level of exploitation is already at the level of around 98 per cent and Haryana follows with 80 per cent. The situation is also precarious in states such as Rajasthan where the level of exploitation is about 62 per cent (CGWB, 2006). Among the selected north Indian states, Punjab and Haryana have more groundwater resources from unconsolidated rocks. Several parts of north Indian states have seen a steep decline in water tables, often implying that water is being 'mined', or extracted at unsustainable rates. The implications of this trend are serious as these states of India that are witnessing the phenomenon of falling water tables, are also India's agriculturally important states with a heavy dependence on groundwater. The area irrigated by groundwater in the states of Punjab and Haryana is over 61 per cent and 48 per cent respectively (Bhatia et al., 1995).

The groundwater utilization is very high in the states of Punjab, Haryana, and Rajasthan. However, states like Himachal Pradesh and Jammu and Kashmir utilize only a small proportion of their groundwater potentials. If the present trend in groundwater utilization in Punjab and Haryana continues, the demands for water would need more supplies and such situation will be detrimental to development and can cause social upheaval and disruptions. The degree of groundwater exploitation has varied widely across north Indian states (CGWB, 2006). Some states have a large number of semi critical, critical and overexploited assessment units. Out of the 237, 137 and 113 assessment units assessed jointly by State Groundwater Departments and CGWB in Rajasthan, Punjab and Haryana respectively, 32 (14 per cent), 25 (18 per cent), and 42 (37 per cent) are safe, and high proportion of them are over-exploited (59 per cent in Rajasthan, 75 per cent in Punjab, and 49 per cent in Haryana) (CGWB, 2006).

In agriculture, water is mainly used for irrigation because of spatio-temporal variability in rainfall. The large tracts of north Indian states are deficient in rainfall and are drought prone. Hence, it is difficult to practice agriculture without assured irrigation during dry seasons. Water need of certain crops also makes irrigation necessary. For instance, water requirement of rice and sugarcane is very high, which can be met only through irrigation. The provision of irrigation makes multiple cropping possible and irrigated lands have higher agricultural productivity than unirrigated land. Further, the high yielding varieties (HYVs) of crops need regular moisture supply, which is made possible only by a well developed irrigation systems. In fact, this is why that green revolution has largely been successful in Punjab and Haryana.

In these states of north India, more than 85 per cent of their net sown area is under irrigation, where wheat and rice are grown. Of the total net irrigated area, 76.1 per cent and 51.3 per cent are irrigated through wells and tube wells respectively in Punjab and Haryana (CGWB, 2006), which shows that these states have utilized large proportion of their groundwater potential and has resulted in groundwater depletion. Besides, the share of area irrigated through wells and tube wells is also very high in these states.

In most parts of the over-exploited areas, the prime cause of over-exploitation is the rising demand for groundwater from agriculture. Further, in groundwater irrigated areas, decisions on cropping pattern and cropping intensity, which are the predominant determinants of agricultural demand for groundwater, are being taken largely independent of the ease of groundwater availability. Thus, water intensive crops have tended to be grown even in the face of scarcity of groundwater, if these crops are perceived to be relatively remunerative. Such distortions occur partly due to the legal/ regulatory regime governing groundwater and partly to the minimum support price policy and agricultural trade policy currently being followed.

The problem has been compounded by the availability of cheap/ subsidized or even free power (for example in Punjab), since power is a main component of the cost of groundwater. Moreover in other states, electric supply is not metered and a flat tariff is charged depending on the horsepower of the pump. This makes the marginal cost of power zero and provides farmers with little incentive to use power or water more efficiently. Power subsidy has undoubtedly encouraged greater use of groundwater. In most of the districts of these states the concentration of dark blocks is more due to overexploitation of groundwater resources for agriculture.

Since 1954, CGWB has been carrying out exploratory drilling for identification of aquifer system, demarcation of potential aquifer zones and evaluation of aquifer characteristics. In Punjab, CGWB has drilled 142 exploratory wells, 154 observation wells, 22 slim holes and 75 piezometers till March 2004 (CGWB, 2006). About 80 per cent of the hydrograph stations fall in all the command areas of various canal systems. The areas falling out of the command are major portions of districts of Hoshiarpur and Ropar, parts of districts of Gurdaspur, Kapurthala, Jalandhar, Ludhiana and Patiala. Water table elevation contours have a maximum value of 476.8 m amsl rising in the northeast along the Himalayas while the minimum value of 173.3 m amsl is in the Punjab plains (Muktsar district). General groundwater flow direction follows the natural slope. There is not much change in the groundwater flow direction which still remains northeast-southwest, but the groundwater gradient between contour level 190m and 180m in Muktsar and Ferozepur districts has become gentle indicating slowing of groundwater movement resulting in spreading of water logged areas to other districts.

The depth to water level lies between 0.97 m bgl in Muktsar district and more than 33.16 m bgl in the northeast in Hoshiarpur district. Deep water levels are observed in the central, eastern and southern parts of the state in parts of Ludhiana, Hoshiarpur, Sangrur, Bhatinda, Ropar, Fatehgarh districts. Deepest water levels (>20m) in about only 4 per cent of wells are prevalent along the kandi areas in the northeastern parts of the state. Very shallow water levels (<2m) in about 3 per cent of wells have been observed in a patch south of Satluj river in Ferozepur and Faridkot districts, which are mainly canal command areas and are water logged. Otherwise about 35 per cent of wells fall in 5-10m and 34 per cent of wells fall in 10-20 m category. Rise in water levels have been reported from south-western parts of the state mainly in Bathinda, Muktsar and Ferozepur districts. The decline in water levels have been reported from central and southern parts of the state mainly in parts of Sangrur, Patiala, Ludhiana, Jalandhar, Moga, and Amritsar districts.

In Haryana also, the CGWB has been carrying out similar exploratory drilling since 1954. CGWB has drilled 341 exploratory wells, 233 observation wells, 21 slim holes and 141 piezometers till March 2003 (CGWB, 2006). The exploratory drilling in Upper Yamuna basin has revealed existence of three major aquifer systems down to depth of 450m. The first aquifer system extends from ground surface to maximum of 167m, the second aquifer system occurs between 197m and 346m and the third aquifer system occurs below 346m and its downward extend has yet to be deciphered by deep drilling. The Upper Yamuna basin and Ghaggar basin have been investigated in detail under the two different water balance projects.

Groundwater occurs in alluvium as well as in hard rocks. In alluvium, sand, silt and gravel beds constitute potential water bearing zones. Groundwater at shallow depths occurs under unconfined conditions, whereas at deeper levels, confined/semi-confined conditions prevail. In hard rocks, weathered/fractured quartzites and cavernous limestone constitute potential aquifers. The flow of groundwater is generally towards southwest. In the north-eastern and eastern parts of the state falling in Ghaggar and Yamuna basins respectively, fairly thick and regionally extensive confined/unconfined aquifers exist down to a depth of 300m to 400m with yield potential of 150-300m3/hr except in Ambala city where the yield is about 40 to 100m3/hr. In Hissar-Sirsa belt, potential aquifers exist within 270m depth with yield potential ranging between 100m3/hr to 200m3/hr for low to moderate drawdown. Shallow aquifers down to 60m to 100m depth occur in the alluvial deposit of Faridabad, Gurgaon and Mahendragarh districts. Wells in these areas yield 30 to 50m3/hr for moderate drawdown. In the parts of southern districts of Mahendragarh, Rewari, Gurgoan and Faridabad, aquifers in the fractured quartzites and cavernous limestone have yield potential of 5 to 50m3/hr for moderate to high drawdown.

III. Groundwater Institutions

An important ingredient in the groundwater institutional framework is the organizational form for groundwater governance. The groundwater is formally managed by government agencies, often at the central and sometimes at a lower administrative level. With increasing groundwater scarcity problems, however, aquifer management organizations, which consist of local stakeholders, have started to develop. This tends to coincide with changes in the laws governing groundwater management, but can also happen spontaneously. Figure 1 illustrates schematically how all of the above constitute the institutional framework that conditions groundwater governance, with the different institutional arrangements, instruments and organizational forms influencing each other.

Looking at the legal framework for management of groundwater in India, there are no *de jure* rights in groundwater; but *de facto*, all landowners having the right to groundwater underlying their land. This is the product of a set of colonial legislation, the Easement Act (1882), which allows private usufructuary rights in groundwater by viewing it as an easement inseparably connected to land. The Transfer of Property Act 1882 provides that easements (groundwater) can be given to one only if the dominant heritage (land) is also transferred. Conversely, the Land Acquisition Act asserts that if someone is interested in getting rights over the groundwater, he would have to be interested in the land.

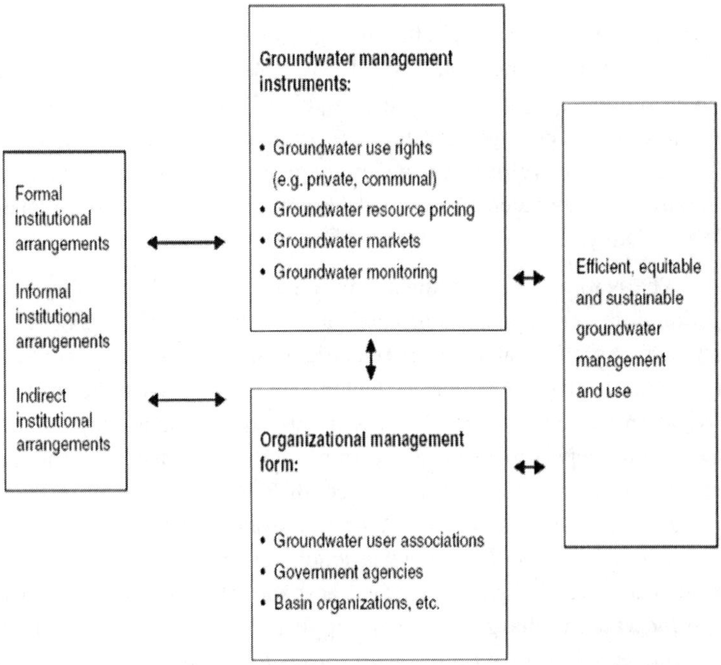

Source: Kemper (2007)

Figure 1: Schematic of Institutional Framework for Groundwater Governance

Thus, groundwater is viewed essentially as a chattel attached to land. There exists, at the same time, no limit to how much water a landowner may draw, in contrast to a legal structure that specifies well-defined property rights setting absolute limits to collective and individual withdrawals.

India is a federal republic and its constitution distributes the legislative power over some subject matters to the States, some to Centre and for some to both Centre and States. The constitutional provisions in respect of allocation of responsibilities between the States and the Centre fall into three categories: (i) The Union List (List I in the Seventh Schedule); (ii) The State List (List II in the Seventh Schedule); and (iii) The Concurrent List (List III in the Seventh Schedule). Under the Constitution, "Water" is a matter included in Entry 17 of List II in the Seventh Schedule i.e. in the State List. "Water" as such is a State subject and that States have jurisdiction to regulate and control groundwater … as Entry 17 of the State List, clearly states "Water, that is to say, water supplies…" … where "water supplies" can be argued to include groundwater. The roles that the Government is expected to play in groundwater development and management are outlined in two important policy statements: National Environment Policy and National Water Policy.

The National Environment Policy has suggested the following action points in relation to groundwater: (a) take explicit account of impacts on groundwater tables of electricity tariffs and pricing of diesel; (b) promote efficient water use techniques, such as sprinkler or drip irrigation among farmers and provide necessary pricing, inputs and extension support to feasible and remunerative alternative crops for efficient water use; (c) support practices of contour bunding and revival of traditional methods for enhancing groundwater recharge; (d) mandate water harvesting in all new constructions in relevant urban areas as well as design techniques for road surfaces and infrastructure to enhance groundwater recharge; and (e) support R&D in most effective techniques suitable for rural water projects for removal of arsenic and mainstream their adoption in rural drinking water schemes in relevant areas.

The National Water Policy (2002) has the following recommendations relating to groundwater: (i) exploitation of groundwater resources should be so regulated as not to exceed the recharging possibilities, as also to ensure social equity; (ii) groundwater recharge projects should be developed and implemented for improving both the quality and availability of groundwater resource; (iii) integrated and coordinated development of surface water and groundwater resources and their conjunctive use should be envisaged right from the project planning stage and should form an integral part of the project implementation; and (iv) over exploitation of groundwater should be avoided especially near the coast to prevent ingress of sea water into sweet water aquifers.

The Model Ground Water Bills have also been framed to form a template for the states in their own regulations of rain water harvesting, notification of areas, requirements for applications for permits prior to digging and drilling of new wells, registration of existing wells and all existing water users. The salient features of the Model Bill are: (i) states to establish a Ground Water Authority; (ii) authority to have powers to notify areas for control and regulation of groundwater development; (iii) authority to grant permit for extraction and use of ground water in notified areas; (iv) existing users in notified areas and new users in non-notified areas to register with the Authority; (v) penalties prescribed for offences; (vi) states to implement rain water harvesting for groundwater recharge. However, once again, the provisions seek only to regulate the creation of water extraction mechanisms, rather than the quantum of water withdrawn. Besides, there has been opposition to the bills on the grounds that like the past record with the system of licensing, they would tend to breed corruption and inequity. Besides, it is felt that such an approach ignores the possibility of successes through localized, participative approaches and adopts a simplistic, centralized approach that fails to consider the wide array of management options suited to diverse sociological as well as hydro-geological contexts. The box 1 summarizes the institutional arrangements and responses for groundwater governance in India.

IV. Groundwater Regulation

Some North Indian State governments have enacted groundwater legislation. An attempt has been made in the following paragraphs to examine the approach to and experience with groundwater regulation in case of Punjab, Himachal Pradesh and Rajasthan. Punjab is a predominantly agrarian state having 85 per cent of its geographical area under cultivation with an average cropping intensity of 188 per cent. The water demand for the kind of agricultural practices followed in the state is very high and a large part of it is for groundwater. Out of the 137 blocks in the state, only 25 are safe; 103 are over exploited, 5 critical and 4 semi-critical. Punjab is not in favour of groundwater legislation as it apprehends that such a step will cause hardship to farmers. Instead, to tackle groundwater over exploitation, the State is in favour of the following initiatives: (i) crop diversification by extending minimum support price to other crops to wean away farmers from paddy cultivation, which is water intensive and contract farming for sowing alternative crop of chick-pea has been successfully tried;

(ii) large scale artificial recharge through construction of check dams, use of drainage water and roof top rain water harvesting; (iii) electricity supply to be controlled, regulated and metered supply in critical areas; (iv) micro irrigation for promotion of drip and sprinkler to conserve water; and (v) alteration in crop calendar by encouraging late sowing of paddy after 16th June to decrease evapotranspiration. The state is also contemplating complete ban on new tube wells and restricting horse power to 10 HP so that the deeper aquifers are not tapped. The pumps need to be replaced with energy efficient pumps. Conjunctive use of saline and fresh water will also help in bringing down the demand for fresh water.

Box 1: Institutional arrangements and responses for groundwater governance

Institutional arrangements	*Institutional responses*
Groundwater institutions	• Cooperative tube well organizations • Emergence of groundwater markets • Groundwater extraction and water trading • Pricing arrangements for groundwater transactions • Check-dams • Common property institutional arrangements • Primarily used for groundwater recharge • Surface irrigation, livestock, and domestic needs • Beneficiary contribute to construction and maintenance

Box 2: Groundwater institutions in Rajasthan

Institutional aspects	*Mechanisms*
Groundwater development	• Regulation of exploitation of groundwater resources as not to exceed recharging possibilities and also to ensure social equity • Periodical reassessment on a scientific basis of groundwater potentials • Amending existing laws/new legislation be enacted • Controlling deep drilling through licensing and control on private operators • Public awareness for self-control in groundwater exploitation from WUAs

(Contd...)

	• Developing a sense of water scarcity and need to conserve • Improving data collection • Preventing detrimental environmental consequences of over exploitation of groundwater • Review and charging rationalistic and realistic water rates • Volumetric measurement of water consumption in all sectors

Himachal Pradesh Ground Water (Regulation and Control of Development and Management) Act, 2005 stipulates for establishment of "The Himachal Pradesh Ground Water Authority" with power to notify areas to regulate and control the development and management of groundwater, maintain database on groundwater, grant permit to extract and use groundwater, register the existing groundwater users and drilling agencies, alter, amend or vary the terms of the permit or certificate of registration, cancel permit or certificate of registration, and collect royalty in respect of use of groundwater. Every user of groundwater in a notified area shall install water measuring device on ground water abstraction structure. Emphasis should be made on rainwater harvesting for conservation and groundwater recharge. The provisions have also been stipulated for cognizance and trial of offences and penalties.

In the context of most driest state of Rajasthan, it has been propagated that the groundwater institutions need to be evolved and strengthened for optimal economic development and social well-being, which calls for an integrated and multi-disciplinary approach to planning, evaluation, approval and implementation of irrigation and drainage projects, including river basin management, of surface and groundwater. There is need for optimisation of groundwater resources exploitation and raising the level of reliability of supplies through conjunctive use of surface and groundwater. Besides, judicious and economically sound allocation of water resources to different sectors has also been called for. The institutional aspects and mechanisms for groundwater governance in Rajasthan are presented in box 2 and groundwater institutions in comparativc perspective are presented in box 3.

In sum, the ownership of the groundwater should be governed by the ownership of the land to the extent the uses (exploitation) of groundwater is not causing depletion in the groundwater levels so the similar rights of the adjoining land owners and public at large are not encroached upon as this natural resource is meant for public use and it should not be allowed to be exploited beyond replenishable level. Therefore, there is a need of an "Act" at the State level to monitor the groundwater levels through scientific methods by piezometers under the advisory guidance of CGWB.

Box 3: Groundwater Institutions in North Indian States: A Comparison

Institutional aspects	*Haryana*	*HP*	*J&K*	*Punjab*	*Rajasthan*
Ownership of tubewells	Private	Private	Private	Private	Private
Ownership of pumps	Private	Private	Private	Private	Private
Overlapping tubewell command area	Yes	Uncertain	Uncertain	Yes	Yes
Competition among pump owners for water sales	Yes	No	No	Yes	Yes
Existence of laissez faire water markets	Yes	No	No	Yes	Yes
Role of village authorities in water regulation	No	No	No	No	No
Registration of GW structures	No	No	No	No	No
Licensing of GW structures	No	No	No	No	No
Conjuctive use	Yes	Limited	Limited	Yes	Uncertain
Social equity	No	Limited	Limited	No	Uncertain
Prevalence of water rates	Yes	No	No	Yes	Yes
Farmers' participation	Limited	Small	Small	Limited	Poor
Monitoring of GW quality	Absent	Absent	Absent	Absent	Absent
Institutionalized incentives	No	No	No	No	No
System of artificial recharge	Yes	Yes	Yes	Yes	Limited
Volumetric allocation	No	No	No	No	No
Pricing of electricity	Subsidized	Subsidized	Subsidized	Nil	Subsidized
Private participation	Small	Poor	Poor	Small	Small

The State Government should also ensure that groundwater levels should not fall below the replenishable level and accordingly take necessary measures for regulation/restriction of the groundwater uses in the area. The enforcement for the regulation/reduction/restriction in the groundwater usage should be made effective by the State Government through the users' group/community participation/ involvement of Panchayat. The users group should be responsible for regulating the groundwater usage among various sectors i.e. irrigation, drinking and industrial. Such regulations by the user group will be made effective on the advice of State Ground Water Board (SGWB).

equity. The detrimental environmental consequences of over-exploitation of groundwater need to be effectively prevented by legislation and its enforcement by local government bodies. To give teeth to their actions the Central and State governments should enact suitable legislation and notify the permissible water depths to which groundwater depletion will be permitted for each region/block/watershed after identifying the special problems of each area. Groundwater recharge projects should be developed and implemented with community participation for augmenting the available supplies.

The Government should transfer the authority for regulating groundwater use to the lowest level, the village panchayat. The Government should have the responsibility of laying down the rules and regulations and then monitoring the implementation. Effective groundwater governance requires (a) awareness of the status of groundwater, both its quality and the quantity available and monitoring is a prerequisite in order to identify whether problems are occurring or are likely to occur; (b) understanding of the aquifer sufficient to be able to identify options (and targets) to remedy a problem situation; (c) water laws and rights in place, widely accepted and clear, or in their absence a practicable system of incentives/disincentives; (d) surveillance, to monitor adherence to regulatory measures or response to incentives/disincentives; and (e) awareness in governmental planning and society at large of the importance of groundwater. Unfortunately these requirements are very rarely met in full. In particular, water rights and laws applied to groundwater can be ambiguous or uncertain in their interpretation. Realistically, changing the situation will take time, but long term goals need to include (a) increasing public and government awareness so that legislation on water issues (like ownership and rights) can be passed and enforcement accepted by society at large; (b) resourcing agencies to actively manage groundwater; (c) encouragement of community management; and (d) incentives (or disincentives) to reduce pollution load.

In brief, the groundwater policy for the future should have the following tenets for achieving sustainable development: economical and efficient use of the water pumped from the aquifers, watershed development and recharge augmentation, conjunctive use, prevention of pollution, more calories per cubic meter of irrigation water, creating a public awareness, pumpage control in overexploited watersheds, and promoting cooperative actions among various groundwater stakeholders.

References

Adelman, Irma, Cynthia Taft Morris, Habib Fetini and Elise Golan-Hardy (1992). "Institutional change, economic development and the environment". *Ambio,* 21(1): 106-110.

Balland, J.N., and Platteau, J.P. (1996). *Halting degradation of natural resources: Is there a role for rural communities?* FAO and Clarendon Press, Oxford.

Bhatia R., Cestti R., Winpenny T.C. (1995). Water conservation and reallocation: Best practiced cases in improving economic efficiency and environmental quality. World Bank paper: UNDP/World Bank Water and Sanitation Programme.

Boyer, Robert and J. Rogers Hollingsworth (1997). "From national embeddedness to spatial and institutional nestedness". In J. Rogers Hollingsworth and Robert Boyer, eds., *Contemporary capitalism: The embeddedness of institutions*, Cambridge University Press, Cambridge.

Central Ground Water Board (2006), *Dynamic Groundwater Resources of India.* Ministry of Water Resources, Government of India, New Delhi.

Commons, J.R. (1934). *Institutional Economics*. Macmillan, New York.

Hanna, S., Folke, C., and Maler, K. G. (1995). "Property rights and environmental resources". In S. Hannah and M. Munasinghe, eds., *Property rights and the environment: Social and ecological issues.* Beijer International Institute of Ecological Economics and the World Bank, Washington, DC, pp. 15-29.

Hardin, G. (1968). "The tragedy of commons". *Science,* 162 (3859), December, pp. 1243-1248.

Hodgson, Geoffrey M. (1998). "The approach of institutional economics". *Journal of Economic Literature*, 36(1): 166-192.

Hussain, Z. and Bhattacharya, R.N. (2004). "Common pool resources and contextual factors: Evolution of a fishermen's cooperative in Calcutta". *Ecological Economics*, 50: 201-217.

Kemper, K.E. (2007). Instruments and institutions for groundwater management. In M. Giordano and K.G. Villholth, ed. *The Agricultural groundwater revolution: Opportunities and threats to development*. CAB International, Oxfordshire.

Marothia, D.K. (2003). "Enhancing sustainable management of water resources in agriculture sector: The role of institutions". *Indian Journal of Agricultural Economics*, 58(3): 406-427.

McCay, B.J. (2002). Emergence of institutions for the commons: Contexts, situations and events. National Research Council. In *The drama of the commons.* National Academies Press Washington, DC. pp. 361-402

McCay, B.J., and Acheson, J.M. (1987). Human ecology of the commons. In B.J. McCay and J.M. Acheson, eds. *The question of the commons.* University of Arizona Press, Tucson, pp. 1-34.

Ministry of Water Resources (1998). *Water Resources Development in India 1947-1997.* Government of India, New Delhi.

Mollinga, P. (2001). "Water and politics: Levels, rational choice and south Indian canal irrigation". *Futures*, Oct-Nov, pp. 733-748.

North, D.C. (1990). *Institutions, institutional change and economic performance.* Cambridge University Press, Cambridge.

Olson, M. (1965). *The logic of collective action.* Harvard University Press, Cambridge.

Ostrom, E. (1990). *Governing the commons.* Cambridge University Press, Cambridge.

Ostrom, E. (1992). *Crafting institutions for self-governing irrigation systems.* ICS Press, San Francisco.

Ostrom, E. (1993). "Design principles in long-enduring irrigation institutions". *Water Resources Research*, 29(7): 1907-1912.

Ostrom, E. and Gardiner, R.W. (1994). *Rules, games and common-pool resources.* University of Michigan Press, Ann Arbor.

Saleth, R. Maria and Ariel Dinar (2004). *The Institutional Economics of Water: A Cross Country Analysis of Institutions and Performance.* Edward Elgar, Cheltenham.

Serageldin, I. (1990). "Water in the 21st century: A dialogue". *Water Policy*, 1(1): 29-137.

Shah, T., Giordano, M., and Wang, J. (2004). "Irrigation in a dynamic economy: What is China doing differently from India?". *Economic and Political Weekly*, July 31.

Uphoff, N. (1986). *Local institutional development.* Kumarian Press, West Hartford.

Wade, R. (1987). "The management of common property resources: Collective action as an alternative privatisation or state regulation". *Cambridge Journal of Economics*, 15: 95-106.

Chapter - 10

Hydro-Power Development and Its Pricing in North Indian States*

— Dr Falendra K. Sudan

Abstract

Hydro-electric projects are the most economic and preferred source of electricity. In India, the share of hydro-power in total installed capacity has been declining steadily since more than five decades. Regional level of hydro potential development (including schemes cleared by the Central Electricity Authority) is expected to be 31% in Northern, 63.71% in Western, 61.26% Southern and 40.5% in Eastern power regions. Though the unexploited hydro-potential (69%) in the Northern power region is substantial, the emerging power supply situation indicates that it may be adequate only for meeting the growing power demands within north India. North Indian states have added huge hydro- capacity in recent past, even than north India would be a net importer of power by the end of 2017. Considering the growing power demand in the North Indian States, there may be little if any surplus for export to other regions. The hydro-power development scenario indicates the need for early development of the Northern Region's hydro potential in order to help meet the future electricity needs of not only the region, but the whole country.

---

* This paper is a part of the research study titled "Comparative Assessment of Power Price Structure in Jammu & Kashmir and Other States of India and Bhutan", sponsored by the Centre for Dialogue and Reconciliation, New Delhi, November 2011- October 2012.

I. Introduction

Unlike other consumer goods, electricity cannot be stored for future use. The generation and consumption of electricity have to be simultaneous and instantaneous. The power generation, transmission and distribution capacity is a complex, time consuming and expensive process. The access to electricity is essential to empower the disadvantaged sections of population. Since early 1950s, the State Electricity Boards (SEBs)/State Electricity Departments were mainly responsible for generation, transmission and distribution of electricity. A few licensees were in the private sector too. In mid-1970s, Central Sector was associated to set up generating stations and high/ extra high voltage transmission lines to bridge the huge gap between demand and supply of power. Now, the States control about 60% of the power generation capacity, 70% of transmission network, and almost cent per cent of the distribution system in India. Electricity is essential for industrialization and improving the quality of life. Harnessing the immense untapped hydro-power potential in north India opens avenues for economic growth and development. It provides an opportunity to improve the well-being of the people and contributes substantially to the economy. Large hydro-power potential of the north India has remained mostly unexploited due to inadequate development of the grid systems, availability of economic and accessible sites closer to load centres of the other regions, low demand for power in the sparsely populated hills and the safety of dam construction in seismically active zone.

The hydro-power gaint the 'National Hydroelectric Power Corporation Limited' (NHPC) is a Government of India owned enterprise. It was incorporated in 1975 with an authorised capital of ₹2000 million. Main objective of NHPC was to plan, promote and organise an integrated and efficient development of hydroelectric power in all aspects. NHPC expanded its objectives to include development of power in all its aspects through conventional and non-conventional sources in India and abroad. Now, NHPC is a Mini Ratna Category-I Enterprise with an authorised share capital of 150000 million. NHPC has an investment base of over 387180 million. In terms of investment, it is among the top ten companies in India. Initially, on incorporation,

NHPC took over the execution of Salal Stage-I, Bairasiul and Loktak Hydro-electric Projects from Central Hydroelectric Project Construction and Control Board. Since then, it has executed 14 projects with an installed capacity of 5295 megawatts (MW) on ownership basis including projects taken up in joint venture. NHPC has also executed 5 projects with an installed capacity of 89.35 MW on turnkey basis. Two of these projects have been commissioned in neighbouring countries i.e. Nepal and Bhutan. With above backdrop, the main objectives of the present study have been to analyze the hydro-power development and its pricing in North Indian States and to suggest policy suggestions to overcome the discrimination in power price structure with Jammu and Kashmir vis-à-vis other North Indian States, where NHPC is operational. The study has widely used published and unpublished data and information from the agencies like Ministry of Power, Central Electricity Regulatory Commission (CERC), NHPC, State Electricity Regulatory Commissions (SERCs), etc. using desk approach.

II. Review of Power Sector Reforms/Laws

In India, electricity is a concurrent subject, wherein both the Central government and the State governments have role to promote power sector and both have the authority to make necessary laws and regulations, and formulate and implement policies and programmes for development of the electricity. In the liberalized era, the Central government has been encouraging and inviting private sector participation for development of power sector. Therefore, the facilitative policy scenario has been provided by modifying the Electricity Act and related policies, laws and regulations.

i. Electricity Act, 2003

The Electricity Act, 2003 received the assent of the President on the 26th May, 2003. It aims to consolidate the laws relating to generation, transmission, distribution, trading and use of electricity. It take measures conducive to development of electricity industry, promoting competition therein, protecting interest of consumers and supply of electricity to all areas, rationalization of electricity tariff, ensuring transparent policies regarding subsidies, promotion of efficient and environmentally benign policies, constitution of CERC, CEA, Regulatory Commissions and establishment of Appellate Tribunal and for matters connected therewith or incidental thereto. The Section 3 of the Electricity Act, 2003 provides that the Central government shall, from time to time, prepare, review or revise the National Electricity Policy and Tariff Policy, in consultation with the State governments and the Authority for development of the power system based on optimal utilisation of resources such as coal, natural gas, nuclear substances or materials, hydro and renewable sources of energy.

There shall be a Commission to be known as the CERC to exercise the powers conferred on, and discharge the functions assigned to it under Section 76 of this Act. CERC established under section 3 of the Electricity Regulatory Commissions Act, 1998 and functioning as such immediately before the appointed date, shall be deemed to be the Central Commission for the purposes of this Act. The Central Commission shall function to regulate the tariff of generating companies owned or controlled by the Central government; to regulate the tariff of generating companies other than those owned or controlled by the Central government; to regulate the inter-State transmission of electricity; to determine tariff for inter-State transmission of electricity; to issue licenses to persons to function as transmission licensee and electricity trader with respect to their inter-State operations; to adjudicate upon disputes involving generating companies or transmission licensee; to specify and enforce the standards with respect to quality, continuity and reliability of service by licensees; to fix the trading margin in the inter-State trading of electricity, if considered, necessary; to discharge such other functions as may be assigned under this Act. In discharge of its functions, the Central Commission shall be guided by the National Electricity Policy, National Electricity Plan and Tariff Policy.

ii. National Electricity Policy, 2005

The Central government notifies the National Electricity Policy on 12th February, 2005. The National Electricity Policy aims at achieving the following objectives: access to electricity - available for all households in next five years, availability of power - demand to be fully met by 2012; supply of reliable and quality power of specified standards in an efficient manner and at reasonable rates; per capita availability of electricity to be increased to over 1000 units by 2012; minimum lifeline consumption of 1 unit/household/day as a merit good by year 2012; financial turnaround and commercial viability of electricity sector; and protection of consumers' interests.

According to the Electricity Policy, maximum emphasis would be laid on the full development of the feasible hydropotential in the country. Harnessing hydro potential speedily will also facilitate economic development of States, particularly North-Eastern States, Sikkim, Uttaranchal, Himachal Pradesh and J&K, since a large proportion of our hydro power potential is located in these States. The States with hydro potential need to focus on the full development of these potentials at the earliest. Hydel projects call for comparatively larger capital investment. Therefore, debt financing of longer tenure would need to be made available for hydro projects.

Central government is committed to policies that ensure financing of viable hydro projects. State Governments need to review procedures for land acquisition, and other approvals/clearances for speedy implementation of hydroelectric projects. Central government will support the State Governments for expeditious development of their hydroelectric projects by offering services of Central Public Sector Undertakings (CPSUs) like NHPC. To facilitate orderly growth and development of the power sector and also for secure and reliable operation of the grid, adequate margins in transmission system should be created.

iii. Tariff Policy, 2006

The Central government notifies the Tariff policy on 6 January, 2006. The tariff policy has been evolved in consultation with the State governments and the CEA and keeping in view the advice of the CERC and suggestions of various stakeholders. The objectives of this tariff policy are to ensure availability of electricity to consumers at reasonable and competitive rates; ensure financial viability of the sector and attract investments; promote transparency, consistency and predictability in regulatory approaches across jurisdictions and minimise perceptions of regulatory risks; and promote competition, efficiency in operations and improvement in quality of supply.

Tariff policy lays down following framework for performance based cost of service regulation in respect of aspects common to generation, transmission as well as distribution. Balance needs to be maintained between the interests of consumers and the need for investments while laying down rate of return. Return should attract investments at par with, if not in preference to, other sectors so that the electricity sector is able to create adequate capacity. The rate of return should be such that it allows generation of reasonable surplus for growth of the sector. The following aspects would need to be considered in determining tariffs. All power purchase costs need to be considered legitimate unless it is established that the merit order principle has been violated or power has been purchased at unreasonable rates.

In the Ministry of Power Resolution on 31 March, 2008 the following proviso is added at the end of Para 5.1 of the Tariff Policy: Provided that a developer, of a hydroelectric project, not being a State controlled/ owned company, would have the option of getting the tariff determined by the appropriate Commission on the basis of performance based cost of service regulations if the following conditions are fulfilled: (a) The appropriate Commission is satisfied that the project site has been allotted to the developer by the concerned State government after following a transparent process; (b) Projects of more than 100 MW design capacity for which sites have been awarded earlier by following a transparent process and on the basis of predetermined set of criteria would also be covered in this dispensation; (c) Concurrence of CEA (if required under Section 8 of the Act), financial closure, award of work and long term power purchase agreement (PPA) (of more than 35 Years) of the capacity specified in (d) below with distribution licensees are completed by 31 December, 2010; (d) Long term PPA would be at least for 60% of the total saleable design energy; (e) Award of contracts for supply of equipment and construction of the project, either through a turnkey or through well defined packages, are done on the basis of international competitive bidding.

In cases, where the conditions mentioned above at (a) to (e) are fulfilled, the Appropriate Commission shall determine tariff ensuring the following: (i) Any expenditure incurred or committed to be incurred by the project developer for getting project site allotted (except free power up to 13%) would neither be included in the project cost, nor any such expenditure shall be passed through tariff; (ii) The project cost shall include the cost of the approved R&R plan of the Project which shall be in conformity with the following: (a) the National Rehabilitation & Resettlement (R&R) Policy currently in force; and (b) the R&R package as enclosed at appendix; and the cost of project developers' 10% contribution towards RGGVY project in the affected area as per the project report sanctioned by the Ministry of Power; (iii) Annual fixed charges shall be taken pro-rate to the saleable design energy tied up on the basis of long term PPAs with respect to total saleable design energy. The total saleable design energy shall be arrived at by deducting the following from the design energy at the bus bar: a) 13% of free power (12% for the host Government and 1% for contribution towards Local Area Development Fund as constituted by the State government). This 12% free power may be suitably staggered as decided by the State government; and b) Energy corresponding to 100 units of electricity to be provided free of cost every month to every Project Affected Family notified by the State government to be offered through the concerned distribution licensee in the designated resettlement area/ projects area for a period of ten years from the date of commissioning".

iv. Electricity (Amendment) Act, 2007

The Electricity (Amendment) Act, 2007, amending certain provisions of the Electricity Act, 2003, has been enacted on 29 May, 2007. It is brought into force with effect from 15th June 2007. Main features of the Amendment Act are: (i) Central government, jointly with state Governments, to endeavour to provide access to electricity to all areas including villages and hamlets through rural electricity infrastructure and electrification of households; (ii) No License required for sale of electricity from captive units; (iii) Definition of theft expanded to cover use of tampered meters and use for unauthorized purpose; (iv) Theft made explicitly cognizable and non-bailable; and (v) The provision for reduction of cross subsidies would continue.

v. National Electricity Fund

The creation of National Electricity Fund (NEF) was announced in the Finance Minister's Budget Speech of Financial Year 2008-09. The objective of the NEF is to provide financial support to the State Power Utilities (SPU) for improving their T&D infrastructure. A Committee constituted under the chairmanship of Member (Power), Planning Commission considered various aspects of establishing the NEF. The Terms of Reference of the Committee are as follows:

- Propose a structure to mobilise funds needed and arrangements for making it available to State Governments.
- Suggest other modalities under which the funds would be disbursed to the States and power utilities. The following are the reasons to setup NEF:
- The focus of investment has been primarily towards generation;
- Commensurate investment not being made in T&D;
- SPU neither have requisite financial resources nor have adequate borrowing capacity;
- The lenders perceive distribution projects of comparatively high risk;
- Borrowing at commercial rates by SPU from financial institutions (FIs), Banks, etc. for different schemes may be difficult;
- Returns linked to AT&C losses;
- Level of reduction in AT&C losses may not be sufficient to service the debt

Following issues need to be resolved in the process of setting up the NEF:

- The Plan scheme for interest subsidy may be extended to loans from the banking sector and other financial institution rather than restricting the subsidy only to loans taken from PFC & REC.
- The interest subsidy scheme be initially made applicable only for distribution work.

- Only non-Restructured Accelerated Power Development and Reforms Programme (R-APDRP) projects and schemes be made eligible under NEF.

PFC shall be the Nodal Agency to process the claim for subsidy received from various financial institutions including commercial banks and would also prepare terms and conditions for release of interest on subsidy amount.

vi. National Policy for Hydro-Power Development

Despite hydroelectric projects being recognized as the most economic and preferred source of electricity, the share of hydropower in our country continued declining since 1963. The hydro share declined from 44% in 1970 to about 25% in 2010. For grid stability the ideal hydro-thermal mix ratio for Indian condition is 40:60. In order to correct the hydro-thermal mix to meet the grid requirements and peak power shortage, in August, 1998 and thereafter in November 2008, the Government of India announced a Policy on 'Hydro Power Development'.

Even if the share of hydro power is to be maintained at 25%, the capacity addition during the 9th and 10th Plan would work out to 23,000 MW. If the share were to be enhanced to 30 per cent, it would require a further addition of 10,000 MW of hydro capacity. The constraints which have affected hydro development are technical (difficult investigation, inadequacies in tunnelling methods), financial (deficiencies in providing long term financing), tariff related issues and managerial weaknesses (poor contract management). The hydro projects are also affected by geological surprises (especially in the Himalayan region where underground tunnelling is required), inaccessibility of the area, problems due to delay in land acquisition, and resettlement of project affected families, law & order problem in militant infested areas.

The Government of India has set the following objectives for accelerating the pace of hydro power development: (i) ensuring targeted capacity addition of 9815 MW from hydel projects in the total capacity addition of 40245 MW in 9th plan; (ii) exploitation of vast hydroelectric potential at a faster pace by taking up for execution all the CEA cleared projects, and take steps to update and obtain clearances for pending DPRs in 10th plan; (iii) promoting small and mini hydel projects potential at a faster pace; (iv) strengthening the role of PSUs/SEBs for taking up new hydel projects such as multi-purpose, projects involving inter-State issues, projects for peaking power and those involving rehabilitation and resettlement; and (v) increasing private investment through joint ventures by providing required atmosphere, incentives and reliefs to stimulate and maintain a trend in this direction.

vii. J&K State Hydel Policy, 2003

In October 2003, J&K government brought out its Hydel Policy to encourage private sector participation in development of hydro projects. Under this policy, ten projects have been awarded to Independent Power Producers (IPPs), which are at various stages of implementation. In April 2008, the State government has approved an implementation framework for development of hydro power projects outlining the following modes of execution:

1. Execution of projects as purely state projects with 100% ownership by JKSPDCL.
2. Execution of large projects through Joint Venture of JKSPDCL with Central Public Sector Undertakings under Memorandum of Understanding (MoU) route.
3. Execution of projects through Public Private Partnership (PPP) mode in the form of Joint Venture of JKSPDCL with private sector for large projects and selection of JV partner through transparent process.
4. Execution of large projects through independent power producers (IPP) on Build, Own, Operate and Transfer (BOOT) basis through International competitive bidding (ICB).
5. Execution of small projects through IPP on BOOT basis through competitive bidding.

viii. J&K State Hydroelectric Projects Development Policy 2011

In order to give further impetus to exploitation of hydro potential, the state Government has decided to revise the State Hydel Policy of 2003 to fulfill the following objectives:

1. Expeditious development of available hydro power of the state.
2. Maximization of benefits to the state by meeting its power requirements and giving a fillip to economic growth.
3. Provide employment opportunities to the people of the state.
4. Develop hydro power projects in an environmentally-friendly manner with minimum dislocation of project affected people.
5. Provide for creation of social and development through private sector participation by removing the implementation related difficulties of IPPs.
6. To accelerate the pace of hydro power development through private sector participation by removing the implementation related difficulties of IPPs.
7. To bring in the investment and associated efficiency from the private sector.

Accordingly, the State government has decided to announce this policy called the "J&K State Hydroelectric Projects Development Policy 2011", which replaces earlier Policy of 2003. Implementation of projects shall be governed by IWT 1960 signed between India and Pakistan and therefore have to be cleared from IWT angle. The policy provides for free power to J&K subject to a minimum of 15% throughout the project confession period, apart from 1% for local area development fund (LADF). IPP shall, after allowing for J&K's share of power including free power, be free to sell the balance power as it deems fit, within or outside the state. In case of sale to the state, it supply shall be metered at inter-connection point. In respect of projects up to 25 MW, J&K shall procure 30% power as per the tariff determined by the regulator. In respect of projects above 25 MW, J&K shall procure quantum of power as indicated in the bid document at the tariff determined through competitive bidding process.

ix. Policy for Development of Micro/Mini Hydro Power Projects

In August 2009, the J&K government had announced 'Policy for the development of Micro/Mini Hydro Power through SHP Projects of capacity upto 2MW. J&K government has endowed J&K Energy Development Agency (JAKEDA) with the mandate to implement all Micro / Mini Hydel projects up to 2 MW station capacity. The main objective of this policy is to attract investors for the development of the state's water resources in an environment friendly manner to provide a solution to the energy problems in remote and hilly areas where extension of grid system is un-economical or un-viable. This will also help in generating revenue for the state and provide employment avenues, in addition to the all round development of the region.

Under the policy, JAKEDA shall invite any agency to bid for identified projects for the development of this sector. These will be termed as IPP and would include any of the private sector entities, central power utilities, state governments or any other government entities and their joint ventures. Only permanent residents of J&K will be entitled to bid and create Mini/Micro Hydel Projects upto 200 kw station capacities. This condition shall, however, be relaxed, in case the bidding process of the projects so reserved does not result in adequate and competitive response and in such cases the projects will be open for all citizens of India.

The IPP shall, after availing for the royalty in the form of free power to the tune of 12% be free to sell the power to the state. In case of sale to the state, this shall be at the tariff to be determined by the JKSERC. This shall be metered at interconnection point. For sale of power to any third party within or outside the state, the IPP shall be required to pay the open access charges, T&D losses as per the regulations of the regulator.

There are several incentives to the power developers. No entry tax will be levied by the State government on power generation/transmission equipment and building material used for MHPs. The government land if required, for power projects shall be allotted on lease for 40 years @ premium of 1 per sq.m. However, in case of non availability of government land, the land required shall be acquired nodal agencies and leased out to the IPP. Mortgage deed in favour of the financing institutions required to be signed by the promoters shall be exempted from payment of stamp duty. The State government has already enabled equitable mortgage in the state. Exemption from court fee for registration of documents relating to lease of land will be granted to the IPPs. 3% interest subsidy shall be payable on the working capital facilities available from the commercial banks to IPPs for a period of 5 years initially from the date of allotment and to be reviewed after 5 years. 10% subsidy on capital investment subject to the ceiling of 60.00 lakhs shall be given in addition to the central subsidy for the power projects from 1 MW to 2MW after successful installation & commissioning of the project. Royalty @ 12% shall be charged after the period of 10 years from the date of commissioning of the Hydel Projects up to 2MW capacity. IPP will be eligible for central financial assistance as per the standing guidelines of the Ministry of New and Renewable Energy, Government of India.

The policy provides various benefits to the state. The state shall avail free power @12% of generation as royalty. IPP shall deposit upfront premium with minimum threshold slab of 50000 per MW for projects upto 1 MW and 1,00,000 per MW for projects from 1-2 MW to the Nodal Agencies within one month from the date of allotment of the site.

x. J&K Water Resources (Regulation and Management) Act, 2010

J&K Water Resources (Regulation and Management) Act, 2010 aims to consolidate the law relating to use of water, the measurement, construction, control and management of works with respect to water storage, conservation and protection, the irrigation, water supply, drainage, flood control and prevention, the improvement in the flow of water, the protection and improvement in the physical integrity of water courses, lakes and springs, the safety and surveillance of dams, the establishment of the State Water Resources Regulatory Authority (SWRRA) for regulating water resources, ensuring judicious, equitable and sustainable management, allocation and utilization of water resources, fixing the rates for use of water and matters connected therewith or incidental thereto.

The act provides that no person, group of persons, government department, local authority, corporation, company, society or any other body, by whatever name called (hereinafter called 'the user'), shall install a unit requiring usage of water of any water source except under a licence issued by the licensing authority. Any user intending to install a unit requiring usage of water for the purpose of generation of electricity shall prepare scheme and submit to the Authority accompanied by such fee and service charges as may be fixed by the Authority for approval. The said scheme shall specifically indicate the location of the unit; the source of water to be used; the purpose for which this unit is to be installed; the type of the unit whether domestic, commercial, industrial or for trading purposes; the quantity of water required for such unit; and the period for which the water is required.

In case of a scheme relating to use of water for generation of electricity, the Government may, on receipt of the recommendations from the Authority, take a decision either approving the scheme with or without modifications or rejecting the same: Provided that no order shall be passed under this sub-section without the agreement of the Power Development Department (PDD) and in case there is no such agreement, the scheme shall be submitted for orders of the Cabinet whose decision shall be final and binding. After the scheme is approved by the Authority under sub-section (2) of section 92 or by the government under subsection (4) of section 92, the Authority shall inform the user accordingly and require him to (a) obtain a licence for use of water under section 96; (b) execute an agreement in such form and manner with the prescribed authority as may be prescribed; and (c) pay such fee and water usage charges as fixed. No user shall install a unit requiring usage of water without adhering to the requirements of section 97. The Authority shall fix the minimum and maximum ceiling of water to be allocated to a user for generation of electricity (hydro-electric project) and construction of dams on any water source.

The Authority shall determine and fix the charges for supply of water to, or use of water by, a licensee. The water usage charges fixed under sub-section (1) shall be reviewed by the Authority after every three years. The prescribed authority shall recover water user charges as per the rates fixed by the Authority from every user or licensee whenever water is supplied or made available or used by a licensee for generation of electricity.

III. Initiatives for Hydro-Power Development in India

India has increased installed power capacity from 1362 MW to over 100,000 MW covering electrification of more than 500,000 villages during last more than six decades. However, the annual per capita consumption is nearly 350 kWh. Large number of rural households has no access to electricity. India has vast geographical area, growing population, and increasing energy needs. However, country is not endowed with large primary energy reserves. In India, coal based power generation dominates the total installed capacity (52%), followed by hydro (25%) and natural gas (10%). The distribution of primary commercial energy resources is quite skewed. Coal is abundant and concentrated mostly in the eastern region (nearly 70% of the total coal reserves). Western region has over 70% of the hydrocarbons reserves of India. More than 70% of the total hydro-potential is located in north and the north eastern regions. Southern region has small coal reserves (6%) and hydro-potential (10%) with of most lignite deposits.

In India, the share of hydro-capacity in total power generating capacity has declined from 34% in 6th Plan to 25% in 9th Plan. By the end of 11th Plan, the hydro-capacity of 26% was envisaged if the targeted capacity addition is achieved. In 2003, a 50000 MW hydro-initiative was launched for accelerated hydro-development and Preliminary Feasibility Reports of 162 projects for 48000 MW power were prepared. Of them, 77 projects with total capacity of 37000 MW were selected for execution, for which the first-year tariff was expected to be less than 2.50 per unit. The tariff level in all the cases is less than 2.00 per kilowatt-hour. Tariff calculations are made at bus bar accounting for evacuation costs of transmission up to the grid pooling stations. Tariff calculations are done using a debt equity ratio of 70:30, interest at 10%, depreciation by straight line method, interest on working capital at 10%, and return on equity at 16% (See Rao, 2006). Tariff calculations were based on CERC tariff notifications prevalent at that time.

During 11th Plan, a capacity addition of 16553 MW has been earmarked and in 12th Plan projects totaling to a capacity of 30000 MW have been identified. Therefore, the effect of 50000 MW initiatives would be visible in the 12th Plan period. However, geological uncertainty, contract management, resettlement and rehabilitation, delay in land acquisition and infrastructure development have been the main reasons for time and cost over-runs in hydro-projects, which needs to be tackled in order to avoid delays in project implementation.

Power sector has a central role in hindering India's competitive cost advantage. Industrial power tariffs are probably the highest among major market peers, which put India at a significant disadvantage position. Power sector has implications for the division of roles, finances and fiscal transfers between the Centre and States. A significant aspect of this sharing includes: sale of power to states by central generators like National Thermal Power Corporation (NTPC) and NHPC. By 2000-01, the unpaid dues (including interest and penalties) of SEBs had reached 415 billion - about 2% of gross domestic product (GDP). Only a debt securitisation package by the Central Government prevented the sector from a default crisis. About two-thirds of the bonds - worth 188 billion - are still outstanding (RBI, 2010). In an effort to obviate a repetition, a tripartite agreement was drawn up between the Central Government, State Governments and the Reserve Bank of India, involving conditionality covenants on sequestering Central Government transfers to States, whose SEBs had defaulted.

There are several channels of Centre-State relationships that manifest through the electricity sector. A deterioration of State finances implies an increasing appropriation of Central transfers meant for commercial operations. Since 2004, one of the big gains of the improving finances of the power distribution segment was a reduction in the need for subsidies. It has lowered States' fiscal deficits, boosted India's savings rate and improved India's credit rating. The irregular payments (defaults) by State government-owned distribution companies (discoms) have influenced the credit ratings of States.

Nearly 44% of rural households have been electrified in India. Six States namely, Punjab, Haryana, Goa, Sikkim, Himachal Pradesh and Jammu and Kashmir have electrified more than 75% of their households. In 2004, the Government of India has launched an ambitious flagship programme called "Rajiv Gandhi Grameen Vidyutikaran Yojana (RGGVY)". Under RGGVY, the government provides 90% of project cost as subsidy for mainly free electricity connections in hitherto non-electrified villages to below poverty line (BPL) households. The government has sanctioned huge sum as capital subsidy for the scheme to provide electricity at below the average cost of supply and the financial implications for state-owned discoms are adverse (See Bhattacharya and Patel, 2008; Patel, 2008).

In 2009-10, power sector in India witnessed capacity addition of 9.6 GW (much of thermal), the highest ever in a single year. In 2010-11, the sector intends to add even more. Nearly 60 GW was added over the 11th Plan period (ending 2011-12). However, it is wrong to say that the power shortages are about to disappear. The peak load deficit was 9.4% during April-October 2010. Over the period, the quality of service has been dramatically altered for the better. At the same time, there is an increasing concern on the deteriorating financial position of State controlled utilities.

There are several "forces" catalysing the relatively upbeat outlook of the power sector. Regulated rate of return on equity on power generation assets has been enhanced from 14% to 15.5% in early 2009. The share of private sector in capacity addition was over 40% compared to 10-15% earlier. There has been an increased exposure of the power sector to market forces. The share of power traded to total power generated has risen to 8%, including bilateral deals and Unscheduled Interchange (UI) trades. Spot power prices have gone up significantly, after declining to a low of 3.39/unit in October 2009 - February 2010, currently a unit costs 5.83 on average.

In 2009-10, total volume of energy approved for open access across States was estimated at 39,000 million units (MUs), which was more than about a quarter from 2008-09. Open access in distribution has been implemented for 7.5 GW, with almost three quarters of this in one State - Gujarat (GoI, 2010a). Power distribution reforms are taking place across States of India on experiment basis. It is being taken as precursor for widespread changes in this key cash-generating segment of the power sector (See Electrical Monitor, 2010; Prayas, 2009). Recently, there have been no reports of defaults by State government-owned utilities to their suppliers. There has also been little evidence of funding constraints (equity and debt) for independent power producers (IPPs).

Aggregate technical and commercial (ATC) losses, although lower than in the past, are not declining fast enough. The scale of commercial losses, 400 billion in 2009-10 was described as "unsustainable" (GoI, 2010b). In early 2010, the losses of state-level T&D utilities at current (2008) tariff levels were projected to increase by 70% from 686 billion in 2010-11 to 1.2 trillion for 2014-15 (GoI, 2010c). Between 2007-08 and 2008-09, the gap between per unit cost of supply and average revenue realized (after accounting for subsidy paid) jumped from 0.35 to 0.60 (PFC, 2010). Technical and commercial losses are more than 40% of electricity produced and reducing these losses to 15% will generate additional revenues of US$ 4.4 billion per year.

There is widespread difference in performance between States. There has been deterioration in the sector's overall financials, with losses doubling to 526 billion in 2008-09 in a couple of years. After relative tranquility, financial losses as proportion of GDP are back to 2002-03 levels. Reduction in ATC loss has not declined much below 30% after a peak of nearly 39% in 2002-03. It is instructive that electricity distribution losses in China are about 6.5%. Aggregate subsidy received from State governments is a fraction of losses and currently lower than in the early 1990s. For some governments, subsidy payments are already acutely felt in their fiscal accounts, as proportion of their respective gross state domestic product (GSDP) in 2009-10, including Punjab (1.9%), Haryana (1.4%), Jharkhand (1.3%), and Kerala, Karnataka, Madhya Pradesh and Rajasthan (nearly 1%). States of Uttar Pradesh, Bihar and Tamil Nadu make subsidy payments at an estimated 0.5% of GSDP. Six governments in 2008-09 and 2009-10, including of large States like Maharashtra (significant losses) and West Bengal (profitable), have not made any subsidy payments to their respective utilities (GoI, 2010b). In some States, fiscal situation will go off the rails due to plunging power sector financials. Keeping this in view, in August of 2010, the Prime Minister constituted a High Level Panel to assess the financial position of state-level electricity utilities, project losses up to 2017, and suggest "corrective measures."

Financial exposure and opportunity cost of State governments to the power sector is considerable (GoI, 2010c). Of the total outstanding guarantees provided by State governments of 1.7 trillion (about 3.5%

of GDP), just over 50% has been extended to power sector utilities (RBI, 2010) The guarantees are primarily on account of governments not in a position to provide budgetary support for investments. Equity investments made in State utilities by respective governments amounted to 713 billion (end-March 2008) and the aggregate return on equity has been deeply negative. There is also considerable debt financing of power utilities by State governments (707 billion), but interest on this is usually adjusted against subsidy and subventions, and is rarely paid for in cash.

The deterioration in the financial conditions of distribution utilities has been fairly steady after 2005-06 and particularly sharply in 2008-09. "Losses with subsidy received" have grown at a compounded average growth rate (CAGR) of 37% during 2005-06 to 2008-09, compared to 15% for India's nominal GDP over the same period and only 9% (in volume terms) for electricity units sold. The primary cause for deterioration was plainly an increase in the cost of power procurement. Power procurement costs account for the largest share of total costs (close to half the total costs), and almost across the board, with few exceptions, power procurement costs have risen by 8-35% over 2007-08.

There has been apparent distortion in the composition of electricity consumption. The share of electricity supply to agriculture in many states is high but the sector's contribution to revenue is not nearly proportional. For instance, in Haryana the share of agriculture is 36%, but contribution to revenue is only 4%. Therefore, it would be unfair to blame solely to the utilities, given the State government (politically) supported mandate to supply designated consumer classes with "affordable" electricity tariffs. Subsidy per unit sold had increased from 0.45 to 0.54 over 2005-06 to 2007-08, before the problems associated with the sharp growth slowdown in 2008-09 post the financial crisis. State-owned distributors are tiding over cash shortfalls by borrowing. For instance, in March 2010, Rajasthan had short-term borrowings of around 145 billion and Uttar Pradesh of around 350 billion (Livemint, 2011).

All the power regions of India have been facing widespread power shortages. Situation in the north India is also further constrained by the inadequacies in transmission, sub-transmission and distribution. In 2004, total installed hydro-capacity was 30,935 MW (26% of national hydro-potential capacity, well below the desirable optimum level of 40%). Central sector contribution to this total was 6,053 MW (19.6%). North India power regions contribute about 10775 MW of the total hydro-capacity.

Regional level of hydro-potential development (including schemes cleared by the Central Electricity Authority (CEA) is expected to be 31% in Northern, 63.71% in Western, 61.26% Southern and 40.5% in Eastern power regions. The unexploited hydro-potential in the Northern power region is substantial (69%). The emerging power supply situation indicates that it may be adequate only for meeting the growing power demands within north India. The draft National Power Plan notified by the CEA in November 2004 covers the 11th Plan (2007-2012) and indicative 12th Plan (2012-2017). Total capacity additions required has been assessed as 61,000 MW and 69,500 MW in 11th Plan and 12th Plan respectively. The hydro component is 22,420 MW and 34,500 MW, which constitutes about 37% and 50% respectively of the proposed capacity additions. The National Power Plan studies indicate that at the end of the 11th Plan, even with a large hydro programme, the Northern power region would be a net importer of power. The hydro resource and power development scenario indicates the need for early development of the Northern Region's hydro potential in order to help meet the future electricity needs of the country.

Large-scale development of hydro-power potential the north India finds justification in the context of the overall power demand in the country. It is also essential to consider and identify avenues for utilization of electricity in the north region. The long term (2016-2017) projections of power demand in India indicate that regional distribution of demand for power would be more or less at the current levels. Special efforts are therefore needed to encourage the growth of demand for power in the northern region. Such an increase in demand would create employment opportunities and economic activity, which would be beneficial to the region. Industrial and agricultural development and total electrification of villages and homes should also form part of this power sector development plan. The subsequent improvement in their personal well-being would enable the inhabitants of the region to view the development of hydro- resources as a venture bringing regional benefit, not merely for export and the benefit of others outside the region. There are also numerous concerns in hydropower development dams in a region. Dams have made an important and significant contribution to human development, and benefits derived from them have been considerable. However, a lack of equity in the distribution of benefits has called into question the value of many dams in meeting water and energy development needs when compared with the alternatives (World Commission on Dams, 2000).

In J&K, there is immense potential for commercial hydro-power generation, which has not been exploited fully due to the restrictions imposed by the IWT, high capital costs, difficult terrain and scarcity of resources. J&K had an installed power capacity of 2,263.6 MW consisting of 1,093.3 MW of State share and 1,170.3 MW of Central share. Upcoming power projects in J&K include five State sector power projects of 453.61 MW and four Central sector power projects of 449 MW. Power sector is suffering from huge revenue losses, structural supply demand gaps, weak infrastructure and high T&D losses. Besides, there is a gross mismatch between load profile and hydro-thermal mix available to J&K. During winter, power demand peaks in the State. At the same time, energy generation falls, which is mainly hydro-power. Thus, there is heavy dependence on Central sector power, which is also in-sufficient to meet winter power requirements of the State.

IV. Review of NHPC Power Projects

Currently, NHPC is engaged in the construction of 10 power projects with total installed capacity of 4502 MW. During 10th Plan, NHPC has added 1970 MW and planned to add another 2230 MW in 11th Plan period. About 12 projects of 9651 MW are awaiting clearances/ approval for their implementation. Detailed project reports are being prepared for 7 projects of 2485 MW. In 2010-11, NHPC has achieved highest ever net profit after tax of 2166.67 crore which is 3.64% higher than the net profit after tax of 2090.50 crore earned during 2009-10. NHPC has registered sales turnover of 4046.59 crore as against 4153.21 crore of 2009-10 (See Annual Report, NHPC, 2010-11).

In 2009-10, sales included an arrear of 844.14 crore. It has achieved 100% sales realization against 97% achieved in 2009-10 and generated 18604 MUs against the target of 18000 MU for "Excellent" MoU rating. In 2010-11, NHPC has achieved 85.2% plant availability factor (PAF) for the operating power stations against the memorandum of understanding (MoU) target of 79.9% for "Excellent" rating. In 2010-11, NHPC has commissioned 120 MW Sewa-II power station in J&K. NHPC signed promoters agreement with J&K State Power Development Corporation (JKSPDC) for formation of Joint Venture Company (JVC) for execution of Pakal Dul and other hydroelectric projects with an aggregate installed capacity of about 2100 MW in Chenab river basin of J&K. In 2010-11, NHPC has also signed agreement with Mangdechhu Hydropower Authority (MHA), Bhutan for providing engineering and design consultancy services to 720 MW Mangdechhu Hydroelectric Project in Bhutan, obtained concurrence of CEA for 520 MW Teesta-IV HE project in Sikkim, submitted revised detailed project reports (DPRs) for Tawang-I with modified installed capacity of 600 MW and Tawang-II with modified installed capacity of 800 MW to CEA, obtained Wild Life Clearance for 1000 MW Pakal Dul HE project in J&K, and received in-principle forest clearance issued by the Ministry of Environment and Forests (MOEF) for 66 MW Loktak Downstream Hydroelectric (HE) project.

NHPC has also initiated the process to develop wind power of 8-10 MW near Salal power station in Bidda, J&K, created an online Project Monitoring Centre at Corporate Office to support video conferencing, live video feeds from cameras installed at strategic location of construction projects, and stablished facilities for online web casting for live broadcasting of important event/announcement/briefing by senior management for all location across the organization in 2010-11. Nearly, 98.5% of the employees relating to operation and maintenance of power stations were trained during 2010-11 against the MoU target of 85%. NHPC has also organized training programme on operation and maintenance for hydropower station for the participants from African Countries in 2010-11. NHPC has also electrified 2667 villages and provided service connections to 7.48 lakh below people line (BPL) households under RGGVY.

NHPC generating stations feed power at the Busbar of power stations to the concerned regional grids. The power is transmitted to 28 beneficiaries (bulk power consumers) through transmission system. This is owned and operated by Power Grid Corporation of India (PGCI) and SEBs in respective regions. Regional Power Committees (RPCs) and Regional Load Dispatch Centres (RLDCs) are apex bodies for integrated operation of power system and proper control and management of Grid. These apex bodies manage transfer of power to respective beneficiaries. Energy available for sale from generating stations is billed to bulk power customers. This is done as per Regional Energy Accounts (REA) issued by respective RPCs based on allocation of power from generating stations to bulk power consumers as per instructions/allocation given by Ministry of Power from time to time. The terms and conditions of sale of energy by NHPC are governed by Bulk Power Supply Agreements/Power Purchase Agreements signed/ being signed by NHPC with the beneficiary States/Bulk Power Consumers.

Each operating power station of NHPC has a station-wise tariff determined by CERC based on Tariff Regulations issued from time to time. CERC determines tariff i.e. Annual Fixed Charges (AFCs) for each station in accordance with tariff regulations applicable for that tariff period. CERC has approved final tariff of Bairasiul, Loktak, Salal, Tanakpur, Chamera-I, Uri, Rangit, Chamera-II, Dhauliganga, Dulhasti and Teesta-V power stations for the period April 2004 to March 2009. The same tariff is approved by CERC for April 2009 to March 2014. CERC has notified CERC (Terms and Conditions of Tariff) Regulations, 2009 on 19 January 2009. It is applicable for a period of 5 years from 01 April 2009 unless reviewed earlier or extended by commission. These regulations also provide that generating companies shall continue to provisionally bill the beneficiaries with tariff applicable as on ending March 2009 till approval of tariff by the CERC in accordance with the Tariff Regulations, 2009. CERC has approved generation tariff of Sewa-II, Dhauliganga, Tanakpur, Dulhasti, Loktak, Bairasiul, Uri, Salal and Chamera-I Power Stations for the period 2009-14 based on the CERC (Terms and Conditions of Tariff) Regulations, 2009.

The tariff (AFC) to be determined by CERC for 2009-14 is to be recovered as capacity charges and energy charges in ratio 50:50 on monthly basis as per provisions of CERC (Terms and Conditions of Tariff) Regulations, 2009. The components of tariff (AFC) are return on equity, interest on loan capital, depreciation, interest on working capital and operation & maintenance (O&M) expenses. Availability based tariff as ordered by CERC has been implemented from 01 July 2002 in western region, 01 December 2002 in northern region, 01 January 2003 in southern region, 01 April 2003 in eastern region and 01 November 2003 north-eastern region.

The Bulk Power Customers of NHPC in North India are power utilities belonging to Haryana, Punjab, Himachal Pradesh, Uttar Pradesh, Uttarkhand, Rajasthan, Delhi and Jammu and Kashmir and Union Territory of Chandigarh. These States are being supplied power from Salal-I and II, Tanakpur, Chamera-I, Chamera-II, Uri, Dhauliganga and Dulhasti Power Stations. Baira Siul Power Station is being supplying power to Punjab, Haryana and Delhi only. In Eastern Region, Rangit and Teesta-V Power Stations are supplying energy to West Bengal, Sikkim, Bihar, Jharkhand, Gridco and Damodar Valley Corporation. In North-Eastern Region, Loktak Power Station is supplying energy to Assam, Manipur, Meghalaya, Tripura, Nagaland, Arunachal Pradesh and Mizoram. Since commencing of commercial generation in 1982, the energy sales and revenues of NHPC have grown significantly. Energy sales from all operating projects of NHPC have risen from 229 million in 1982-83 to 40466 million in 2010-2011.

NHPC has adopted a monthly billing cycle based on Regional Energy Accounts (REAs) issued by respective RPCs based on data provided by RLDC. Billing is done centrally at Corporate Office on monthly basis in accordance with CERC Tariff Regulations 2009 in vogue and as per tariff notification issued by CERC for that particular power station from time to time. Payments are received through confirmed, revolving, irrevocable "Letters of Credit" opened by beneficiaries in favour of NHPC and also directly through transfer to NHPC account/through Demand Draft/Cheques. Operation of receipt of payments through letters of credit from beneficiaries, adopting NHPC rebate scheme and with persistent follow up with them by Commercial

Division, 100% realization of current dues has been achieved in 2010-11. A surcharge @ 1.25% per month is levied if the payments are not made by beneficiaries beyond a period of 60 days from date of billing as per CERC Tariff Regulation 2009.

V. Hydro-Power Development in North Indian States

NHPC is India's largest hydropower producer. The hydropower plants of the NHPC are mainly based in north and north-east India. Nearly 70.6% of the installed capacity is in these regions. The higher capacity index enables the NHPC to earn incentives. NHPC had completed Chamera –II, Dhauliganga – I, Indira Sagar and Omkareshwar projects ahead of the schedule. NHPC sells its entire power to the SEBs under the long term PPAs. About 12% of the generation is sold as free power to the SEBs in the respective States in which the plants are located. The power is sold as per the CERC guidelines for the determination of tariff which ensures 15.5% ROE on its total regulatory capital.

i. Power Supply in North India

In India, total ex-bus energy availability has increased by 5.6% in 2010-11, over the previous year. The peak met increased has by 6.0%. The shortage conditions prevailed both in terms of energy and peaking availability. Energy requirement registered a growth of 3.7% in 2010-11 against projected growth of 5.6% and peak demand registered a growth of 2.6% against the projected growth of 6.5%.

All the regions continued to experience energy and peak power shortage of varying magnitude. There were also short-term surpluses depending on the season or time of day. The surplus power was sold to deficit States or consumers either through bilateral contracts, power exchanges or traders. Energy shortage varied from 4.3% in the eastern region to 13.3% in the western region in 2010-11. Northern and north-eastern regions have experienced energy shortage of 8% and 8.8% respectively (See Central Electricity Authority, LGBR: 2011-12).

The forecast of energy requirement, energy availability, peak demand and peak met in the northern region were quite close to the actual in 2010-11. Actual energy requirement and peak demand were lower by 4.5% and 6.4% respectively. Actual energy availability and peak met were higher by 0.2% and 2.7% respectively than the forecast. Actual energy shortage was 8.0% as compared to forecast of 12.4%. Actual peak demand of the northern region was less than the anticipated due to heavy rainfall in the region resulting in lower demand of irrigation pumping.

Annual power supply position in terms of energy requirement vis-a-vis energy availability of north Indian States in 2010-11 reveals that Chandigarh, Delhi and Rajasthan faced negligible energy shortage, whereas Himachal Pradesh, Haryana, Punjab and Uttarakhand experienced energy shortages of 3-6%. Energy shortage in Uttar Pradesh was 15%. Maximum energy shortage was at 25% in J&K.

There was no energy shortage in Chandigarh against a forecasted shortage of 9.1%. Delhi had marginal shortage against projected surplus of 36.3%. Haryana had energy shortage of 5.6% which is lower than the forecasted 24.5% due to lower energy requirement and higher energy availability as compared to the forecast. Actual energy shortage in Himachal Pradesh was 3.4% as against anticipated energy surplus of 15.9% due to sale of power to other parts of the country. Actual shortage in J&K was 25.0% against anticipated shortage of 21.5% due to lower energy availability than anticipated. In case of Punjab, actual energy shortage was 6.0% against a forecast of 14.4% due to lower energy requirement. Rajasthan had marginal energy shortage of 0.9% against a forecast of 0.8%. Uttar Pradesh had energy shortage of 15.0% against a forecast of 28.4% due to lower requirement and higher availability than anticipated. Uttarakhand experienced a shortage of 6.0% against anticipated energy shortfall of 14.8% during 2010-11.

ii. Power Supply by NHPC

The performance of the hydropower plants of NHPC has been satisfactory with the achievement of 98% of the planned electricity generation in 2009-10. NHPC has major expansion plans over the next few years. It is expected to continue to maintain its leading position in the hydroelectric power segment. It has been proposed to maximize hydro capacity addition during 12th Plan (2012-17) for reducing CO2 emissions and energy security of the country. A shelf of 109 hydro electric schemes aggregating to 30,920 MW has been identified.

Even though the cost per MW in case of the projects located in J&K viz., Uri-II, Kishenganga, Nimmo Bazgo and Chutak are on the higher side, the overall cost of the capacity expansion is within the industry benchmarks of 5 Crore per MW which is satisfactory. The major contributor to this factor is the Subansiri (Lower) project in Assam of 2000 MW capacity which is being constructed at the per MW cost of only 3.1 Crore per MW. The ROE as per CERC guidelines has been revised to 15.5% (additional 0.5% for timely commissioning of the project) for 2009-2014 as against 14% for 2004-2009. The higher ROE entitlement would result in the better return to the company. NHPC has major capex plans over the next few years with capex being 4,008 Crore for 2010, 4,894 Crore for 2011 and 6,542 Crore for 2012. The total planned capex for the 12th Plan is 29,000 Crore. The huge capex corresponding with the huge capacity enhancement plans means that the eligible regulatory capital base of the company which is at present is about 8,500 Crore would continue to rise. Consequently, EPS is expected to register the CAGR of 20.4% over 2009-2013.

NHPC has also about 14,156 MW of capacity under various stages of development. Even though it is too early to gain growth visibility aided by these plants, the visibility may improve going forward as and when these projects achieve sanctions and clearances. The total installed capacity in hydro segment in January 2010 was 36,885 MW which is only 25% of the total potential capacity of 1,48,000 MW of the country. The share of hydropower in the total installed capacity has continued to decrease over the years on account of the high growth in the thermal based power capacity as compared to capacity addition in hydropower sector. Ideally, the mix between the hydro and thermal based power generation should be 40:60. However, in India, the capacity mix is heavily skewed in favour of thermal based capacity and the hydro segment contributing only 23.5% to the overall installed capacity in the country as against 66.6% by the thermal segment in 2010. During the 11th Plan, the total capacity addition target is 10,347 MW; out of which, 3,431 MW has been commissioned so far. For the 12th Plan the targeted addition is 30,000 MW out of which 3,431 MW is to be set up by NHPC.

NHPC has the highest operating margins among the major power sector players as it is into the hydropower segment which does not require any fuel expenses. However, the return ratios for the company are low vis-a-vis the other major players. The installation of the hydropower plants is subject to many environmental, regulatory as well as topographical hurdles. The plants of NHPC have also in past faced the delays of up to 8 to 10 months on account of these factors. However, any substantial delay beyond the estimates may adversely impact the valuations. The improvement in the allowable ROE to 15.5% from 14% has been the positive development for the company. However, any adverse regulatory changes may impact the profitability of the company.

iii. Hydro-Power Development in J&K

The development of hydro potential in J&K is expected to usher in huge economic benefits in the form of infrastructure development, industrialization and employment generation. With increase in hydropower generation and improved efficiency in T&D of electricity, the State aims to provide energy at affordable cost for industrial development and also become a net exporter of energy. Availability of electricity at competitive rates will also help improve the growth of basic infrastructure of the economy and better quality of life of the masses.

In J&K, power projects of 2 MW and above is the responsibility of JKPDCL. The T&D is vested to J&K Power Development Department (JKPDD). JKPDCL was carved out of JKPDD in 1989 and incorporated as a company in 1995 with the mandate to plan, execute, operate and maintain all generating stations including such stations that existed at the time of creation of the Corporation. The installed capacity of 21 operational power houses of JKPDCL is 929.70 MW comprising of 754.70 MW of hydro power stations with the largest being 450 MW Baglihar HEP Stage I and 175 MW of Gas turbines. In addition, installed capacity of the projects under operation with NHPC is 1680 MW from which free power to the extent of 12% of the installed capacity is available to the State.

At present the unrestricted demand in the State is 2425 MW, while suppressed demand is 1492 MW with scheduled curtailment. Thus, there is deficit of 933 MW against the restricted demand. However, this deficit does not capture the grim situation adequately. The peak demand in the harsh winter conditions surges up and that is precisely the period when generation from hydro stations dwindles substantially due to lean discharge in the rivers. Consequently the State has to rely mainly on the allocation from Central Power Stations. J&K is often forced to withdraw from the grid, attracting UI and panel rates. Due to purchase of considerable amounts of power from the northern grid and overdrawals under UI regime, the State suffers substantial drain of its resources on this account. Harnessing of available hydro-potential, shall, therefore, automatically result in improving of power situation in the state.

The demand pattern in the State comprises 35% domestic and 65% non-domestic consumption. On per capita basis, the State consumes 750 units compared to 872 units in Himachal Pradesh, 706 units in Uttarakhand, 1506 units in Punjab, 1208 units in Haryana and 671 units national average. Going by the projected growth pattern, the power demand in the state is estimated to be about 2600 MW in 2012-13 and about 5500 MW in 2025-26.

J&K government has approved Hydroelectric Project Development Policy 2011 to harness State's huge hydropower potential of 20,000 MW of power. Under the policy, Government has approved a multi-pronged strategy for setting up the power projects purely as State projects, through the joint venture mechanism in public-private partnership (PPP) mode and on Built, Own Operate and transfer (BOOT) basis. A roadmap has been drawn up for generating around 6000 MW of power during next 10 years in J&K. Three projects with a total capacity of 329 MW were expected to be commissioned in the State during 2011-12.

The power projects being executed in the State are the 2120 MW Pakadul, Kiru and Kawar projects as joint venture with NHPC and

PTC. The JVC has been incorporated and it has started functioning. The 820 MW Rattle project allotted to one IPP through international tariff based bidding on fast track, is likely to be commissioned in 2017. With a view to overcome the operational inefficiencies leading to high AT&C losses, the State government has engaged a national reputed consultancy M/S Energy and Resources Institute, New Delhi for preparing a blue print for bringing about a 'Turn Around' in the power sector. The State government has initiated multi-pronged action for implementation of the recommendations of the consultancy. J&K government has enacted its own Electricity Act 2010 and Conservation Energy Act 2011 on the lines of Central Electricity Act for bringing about reforms in the power sector besides to address the demand side management issues of the power sector. The State Electricity Regulatory Commission (SERC) has been made fully functional to ensure metering of all connections and recovery of revenue for power supplied at tariff and tariff petitions are being filed regularly before the commission.

In sum, there is tremendous hydro-power potential in J&K. Besides the IWT, the shortage of capital is the major constraints in tapping hydropower potential of the State. IWT put constraints on water storage on major rivers, thereby limiting the scope of hydropower generation. The topography of the State also adds to the problem of power deficiency in unreachable regions specifically during winter as operation and maintenance of transmission lines are un-economical in these areas. At the same time, J&K is facing acute power shortage. Up to 2007-2008, total production of electricity was 788.77 MW against the total peak requirement of about 2000 MW. Nearly 2000 villages/hamlets are without accessibility to electricity. Therefore, there is urgent need to tap and develop the hydropower potential to meet the unmet needs of electricity of small community living in difficult terrain and isolated locations. Micro/Mini Hydel projects may be built in isolated geographical regions with no electrical distribution network. There are numerous advantages of Micro/Mini Hydel projects such as minimal reservoirs and civil construction work, relatively low environmental impact and use of less capital. There is tremendous potential for generation of electricity using extensive network of canals and streams through Micro/Mini Hydel power projects in J&K.

VI. Hydro-Power Pricing in North Indian States

In India, the National Power Grid (NPG) system has been evolved to facilitate free flow of power across regional boundaries. NPG has been responsible to meet the short fall of deficit regions from a surplus region. It has also been used for evacuation of power from project(s) located in one region to the beneficiaries located in other region(s). It has also facilitated trading of electricity among buyers and sellers in various regions across the country. NPG has been developed in phased manner. All the regional grids have already been interconnected. Total transmission capacity of inter-regional transmission system was 20750 MW in March 2010. Except southern region, all other four regions are inter-connected in synchronous mode and are operating in parallel. Total inter-regional transmission capacity was 5750 MW by the end of 9th Plan. During 10th Plan, a total of 8300 MW of inter-regional capacities have been added. Thus, total inter-regional transmission capacity was 14050 MW by the end of 10th Plan. During 11th Plan, inter-regional transmission systems of 18600 MW capacity have been planned. By the end of 11th Plan, total inter-regional transmission capacity of the NPG was increased to 32650 MW.

i. Cost, Losses and Dues Outstanding of Power Supply

In 2001-02, average cost of supply of electricity was 2.46 per unit. It decreased to 2.38 per unit in 2002-03. Thereafter, it gradually increased to 2.93 per unit in 2007-08. During 2001-02 to 2007-08, average realization from power sale has gradually increased from 1.81 to 2.39 per unit. Various power utilities in India have been suffering losses over the years without subsidy. Gap between average revenue realization and average cost of supply remained constantly high over the years. It has caused erosion in internal resources generation by the SEBs and led many of them to virtual bankruptcy. Level of commercial losses of the SEBs/utilities depended inter-alia on unaccounted energy losses, effective subsidies incurred towards sales to agriculture and domestic sectors, efforts to neutralize them through cross subsidization and level of subventions provided by State governments.

Gross subsidy on energy sales had been increasing over years due to supply of electricity to agriculture and domestic consumers at subsidized rates. As a result, SEBs have been unable to make full payments to Central Power Sector Utilities (CPSUs) for purchase of power. This has caused accumulation of huge outstanding amount to be paid by SEBs to CPSUs and adversely affected growth and performance of CPSUs. This deficit continues to rise and threaten the viability of the CPSUs. Poor creditworthiness of SEBs have also effectively blocked investments by private sector. Managerial and financial inefficiency in SEBs have also adversely affected capacity addition and system improvement programmes. During reforms process, the Expert Group constituted by the government recommended a scheme for one-time settlement of dues payable by the SEBs to CPSUs and Railways. Considerable progress has been made in the settlement of dues payable by SEBs to CPSUs and the Railways. CEA has been monitoring the status of the outstanding dues payable by SEBs to CPSUs. Total dues outstanding to various CPSUs by J&K stood at 99.56 Crores, of which 75.83 Crores was due to NHPC up to 2009-10.

ii. Composite Tariff of Hydropower

The composite tariff rate for Indira Sagar hydro station (8x 125=1000MW) of NHDC in 2006-07 was 2.10 per kWh. CERC had approved the provisional tariff @ 1.83 /kWh for Dauliganga HE station stage-I (4x70 MW) of NHPC upto 31.03.2007. Nathpa Jhakri HE Project (6x250 MW) of SJVNL was commissioned in May, 2004. CERC had approved the provisional tariff @ 2.35/kWh from 01.04.2004 to 31.03.2006. Two units of Dulhasti HE station (3x130 MW) of NHPC in J&K were synchronised in 2006-07. CERC approved the provisional tariff @ 3.00 /kWh from date of commercial operation of generating unit(s). In case of Tehri Stage-I, the power generated was being billed provisionally @ 3.50/kWh till the provisional tariff was approved by CERC. However, it was difficult to supply energy @ 3.50/kWh and that the rate of supply of energy was proposed to be 6/kWh, if the actual expenditure incurred till commissioning of the generating unit was taken into account.

CERC approved generation tariff of Bairasiul, Chamera stage -I, Chamera stage-II, Salal, Uri, Tanakpur, Rangit and Loktak hydropower stations of NHPC for the period 2004-09. Subsequently, NHPC filed review of CERC orders in respect of Bairasiul, Chamera stage -I, Salal, Uri, Tanakpur and Rangit hydropower stations. The composite tariff of hydro-stations of NHPC under purview of the CERC in 2008-09 was as high as 5.09 for Dulhasti in J&K followed by 2.67 for Chamera - II and 1.81 for Dhauliganga in H.P, 1.59 for Rangit and 1.50 for Teesta - V in Sikkim, 1.39 for Chamera – I in H.P, 1.28 for Loktak in Manipur, 1.22 for Uri - I in J&K, 1.20 for Tanakpur in Uttrakhand, 0.78 in Baira Sul in H.P and 0.66 for Salal in J&K. Thus, both the high and low tariffs of hydropower stations were reported from J&K. in 2009-10, the more or less the same picture remains with minor variations in tariff structure across the hydrostations of NHPC.

In 2009-10, the composite tariff of NHPC hydrostations under purview of the CERC was high at 6.01 for Dulhasti in J&K, 2.72 for Dhauliganga – I and 2.66 for Chamera – II in H.P, 2.17 for Loktak in Manipur, 2.00 for Uri – I in J&K, 1.89 for Tanakpur in Uttrakhand, 1.65 for Rangit and 1.62 for Teesta – V in Sikkim, 1.38 for Chamera – II and 1.25 for Baira Sul in H.P and the lowest for Salal in J&K at 0.66. Therefore, there has been an increase in composite tariff of all hydrostations at varied levels except Chamera – I and II in H.P, where there has been negligible decline in composite tariff by 0.01 and in case of Salal in J&K, the composite tariff remined at the same level.

iii. Power Transactions and Tariff

In all the power generating stations of NHPC except Loktak in Manipur and Dulhasti in J&K, the rate of sale of power per Kwh was higher than the corresponding composite tariff fixed by the CERC. This results in significant profits to the hydro-generating stations. The data further reveals that the composite tariff fixed by the CERC and the rate of sale of power per Kwh also varied by hydro generating stations of NHPC across States of India. Not only this, the rate of sale of power per Kwh by hydro generating stations of Uttar Pradesh Jal Vidyut Nigam Limited, Uttarakhand Jal Vidyut Nigam Limited, and Orrisa Hydro-power Corporation Limited were significantly more or less lower compared to the hydro generating stations of NHPC. In case of J&K, the difference between the rate of sale of power per Kwh by hydro generating stations of NHPC and the composite tariff fixed by the CERC stood at 0.16 for Uri, 0.09 for Salal and minus 1.63 for Dulhasti in 2008-09.

iv. Impact of Water Usage Charges on Power Cost

J&K Water Resources (Regulations and Management) Act, 2010 has resulted in increase in tariff of hydropower plants in J&K due to introduction of water usage charges. The Act further provides to establish SWRA whose function among other functions shall be to establish a water tariff system and fix water usage charges for use of water on account of generation of electricity also. Levy of water usage charges will have substantial impact on tariff of the all operating hydropower stations located in J&K and small impact on tariff of thermal power stations. Though the exact financial implications shall be known after the usage tariff is notified by the authority established under this Act, anticipated hike already calculated by NHPC is 25 paise per cu meter.

In case of the existing hydropower plants, the tariff per unit without water charges was 0.66, 1.70, 5.12, and 4.78 for hydro generating stations of Salal, Uri, Dulhasti and Sewa II respectively, which has been increased to 1.89, 2.20, 5.70, and 5.00 per unit due to water charges levied under J&K Water Resources (Regulations and Management) Act, 2010. Therefore, there has been significant impact on tariff of NHPC hydro generating stations in J&K. As a result, the power purchase cost has increased increased to 429.54 Crore with water usage charges compared to 298.54 Crore without water usage charges, thereby increasing the net power purchase cost to the tune of 131.00 Crore (an increase of 43.88%).

There has been recovery of 317.38 Crore from JKPDD due to implementation of water usage charges on existing Hydro plants in J&K after enactment of J&K Water Resources (Regulations and Management) Act, 2010. These charges have created unnecessary burden on JKPDD, which will be ultimately passed on to the consumers. Therefore, the State Government should remove these charges from ARR, so that less power tariff hike may be possible.

In case of upcoming hydroplants in J&K, the tariff per unit without water charges of 7.02, 6.93, and 3.25 for Nimmo Bazgo, Chutak and

Uri II respectively will increase to 10.25, 8.66, and 4.02 respectively with water charges of 3.23, 1.73, and 0.77 per unit due to J&K Water Resources (Regulations and Management) Act, 2010. This will result in net increase in power purchase cost to the tune of 176.44 crores. The anticipated increase in average per unit power purchase cost of the hydro plants due to implementation of water usage charge in J&K has been analyzed in this paragraph. Hydroplants accounts for almost 50% of the total power purchase by JKPDD. On an average, there has been increase of 81 paise/unit in power purchase cost from existing hydroplants in J&K due to imposition of water usage charges. This will put an additional burden of 186.78 Crore on JKPDD from hydel sources located in J&K as the power cost with water usage charges will be 815.60 Crore against the power cost of 628.82 Crore without water usage charges.

The CERC has approved the cost of power purchased from JKSPDC based on the tariff approved for 2011-12 at 592.25 Crore. The approved per unit cost of power and total cost of power purchase from JKSPDC stations for 2011-12 has been analyzed as under. The total power purchase cost from NHPC was approved at 359.26 Crore with per unit average cost of 1.33, whereas the power purchase cost from hydel stations of JKSPDC was approved at 592.25 Crore with per unit cost of 2.11 in 2011-12. In case of Baglihar hydel station, the power purchase cost was approved at 438.40 Crore with per unit cost of 3.51. Therefore, the per unit cost of power from non-NHPC hydel stations was comparatively higher than NHPC run hydel stations in J&K. In case of other non-NHPC hydel stations also the per unit power cost was higher than the average of NHPC hydel stations. For instance, the per unit power cost was approved at 5.89 (Pahalgam) followed by 5.25 (Marpachoo), 5.09 (Haftal), 4.97 (Igo-Mercellong), 2.89 (Sewa III), 2.14 (Chenani – III), 1.70 (Bhaderwah), and 1.69 (Bazgo).

A comparative power pricing scenario for thermal, hydro and nuclear power per unit of energy and NHPC and non-NHPC power stations have been presented in this paragraph for the year 2011-12. The approved per unit power purchase cost of NHPC was 1.33 against 2.69 for NTPC, other hydel stations at 2.41, and nuclear power at 2.20 per unit of energy. In case of hydel stations run by NHPC, the approved power purchase cost was as high as 5.96 for Dulhasti followed by Sewa II (5.48), Chamera II (2.86), Dhauliganga (2.81), Tanakpur (2.08), Chamera I (1.99), Uri (1.46), and Salal (0.94). The per unit power purchase cost was approved at 2.41 for other hydel stations. Therefore, it is clear that the approved power purchase cost of NHPC run hydel stations was comapartively low in J&K than in other north Indian States, except Sewa II. Even for the other non-NHPC hydel stations outside J&K, the approved power purchase cost stood at 3.71 (PTC – BHEP), followed by 2.58 (Tehri HEP), 2.16 (NJPC – Satluj) and 1.84 (Tala HEP), which are higher than the approved average cost of power purchase of NHPC run hydel stations.

The summary of power purchase cost proposed by JKPDD and approved by the Commission for 2011-12 is analyzed in this paragraph. The average cost of one unit of energy for the utility, based on the approved power purchase quantum and cost for 2011-12 is 2.48/unit. The proposed and approved power purchase cost stood respectively at 2.64 and 2.13 for hydel stations of JKSPDC and 2.38 and 2.20 for CPSUs respectively. Therefore, the approved power purchase cost of CPSU was marginally higher by 0.07 only. The proposed power purchase cost from outside J&K stood at 2.37 against the approved cost of 2.20. However, the net power purchase cost per unit from CPSUs stood at 2.76 (proposed) and 2.57 (approved). Thus, both the proposed as well as approved power purchase cost per unit from the CPSUs outside J&K was also higher than the average power purchase cost of NHPC stations (1.33).

VII. Conclusion and Policy Options

Hydropower is a renewable and economic energy source. It is less subject to price fluctuations than energy sources using fossil fuels. Hydro-stations can be started and stopped quickly. They are able to accommodate system load variations, making them ideally suited for meeting system peak loads. They enable the thermal and nuclear capacities to operate at base load, allowing the overall system to operate more economically and contributing to system reliability. Hydro-projects are generally located in hilly and remote areas. Development of hydro-projects can help create such infrastructure as roads, communications, and electricity. Storage hydro schemes can also useful for irrigation, flood control, and navigation. Hydro-projects avoid most of the greenhouse gas emissions associated with thermal projects. Presently, small hydro-schemes are eligible for carbon trading benefits. However, there is no difference in technology of power generation between small and large hydro-projects or their basic parameters and features, other than size and installed capacity.

Regional level of hydro potential development (including schemes cleared by the Central Electricity Authority) is expected to be 31% in Northern, 63.71% in Western, 61.26% Southern and 40.5% in Eastern power regions. Though the unexploited hydro-potential (69%) in the Northern power region is substantial, the emerging power supply situation indicates that it may be adequate only for meeting the growing power demands within north India. North Indian states have added huge hydro- capacity in recent past, even than north India would be a net importer of power by the end of 2017. Considering the growing power demand in the North Indian States, there may be little if any surplus for export to other regions. The hydro-power development scenario indicates the need for early development of the Northern Region's hydro potential in order to help meet the future electricity needs of not only the region, but the whole country.

While large-scale development of the north India hydro-power potential finds justification in the context of the overall power demand in the country, it is also essential to consider and identify avenues for utilization of electricity in the region. The regional distribution of demand for power is likely to be more or less at the current levels. Special efforts are therefore needed to encourage the growth of demand for power in the Northern region. Such an increase in demand would create employment opportunities and economic activity, which would be beneficial to the region. Industrial and agricultural development and total electrification of villages and homes should also form part of this power sector development plan. The subsequent improvement in their personal well-being would enable the inhabitants of the region to view the development of hydro- resources as a venture bringing regional benefit, not merely for export and the benefit of others outside the region.

Power supply is essential for speedier economic development and better quality of life, for which there is need to harness the immense untapped hydro-power potential in north Indian states. There is need to tap the commercial hydro-power generation potential of the hilly states of Himachal Pradesh and Jammu and Kashmir. In Jammu and Kashmirm hydro-power generation potential has been exploited up to 10% due to the Indus Water Treaty (IWT), high capital costs, difficult terrain and financial scarcity. Therefore, the IWT - that safeguards interests of downstream population and not upstream population needs to be reviewed to ensure sustainable hydro-power development of the State.

Power sector in hilly states is suffering from huge revenue losses. For instance, in Jammu and Kashmir, the revenue gap between aggregate cost of electricity supply and aggregate tariff charged stood at more than 2 per kWh and electricity metering is very low at 30-40% resulting in highly unsustainable power sector. There is peak energy deficit of around one-fourth and energy deficit of one-third and only one-fourth of the domestic energy requirement is met by the hydro-power in the State. State has resorted to drawing heavily under UI by paying higher power price to meet the growing electricity demand. Therefore, steps need to be taken to get balance energy at reasonable price from ongoing hydro-power projects in the State.

Power deficit is also due to power thefts and poor T&D network, which results in electricity losses as high as 60%, which needs to be plugged by various means to generate revenue for the public exchequer. North Indian States should undertake robust power reforms in T&D through its regulatory authorities and concerned departments. There is need to reduce tariff subsidy and power sector losses by setting up performance standards for PDD. PDD needs to be restructured completely to function on commercial lines. There is need to develop a long-term transmission plan, which require more funds for strengthening T&D infrastructure. Energy audits need to be carried out to assess technical and commercial losses and metering should be made mandatory to correctly identify leakages and billing and collection have to be improved and losses reduced substantially.

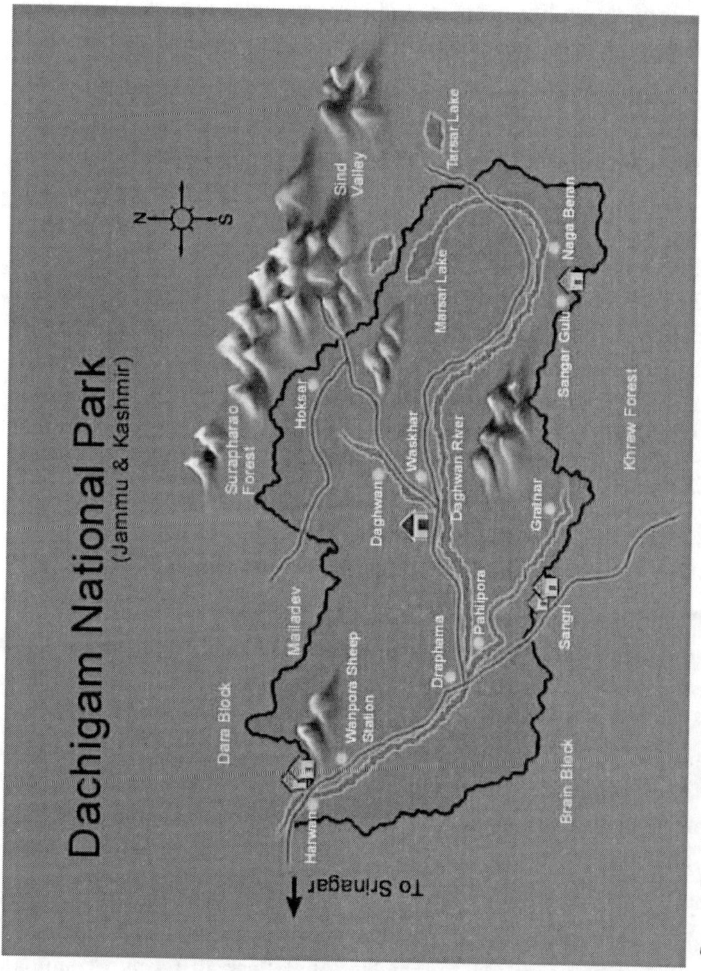

Source: Dachigam Management Plan, 2011-16.

extremely limited if not almost non-existent because people mostly equate recreational services of park with amusement and overlook its total value for humans. There is inadequate endeavor to compute the true value for scarce resources including water, beaches, parks land, and forests for its provision. Stemming from increasing population, income and mobility, the demand for recreational areas has been ever-increasing in many developing countries (Clawson et al., 1996).

Dachigam National Park is endowed with various use and non-use values which benefit its key stakeholders, both tourists and local people. Tourists are attracted by recreational activities like watching endemic and endangered plant and animal species, bird watching, trekking and scenic beauty etc. Flow of tourists has displayed a persistent increase over the years (Tourist flow has increased from 8807 in 2014 to 12754 in 2015)[1]. Accordingly we need to impute values that reflect the true social costs and benefits of activities. Failure to incorporate the true social costs and benefits may underestimate net conservation benefits and overestimate net development benefits which in turn might impose an irreversible damage to recreational resources in favor of other development activities. This is due to the discrepancy between the level of national park service enjoyed by people and the low value/attention attributed to them. Since ecotourism services are not traded in the market, their economic values are not actually known.

Additionally, despite the fact that the park houses multiple landscapes of attraction, the site has been unable to improve its ecotourism attributes and expand types and variety of its recreational services for a long time. In essence, flora and fauna (i.e biodiversity) is persistently deteriorating mainly because of widespread deforestation, anthropogenic pressures, encroachment, poaching and inadequate management. Thus quantifying their values and productive capacities assumes significance. This may serve as a base for raising social awareness, educating people and modeling public policy.

Against this backdrop present study is an attempt to estimate economic value of Dachigam National Park in terms of annual recreational value to onsite visitors, direct benefits from its provisional services and conservation values of the park.

Travel Cost Method: Design And Application

Theory of TCM and its application is relatively straightforward. It is based on the microeconomic theory of consumer behaviour i. e. maximization of consumers utility derived from consumption of marketable goods and services subject to budget constraint (see Gravelle and Rees 2004). This analogy can also be applied to environmental goods and services such as wetlands, parks, hill stations, tourist places etc. TCM, as an appropriate and widely used method for estimating recreational demand of natural resources, was first suggested by Harold Hotelling in 1947 (Haab and McConnell 2002). It is assumed that individual's utility under TCM depends on number of visits to site, quality of site and bundle of other goods (McConnell 1992).

The Survey

Target population of the present study for estimating Individual Travel Cost was defined as onsite visitors. According to unpublished sources of Department of wildlife protection (Jammu & Kashmir) 12754 visitors visited Dachigam National Park during March to December, 2015. This population is assumed as reference population for determining sample size. Following from Krejcie and Morgan (1970) we used following formula to work out sample size:

$$s = \chi^2 NP(1-P) \div [d^2(N-1) + \chi^2 P\,(1-P)] \qquad \ldots\ldots (1)$$

Whereas, s = Sample size required.

x^2= Table value of chi-square for 1 degree of freedom at the desired confidence level (1.96 × 1.96 = 3.841).

N = Population size. (i.e. 12754)

P = the population proportion (assumed to be 0 .83).

d = Degree of accuracy expressed as a proportion (.04).

Thus a sample of 336 was selected at different spots of the park. Out of 336, only 301 filled questionnaires were finally used for TCM as the remaining 35 provided partial information.

Since target population of the present study was predefined where every sampling unit (a visitor who was interviewed) had visited the site for the purpose of recreational benefits. In view of the main objectives of the present study, purposive sampling technique was employed to choose onsite respondents (visitor). A face-to-face interview method was used to elicit information from onsite visitors. For collecting data highly trained and experienced enumerators were employed. Data was collected during months of May, June and July (2015) on weekdays only[2]. A survey questionnaire was developed after consultations with stakeholders and discussions with experts. Questionnaire thus designed was administered to potential respondents for pre-testing. Process of pre-testing questionnaire was started in earlier May, (2015) for a week to gauge respondents reactions and feasibility of questionnaire. Field survey was carried out from 10th of May 2015 to ending July 2015. Since an Individual Travel Cost Method (ITCM) has been used for estimating recreational benefits accruing to biological resource (Dachigam National Park) in the present study, questionnaire was designed in that direction to get the required data. It was divided into four sections; with some follow-up and multiple choice type questions to extract most required information.

First part of the questionnaire covered demographic and socio-economic profile of the visitor. It included questions on name, age, sex, level of education, marital status, family size, personal income, and occupation etc. Second part included key questions related to the origin of visitor, mode of journey (by car, train, plane, bus, auto, cycle or foot etc.), travel time, onsite time spent, and other expenditures related to trips. Part third contained questions related to the visitor's various on-site activities, related expenditures and time requirements. These included activities like bird-watching, trekking, watching endemic and endangered species, site-seeing, spending time in a beautiful place with family or friends etc. and their expenditures and time spent. Last part of Questionnaire was related to understanding respondents' perceptions and attitudes about existing state of environmental quality of the site, their suggestions and preferences for further improvements of facilities which may attract more tourists. This section also posed questions regarding management and preservation issues of the site and possible stake-holders' initiative for its conservation.

Econometric specification

Various studies have been attempted to estimate value of recreational sites either with single travel cost models or with multiple-site models. Later is mostly practicable with random utility models, whereas former includes Individual or Zonal Travel Cost methods. In the present study a single site Individual Travel Cost Model has been applied to estimate recreation value of Dachigam National Park. Following from Garrod and Willis (1999) we estimated following Trip Generation Function (TGF):

$$NV_{ij} = f\left(RTTC_{ij}, RDHS_{ij}, Q_j, S_i, Y_i\right) \qquad \text{.................(2)}$$

Where, i =1, 2, 3.......n,

NV_{ij} = Number of visits made by individual 'i' to site 'j' in last one year.

$RTTC_{ij}$ = Round Total Travel Cost including time cost incurred by individual 'i' to site 'j'

$RDHS_{ij}$ = Round distance from home of individual 'i' to site 'j'

Q_{ij} = Vector of environmental qualities of the site 'j'

S_i = Vector of socio-demographic characteristics of the respondent 'i'

Y_i = Monthly income of the individual 'i'

Based on variables used in models in this study, proposed demand function is as:

$$NV = exp\,(\alpha + \beta^1 RTTC + \beta^2 RDHS + \beta^3 Q + \beta^4 Age + \beta_5 Flyz + \beta_6 Edu + \beta_7 MI + \varepsilon) \qquad \text{.........................(3)}$$

After taking natural Logarithms, we have:

$$Ln(NV) = \alpha + \beta_1 RTTC + \beta_2 RDHS + \beta_3 Q + \beta_4 Age + \beta_5 Flyz + \beta_6 Edu + \beta_7 MI + \varepsilon \qquad \text{.........................(4)}$$

Once TGF is estimated, a demand function can be derived which is used to estimate consumer surplus/welfare of the society.

Consumer surplus (in absolute terms) is an amount of 'access value' which a consumer 'i' gets from a trip to the site 'j'. It is calculated by the following method given by Garrod and Willis (1999); Creel and Loomis (1990):

$$CS = -\frac{1}{\beta_1} \qquad \text{.........................(5)}$$

The Total Consumer Surplus (TCS) generated by site 'j' to the users during a particular period of time is estimated by:

TCS = Average CS × Total number of visitors to site 'j' in last one year. (OR)

Average Consumer Surplus (Av. CS) per-year for a visitor was estimated by Adamowicz et al. (1989) as:

$$Av.CS = \frac{E(r)}{(-\beta_1)} \qquad \text{.........................(5)}$$

Where CS = Consumer Surplus per-visitor per-year to site 'j' by individual 'i'

β_1 = Coefficient of $RTTC_{ij}$ and

E(r) = Average Annual visits

Annual consumer surplus can be calculated as multiply consumer's surplus per-visit with total number of visits during a particular time period (say one year). This is estimated as:

CS_{annual} = CS per visit x Annual visits

$$CS\ annual = \left(\frac{1}{-\beta_1}\right) \cdot Annual\ visits \qquad \text{.........................(5)}$$

Results: Empirical Estimates From Econometric Models

Poisson and Truncated Poisson Econometric Models were used to estimate the results in present study. Results obtained by Poisson Model were estimated by using Pseudo Maximum Likelihood Estimation (PMLE) approach using STATA version 12.0. Recreation Demand

Function was estimated with number of visits taken to the study site regressed on travel cost variable along with other socio-economic variables. Based on the significance of each variable, the relevant variables that help to explain the recreation demand function were identified. Coefficient of model can be interpreted as semi-elasticity given the exponential conditional mean. The overall signs and significance of estimated coefficients were consistent with both economic theory and the existing empirical literature on this subject.

Poisson Model Results

Poisson Regression (PMLE) model shows that estimated coefficient of travel cost (RTTC) variable not only had expected negative sign but also found to be significant at 1% level. In the present study, travel cost acts as a proxy for the price of access which includes expenses on travel, time cost (travel and onsite time cost), and other expenses on food and accommodation etc. Coefficient of RTTC was -0.01556 which implies that, with a thousand rupee increase in travel costs the expected number of visits (NV) to the site decreased by 0.015% (in terms of semi-elasticity) while holding all other variables constant in the model. The RDHS variable, residence from home to the site, measured in Km (Kilometres) showed a negative sign with significance at 1% level. This indicates that farther the place of residence from site, lower will be the number of visits made by visitor to the site. Coefficient of RDHS was -0.00015. This implies that with a one km increase in distance the number of visits increased by 0.01%, ceteris paribus. Similarly, negative relationship with age suggests that younger people are more likely to visit the site than older people. Coefficient of this variable was -0.0071. The effect of various socio-economic and demographic factors on recreational demand of visits showed contradictory results as shown in past literature. In the present study, the variable Sex included as a dummy variable (Male=1, Female=0), had positive coefficient which implies that males were more likely to visit the site than female. Family Size (Flyz) had positive coefficient but was found insignificant in the Poisson Regression Model. It implies that more visitors were likely to come with family members to the study area. The value of income co-efficient worked out to be 0.007168 at significant of 5% level. Its sign accords with a priori expectation. It implies that visitor's income (MI) had a positive and significant influence on recreational demand for visits to the site.

The sign of the estimated coefficient of education variable (Edu) was found positive and complying with a priori expectations. It implies that people who were well educated undertook more visits to the site, as they have more knowledge about environmental resources and their recreational values than uneducated. We found the variable (Edu) significantly influences (at 1% level) demand for recreational visits to the site with a coefficient of 0.061689. Keeping the other variables constant in the model, a one year increase in schooling will increases number of visits by 6.1%.

Table-I: Results from Poisson regression

Variable	*Coef.*	*Std. Err.*	*Z*	*P>z*
Age	-0.00353	0.019597	-0.18	0.857
Age2	5.73E-05	0.000231	0.25	0.804
Gen	0.214397***	0.080905	2.65	0.008
Flyz	0.000571	0.010869	0.05	0.958
MI	0.007168***	0.001452	4.94	0.000
RDHS	-0.00015***	2.28E-05	-6.76	0.000
RTTC	-0.01556***	0.006003	-2.59	0.010
Edu	0.061689***	0.021523	2.87	0.004
Constant	0.473344	0.399159	1.19	0.236
Model statistics summary				
Log pseudo likelihood	-453.249			
Wald chi2(8)	281.84			
Prob> chi2	0.000			
Pseudo R2	0.1002			
N	301			

Source: Field Survey, (2015)
*** indicates the coefficient is statistically significant at the 1%, level or less.
df = Degree of Freedom, N = No. of Observations

Summary of Model fit: The overall findings from the Poisson Regression Model reveal that co-efficient of independent variables were found to be quite expected and in line with established literature and economic theory. The outcome of the Log Pseudo Likelihood of the Model (Poisson PML) was -453.249. While as the Wald Test Statistics of the model with 8 degree of freedom was 281.84which reject the null hypothesis of zero effects for all predictors in the model at 1% level of significance. The R-square [which was squared correlation between fitted and observed values of dependent variable, Y and$\hat{Y}$ and (Y=NV)] was estimated in the model as 0.1002.

Truncated Poisson Regression Model (TPRM)

When the dependent variable has only integer values which are greater than or equal to one, a Truncated Poisson Model is used to estimate the demand function. In the present study same method has been used, as the data have been collected from only onsite visitors (excluding offsite visitors) and the number of visits (dependent variable) of a visitor was truncated at zero. Even though non-truncated model Poisson PMLE reported significant results, the main problem with this model is that it overestimates consumer surplus due to the greater value of coefficient of Round Total Travel Cost Variable (RTTC) which is mostly created by the presence of truncation bias in the data. Results from Truncated Poisson Model are presented in the Table-II.

It is obvious from the table that coefficient of Round Total Travel Cost (RTTC) is negative and significant at 1%. This is consistent with a priori expectation. Coefficient of RTTC worked out to be -0.08019, which implies that, *Ceteris Paribus*, with a thousand rupees increase in total travel cost the expected number of visits (NV) decreased by 0.08% (in terms of semi-elasticity). Coefficient of Age was found negative though insignificant and positive sign of coefficient of variable Sex with significance at 1 % showed similar type of direction as found un-truncated models. Family size (Flyz) variable coefficient is positive but insignificant. The coefficients of monthly income (MI) and education (Edu) of the visitor in truncated poisson model also have the positive sign same as in un-truncated models with a significance of 1%. The positive relation of monthly income and education of the visitor with the demand for recreational visits in this model were followed in the same line with some other studies in the valuation literature.

Truncated Poisson Regression Model (TPRM) was quite fit for this data as compared to untruncated models as shown by the model

Table-II: Truncated Poisson Regression (Truncation Point=0)
Dependent Variable = No. of visits last one year (NV)

Variables	*Coef.*	*Std. Err.*	*Z*	*P>z*	*[95% Conf. Inter]*	
RTTC	-0.08019*	0.012113	-6.62	**0.000**	-0.10393	-0.05644
Age	-0.0001	0.00469	-0.02	0.982	-0.0093	0.00909
Sex	0.389306**	0.154713	2.52	0.012	0.086073	0.692539
Flyz	0.006286	0.017439	0.36	0.718	-0.02789	0.040466
MI	1.25E-05*	2.03E-06	6.17	**0.000**	8.53E-06	1.65E-05
Edu	0.133168*	0.036568	3.64	**0.000**	0.061496	0.20484
Constant	-0.34496	0.345165	-1.00	0.318	-1.02147	0.331555
Model Statistics Summary						
Log pseudo likelihood	-398.579					
LR chi^2	137.03					
Prob> chi^2	0.000					
Pseudo R^2	0.1525					
N	301					

Source: Field Survey, (2015)

* and **indicates the coefficient is statistically significant at the 1%, and 5% level respectively.

statistics. The R^2 (Pseudo R^2)[3] was 0.15 with 6 degree of freedom, which is an improvement than un-truncated poisson models.

Other results showed that the proportion of men and women who answered the questionnaire was 79 and 21 respectively. The average age of respondents was 35.52 years. The monthly household income of respondents ranged between Rs. 3,000 to Rs. 150,000 with mean income equal to Rs. 32,951. The average number of trips undertaken to the park (including the present one) was 2.25.

Benefit/Welfare Estimates for Dachigam National Park

Poisson MLE and Truncated Poisson Model were used to estimate the recreational demand function for number of visits to the site. After estimating the demand function the results were used to estimate welfare measures/consumer surplus (CS) of visitor's visits to the Dachigam National Park. Only the visitor's to Dachigam National Park were used for the calculation of welfare measures in the present study. The estimated coefficients of the travel cost covariates (for Poisson PMLE and Truncated Poisson Model) were used to calculate the consumer/welfare surpluses (see in table-III).

Consumer surplus per visitor per visit can be calculated by $1/\text{-}\beta_{RTTC}$ (Creel and Loomis, 1990), which in present study is equal to Rs. 64267.35 (US$1020.12) and Rs. 12470.38 (US$197.94) by using estimated coefficient of RTTC (β_{RTTC}) of Poisson PMLE and Truncated Poisson Regression Model respectively. Since the average recreationists/visitors visit per year in our study was 2.25. Thus the average annual consumer surplus per visitor is calculated by multiplying the average annual visits by consumer surplus per visitor per visit, which is equal to Rs. 144601.54 (US$2295.26) and Rs. 28058 (US$445.37) from the respective models. Similarly, the annual recreational value of the Dachigam National Park for our sampled visitors (301) was calculated by multiplying average annual consumer surplus per year per visitor by the total number of sampled visitors (i.e.301), which is equal to Rs. 43,525,063.54 (US$6,90,874.02) and Rs. 8,445,564.86 (US$1,34,056.59) from the respective models. This implies the Dachigam National Park visitors received a substantial amount of monetary benefit from the recreational use of Dachigam National Park ecosystem. It indicates that the Park has a great unseen economic value and it is a valuable asset for the society.

Table-III : Welfare Measures for Dachigam National Park

	Poisson PMLE	***Truncated Poisson Model***
β_{RTTC}	-0.01556	-0.08019
CS/visit per visitor	Rs. 64267.35 * (US$1020.12)	Rs. 12470.38 (US$197.94)*
Average Consumer Surplus per year†	Rs. 1,44,601.54 (US$2295.26)*	Rs. 28058 (US$445.37)*
Total Annual Consumer Surplus/Recreational Value of Dachigam National Park††	Rs. 43525063.54 (US$6,90,874.02)*	Rs. 8445564.86 (US$1,34,056.59)*

Source: Field Survey, (2015)
β_{RTTC}= Coefficient of Round total travel cost
*1US $ = Rupees 63 on the basis of exchange rates on June 2015
†Based on the sample mean of the visits (i.e. 2.25)
††Based on the sample (total number of visitors i.e. 301)

The total social welfare value of the recreational activities of the Dachigam National Park is estimated by multiplying the total annual population of visitors to the park by average annual consumer surplus per visitor. The only available estimate of the annual population of visitors/tourists to the park in (2015)[4] was 12754, which includes domestic as well as foreign tourists. On the basis of this estimation of total tourists/visitors flow to Dachigam National Park, the total consumers surplus of Dachigam National Park are equal to [Rs.64267.35 × 12754] Rs. 81,96,65,781.9 (US$1,30,10,567.97)[5] and [12470.38 × 12754] Rs. 15, 90, 47,226.52 (US $ 25, 24,559.15)1 per annum for Poisson PMLE and Truncated Poisson Models respectively. It is observed from the estimation that due to the truncation effect, the total consumer surpluses obtained from the Poisson PMLE Model showed upward biasness as compared to Truncated Poisson Regression Model. This could be indicative of the fact that Truncated Poisson Regression Model performs better than the Poisson MLE Model, even though it showed downward bias in consumer surplus. However, it overcomes the problem of truncation bias.

Recreational Value of Dachigam National Park

The total recreational value equals the consumer surplus plus total cost of the visit. The total annual monetary recreational value of the Dachigam National Park worked out to be Rs. 24,76,14,828 (approximately US$39, 30,395) for given number of visitors (12754)2 as shown in table-IV.

Table IV: Total Recreational Value Per year of the Dachigam National Park on the basis of Visitors Data from the office of Warden Department of Wildlife J &K (2015)

Consumer Surplus		Total Expenditure		Total Recreational Value
Per visitor (A)	Per Year Visitors (B) = (Ax12754)	Per Visitor (C)	Per Year Visitors (D)= (Cx12754)	Per year Visitors (B+D)
Rs. 12470[a] (US$197)*	Rs.15,90,42,380 (US$81,455)*	Rs. 7775[b] (US$123)*	Rs. 9,91,62,350[b] (US$15,74,006)*	Rs. 24,76,14.828 (US$39,30,395)*

Source: Field Survey, (2015)

[a] Calculated on the basis of Truncated Poisson Regression model

* 1US $ = Rupees 63 on the basis of exchange rates on June, 2015

[b] Without inclusion of time cost.

This estimated recreational value of the park is sum of the consumer surplus (benefit) of visitors and the total expenditure of the visitors to the site in the form of transportation charges, hotels and other accommodation charges, expenditure on food, and other expenses on site like expenses on site seeing, watching endemic and endangered species and trekking etc. Thus the total expenditure of recreational visitors either during travelling or on the site and consumer surplus provides market signals to the people who were engaged in some form of economic activity such as providing services (like, tourist guide, accommodations etc.) to serve visitors. This would help them to improve the standard of living by providing some form of livelihood and give them opportunity to generate income and employment.

From TCM estimates total welfare gain (consumer's surplus) of Dachigam National Park was found to be Rs. 24 Crores per-annum given a tourist inflow of 12754 to park (Department of Wildlife, J&K). This considerable recreational value of the Park indicates its importance as a tourist destination. Inferences from TCM suggest that developing alternative means of transport and moderating other facilities like accommodation, food etc. for accessing this site can considerably decrease travel cost leading to an increase in visit frequency. This in turn will increase state revenue.

Policy Implications and Conclusions

The findings from the study indicated that the direct use values (Provisional, recreational and conservation values) of Dachigam National Park are quite high. By using the Poisson Regression (PMLE) and Truncated Poisson Regression Models, the annual consumer surplus of the visitors were estimated as Rs. 4,35,25,063 (US$6,90,874)[6] and Rs. 84,45,564 per year (US$1,34,056)[7] for given number of visitors (12754)[8] respectively from the site. It is observed from estimated results that various socio-economic (like age, education, income etc.) and other determinants of visitor like travel cost, travel distance etc., determines the visitors recreational demand for site. The representative values determine that park has huge potential of tourism (recreational) value. Thus provisioning of more recreational facilities on park will increase tourist inflow which in turn not only to generate income and employment of local people but also boost the welfare of state economy. Estimated direct use value of Dachigam National Park reincarnates its significance as a precious natural asset providing varied functions and services to people. Hence its preservation, overall development and sustainable management should be an important policy objective and a national priority. Empirical analysis of socio-economic variables and estimates of consumer surplus in this study can help in formulation of policies with respect to its management. For example, visitors to the site will increase frequency of their visits if its attributes are improved in future. This in turn may increases state domestic product.

References

1. Ali, M. Recreation Use Value of Wondo Genet Wetland Ecosystem-Ethiopia. Masters of Science Thesis Submitted to the Department of Forest Resource Management, Faculty of Forest Sciences of the Swedish University of Agricultural Science (SLU), Umea, 2007.

2. Ankomah, E. and Adu, K.O. Recreational Value of National Parks in Ghana: A Case of Kakum National Park, *International Journal of Ecological Economics and Statistics*, 2015; 36(3): 125-133
3. Belkayali, N., Atan, M., Talay, I., and Akpinar, N. Determination of economic value of Goreme Historical National Park via contingent valuation method. *Scientific Research and Essays*, 2010; 5(9): 934-940.
4. Abinash B, Ritwik M. Application of Travel Cost Method to Asses the Pricing Policy of Public Parks: The Case of Kaziranga National Park. *Journal of Regional Development and Planning.* 2012; 1(1): 41-50.
5. Chape, S., Spalding, M., Taylor, M., Putney, A., Ishwaran, N. and Thorsell, J. History, Definitions, Values and global perspective. In S. Chape, M. Spalding and M. Jenkins (Eds.). *The world's protected areas: status, values and prospects in the 21st century* (pp. 1-35). Berkeley: University of Calfornia Press; 2008.
6. Chopra, K. *Economic Valuation of Biodiversity- The Case of Keoladeo National Park* (Edited book) Gopal K. Kadekodi 2004. Environmental Economics in Practice- Case Studies from India. Oxford University Press, New Delhi; 1998.
7. Clawson, M., and Knetsch, J.L. Economics of Outdoor Recreation, Washington, DC. Resources of the Future; 1966.
8. Creel, M and Loomis, J.B. Theoretical and Empirical Advantages of Truncated Count Data Estimators for Analysis of Deer Hunting in California. *American Journal of Agricultural Economics.* 1990; 72(2): 434–441.
9. Davis, R. *The value of outdoor recreation: An Economic Study of the Maine Woods*. Ph. D. dissertation, Department of Economics, Harvard University; 1963.
10. Dobson, A. *Conservation and biodiversity*, Scientific American Library, New York; 1996.
11. DeGroot R.S., Stuip, M., Finlayson, M. and Davidson, N. Valuing wetlands: guidance for valuing the benefits derived from wetland ecosystem services. Ramsar Technical Report No. 3/ cbd Technical Series No. 27, Ramsar Convention Bureau Gland Switzerland. *http://www.ramsar.org/pdf/lib/lib_rtr03.pdf. Cited 21 March 2011;* 2006.
12. Dixion, J.A and Sherman, P.B. *Economics of Protected Areas: A new look at benefits and costs.* Island Press, Washington DC, USA; 1990.
13. Englin, J. and Shonkwiler, J.S. Estimating Social Welfare Using Count Data Models: An Application to Long-Run Recreation Demand under Conditions of Endogenous Stratification and Truncation. *The Review of Economics and Statistics*. 1995; 77(1): 104–112.
14. Freeman, A. M., III. *The Measurement of Environmental and Resource Values: Theory and Methods*, 2nd edition, Washington, DC: Resources for the Future; 1993.

15. Garrod, G., & Wills, K. G. *Economic Valuation of the environment: Methods and case studies*. Northampton, MA: Edward Elgar; 1999.
16. Gravelle, H., and Rees, R. *Microeconomics*. Longman, London, 1992, pp. 139-140
17. Haab, T. C and McConnell, K. E. *Valuing Environmental and Natural Resources: The Econometrics of Non-market Valuation*, Edward Elgar Publishing; 2002.
18. Hadker, N et al. Willingness-to-pay for Borivli National Park: evidence from a Contingent Valuation. *Ecological economics.* 1997; 21(1):105-122.
19. Harmon, D and Putney, A.D (Eds.). The full value of parks: From economics to the intangible (pp. 3-11). Lahman: Rowman and Littlefield Publishers; 2003.
20. Hellerstein, D and Mendelsohn, R. A Theoretical Foundation for Count Data Models. *American Journal of Agricultural Economics*. 1993; 75 (3): 604–611.
21. Hearth, G., and Kennedy, J. Estimating the economic value of Mount Buffalo National Park with the travel cost and contingent valuation methods. *Tourism Economics*. 2004; 10(1): 63-78.
22. Jungho Suh, J. and Steve Harrison, S. Management Objectives and Economic Value of National Parks: Preservation, Conservation and Development. Discussion Paper No. 337, School of Economics, the University of Queensland; 2005.
23. Khan, H. Economic Valuation of the Environment and Travel Cost Approach: The Case of Ayubia National Park. *The Pakistan Development Review*. 2003; 42(1): 537-551.
24. Krejcie, R.V., & Morgan, D.W. Determining Sample Size for Research Activities. *Educational and Psychological Measurement;* 1970.
25. Lee, C.K., and Han, S. Y. Estimating the use and preservation values of national parks using contingent valuation method. *Tourism Management*. 2002; 23(5): 531-540.
26. Mahmud M.Y. Measuring Environmental Benefit of a Recreation Site: An Economic Estimation of Sodere Recreation Area, Unpublished MSC. Thesis, Addis Ababa University; 1998.
27. Management Plan, 2011-16. Department of Wildlife, Jammu and Kashmir; 2011.
28. Mangan, T., Brouwer, R., Lohano, H.D. and Nagraj, G.M. Estimating the Recreational Value of Pakistan's Largest Freshwater Lake to Support Sustainable Tourism Management Using a Travel Cost Model. *Journal Sustainable Tourism*. 2013; 21(3):473-486.
29. Martýnez-Espineira, R. and Amoako-Tuffour, J. *Multi-destination and Multi-purpose Trip Effects in the Analysis of the Demand for Trips to Remote Recreational Site*. EERI Research Paper Series No. 19/2008. Brussels: Economics and Econometrics Research Institute; 2008.

30. McConnell, K.E. On-Site Time in the Demand for Recreation. *American Journal of Agricultural Economics*. 1992; 74(4): 918-925
31. Mitra, A. Environment and Nature-Based Tourism: An Endeavour at Sustainability, Kaniskha Publisher, New Delhi; 2003.
32. Nuva, R. and Shamsudin, M.N. Willingness to Pay towards the Conservation of Ecotourism Resources at Gunung Gede Pangrango National Park, West Java, Indonesia. *Journal of Sustainable Development*. 2009; 2(2): 1 -2.
33. Pak, M. and Turker, M. F. Estimation of Recreational Use Value of Forest Resources by Using Individual Travel Cost and Contingent Valuation Methods (Kayabasi Forest Recreation Site Sample). *Journal of Applied Science*. 2006; 6(1): 1-5.
34. Pearce, D. and Moran, D. 1994. The Economic Value of Biodiversity. London, UK: Earthscan.
35. Preez, M.D; Dicken, M and Hosking, S.G. The Value of the Tiger Shark Diving within the Aliwal Shoal Marine Protected Area: A Travel Cost Analysis. *South African Journal of Economics*. 2012; 80(3): 387-399.
36. Singh, G., and Kachroo, P. Forest Flora of Srinagar. Natraj Publishers, Publications Division, Dehradun, 1977.
37. Singh, G., and Kachroo, P. (1978). Plant Community Characteristics in Dachigam Sanctuary, Kashmir, Natraj Publishers, Publications Division, Dehradun. 434pp.
38. Stolton, S., Dudley, N. (Eds.) *Arguments for protected areas: Multiple benefits for conservation and use*. London; Washington: Earthscan; 2010.
39. Suh, J., Harrison, S.R. Preface. In: J. Suh, S. Harrison, J. Herbohn, E. Mangaoang and J. Vanclay, ACIAR Smallholder Forestry Project ASEM/ 2003/052 Improving Financial Returns to Smallholder Tree Farmers in the Philippines Proceedings from the ACIAR Project Planning Workshop Held in Ormoc City, the Philippines 15-17 February 2005. ACIAR Smallholder Forestry Project ASEM/2003/052 Improving Fin, Ormoc City, the Philippines, (1-1). 15-17; February 2005.
40. Twerefou, D.K and Ababio, D.K.A. An Economic Valuation of the Kakum National Park: An Individual Travel Cost Approach. *African Journal of Environmental Science and Technology*. 2012; 6(4): 199-207.
41. WCPA-IUCN. Economic values of protected area managers; Cambridge: IUCN; 1998.

Notes

1. Department of Wildlife, Jammu and Kashmir (2015)
2. Avoids collecting the data on holidays, because there is a probability of visiting those visitors whose estimation of time value is very difficult (e.g. the fixed income group of people, whose income could not be deducted during, holidays).

3. R2 or Pseudo R2 showed the correlation between Y and $\bar{Y}$
4. Department of Wildlife, Jammu and Kashmir, Srinagar (2015)
5. 1US $ = Rupees 63 on the basis of exchange rates on June, 2015
6. 1US $ = Rupees 63 on the basis of exchange rates on June 2015
7. 1US $ = Rupees 63 on the basis of exchange rates on June 2015
8. *Data from Department of Wildlife Protection, J &K (2015)*

Chapter - 12

Reviving the Era of Interdependence: An Appraisal of India-Pakistan Trade from 1947 to 1965

— ***Sajad Padder***

Until India and Pakistan became independent from the British, they not only formed one political entity but also one integrated economy. Greater Punjab was one economic entity for centuries before partition bi-furcated it into two in 1947. Karachi and Bombay were tightly knit sister cities on the sea under the same administrative unit of Bombay Presidency. Today these regions are all but severed. At the time of partition, both India and Pakistan were highly dependent on each other for trade. Both countries had bank branches in each other's country. In 1965, war broke out between the two countries. Trade and economic relations became causalities of war. The aim of this paper is to look into the nature of bilateral trade relationship from 1947 to 1965. Even the 1947-48 war between India and Pakistan had limited impact on bilateral trade. It is intriguing to know how the two countries, irrespective of economic complementarities, continue to squeeze bilateral trade, given the strategic location of the north-west states of J&K, Punjab and Rajasthan, this revival is expected to have immediate positive spill-over effect over peace and prosperity over this region and the referred to states in particular. Reviving the pre-1965 trade arrangements including the cross-LoC trade will bring peace and prosperity to both countries and principally to the North-Western states of India.

Key Words: *India-Pakistan Relations, Trade, War, Peace, Kashmir.*

In the beginning of the period 1947-1965, economies of India and Pakistan were reasonably integrated, sustained by the Standstill Agreement under which goods from one country to another were exempted from customs duty. In addition, there were few visa restrictions. The closeness of ties is reflected by the fact that in the immediate aftermath of independence, the volume of trade between the two countries was quite high. This is reflected in the high shares in total import and export of the two countries towards each other. It can be attributed to a high level of people to people contacts, a shared history, cultural similarities, geographical proximity, relatively open and accessible land routes to cross either side of the border and relatively low accessibility to foreign markets. Existence of a number of land routes was perhaps the most important factor that facilitated easy movement of people and goods across the border that translated into high trade volumes. It is observed that a number of land routes were operational for movement of goods across borders till 1965.[1]These land routes had a direct impact on the volume of trade. The closing downof such routes resulted in a drastic decline in trade volumes.

Table 1: Important Trade Routes (before 1965)

Important Trade Routes (before 1965)				
India	***Indian States***	***Pakistan***	***Pakistan States***	***Train Services***
Munabao	Rajasthan	Khokhrapar	Sindh	Train service started in 2005, but the route is yet to re-open for trade
Attari	Punjab	Wagah	Punjab	Re-opened
Hussainiwala/ Ferozepur	Punjab	Ganda Sindhwan/Kasur	Punjab	Closed since 1965

Source: Mohan Bhuyan, "International Links from India". Retrieved from: http://irfca.org/docs/international-links.html

The data regarding trade between India and Pakistan during 1947-48 are incomplete on account of the omission of direct sea-borne trade of Sind and East Bengal.[2] Moreover, it was an abnormal year with all the adverse effects of partition. With imports valued at Rs. 1,093 million into India from Pakistan and exports valued at Rs. 770 million from

India to Pakistan, the year 1948-49 saw probably the largest volume and value of trade compared to the subsequent years.[3] It is difficult to say much about the accuracy of the data of that year. The entire land-frontier of thousands of miles was not marked and adequate numbers of offices for collecting customs duties on land routes were not yet opened. Economic life in the border districts was not settled. Under these circumstances, 1948-49 has not been taken as the base year for studying the trends in trade between India and Pakistan.

In 1949, the U.K. and many other countries in the sterling area devaluated their currencies. In September 1949, India devalued its currency by reducing the dollar value of the Indian rupee from 30.225 cents to 21.00 cents, the degree of devaluation being the same as in the case of the pound sterling. Pakistan did not to resort to devaluation of its currency. The problem of an adverse balance of payment facing other countries was non-existent in case of Pakistan. Moreover, its main exports were raw materials. Had Pakistan devalued the rupee it would not have been able to expand its markets in the hard currency area. The dollar area was an important source of capital goods and with devaluation, these goods would have been costlier and less easy to obtain. This would have inevitably retarded the pace of Pakistan's industrial advance.[4] Consequently, Pakistani commodities became dearer in India and Indian commodities cheaper in Pakistan. As India was an important customer of Pakistan's raw jute, Pakistan's decision not to devalue her currency affected Pakistan's jute trade adversely. During the year 1950-51, imports from Pakistan into India were of the order of Rs. 440 million, while exports from India to Pakistan were of the order of Rs. 306 million. 80 per-cent of the imports came from East Pakistan and 20 per-cent from West Pakistan. About 55 per-cent of India's exports went to West Pakistan[5]exclusively by land. 90 per-cent of the imports of India came by land. Raw jute, raw cotton, raw hides and skins, among other items constituted 71 per-cent of Indian imports. However, grains, pulses, flour, fish, fruits and vegetables were also significant among the various commodities imported into India. The other commodities imported from Pakistan were jute manufactures, cotton textiles, leather, vegetable oils, small quantities of cement, chemicals and machinery. 16.5 percent of India's exports were unmanufactured tobacco, wood and timber, leather, coal, etc.[6]

Irrespective of trade complementarity between India and Pakistan, we find a declining trend in between them. The percentage of imports into India from Pakistan to India's total imports decreased gradually from 9.3 in 1951-52 to 3.03 in 1952-53, 1.3 in 1961-62 and 1.0 in 1964-65. The percentage of exports from India to Pakistan to India's total exports decreased from 6.3 in 1951-52 to 4.2 in 1952-53, 1.5 in 1953-54 and about 1.2 in 1964-65.[7] From 10th September 1965 the trade between India and Pakistan was suspended because of the war.

On the basis of these temporal fluctuations in quantum of trade between India and Pakistan, it is convenient to divide this phase into three periods. The base year starts for the analysis is 1950-51.[8] The three periods spawn over:

(i) 1950-51 to 1954-55

(ii) 1955-56 to December, 1959 and

(iii) January 1960 onwards.

In August, 1955 Pakistan devalued its currency whereby exports of jute manufactures and cotton goods increased sharply. In July 1955, India and Pakistan signed an agreement for facilitating trade in coal, raw jute, raw cotton, mica, bauxite, lime, limestone, books, periodicals, betel leaves, betelnuts etc. This agreement came into force from September 1955. It gave a fillip to the dwindling Indo-Pak trade, mainly in increased exports by Pakistan to India.[9] Similarly, another agreement was entered into in January 1957. In yet another effort to revive the trade relations, a new agreement was signed between the two countries on 21 March 1960.[10] In September 1963 the representatives of the Governments of India and Pakistan entered into yet another trade agreement. Two protocols of this agreement were signed in July 1964 and in January 1965. But in September 1965 an armed conflict between India and Pakistan broke out and trade between the two countries was banned with effect from 10th September 1965.

First Period—1950-51 to 1954-55

In August 15, 1947, when the Indian subcontinent was partitioned and two separate states of India and Pakistan came into being, trade between territories which were until then parts of the same economic and political unit became international in character. The inter-dominion boundary line had cut across railways, waterways and road-ways. It resulted in the division of provinces, districts and even individual dwelling houses in certain cases, thus, creating socio-economic problems both immediate and ultimate. These problems could only be solved by mutual co-operation and long-term understanding between the two countries. Prior to partition, an Expert Committee consisting of the representatives of the two governments, which had still formally, to come into existence was constituted. This expert committee had studied the problem of inter-dominion commercial relations and did make certain recommendations which were approved by the Partition Council. It recommended that the two governments should agree to maintain the *status quo* as far as possible regarding all matters affecting trade and movements between the two dominions up to the 29th February 1948 and in particular that they should not:

- impose customs barriers between the two Dominions;
- change existing import and export polity;
- change existing customs, tariffs, excise duties and cesses;
- impose any restrictions on the free movement of goods and remittances including capital and capital equipment
- levy transit duties or taxes on goods passing across the territory of the other;
- interfere with existing trade channels by monopolistic government purchases;
- modify existing controls or introduce new controls;
- interfere with contracts between nationals of the two states.[11]

The agreement was generally referred to as the Standstill Agreement and was merely intended to provide a breathing time in which a more lasting arrangement could be arrived at between the two governments after they had started functioning as separate units. Even during the pendency of the agreement, however, difficulties began to arise. Within two months of partition, the Sind government imposed certain restrictions on the movement of a large number of commodities, with the result that not only was the free flow of goods stopped but even those goods intended for consumption in territories forming part of

India which had, according to normal practice, been imported through the port of Karachi were held up. The protests of the government of India to the government of Pakistan did not succeed in securing the repeal of these restrictions so as to permit the kind of freedom of movement which was possible for indigenous as well as imported goods going from India to Pakistan and which enabled East Bengal, for example, to receive from Calcutta not only goods originally meant for East Bengal but also those which were imported into the Calcutta market for local sale.[12]

Negotiations again started in June 1949 for a fresh agreement for the supply of commodities during the twelve months—July 1949 to June 1950. These negotiations followed the inter dominion conferences at Kolkata in 1948, and a follow up conference in Karachi in May 1948 as well as a review conference held in Delhi in December 1948. These conferences *inter-alia* had discussed major issues related to trade interrelations, and transit measures. A delegation of the representatives of the Government of India visited Karachi for the same purpose in the third week of June 1949 and a Trade Agreement was signed on 24th June 1949. India, having suffered a substantial adverse balance of trade with Pakistan in 1948-49 because of Pakistan importing a fraction of the cotton textiles quota agreed upon in the previous year's agreement, emphasized, that it could not afford to carry such substantial unfavorable balance in the following year. It was accordingly agreed by both sides that the proposed agreement should be more realistic and implemented in full.[13]

Under the new agreement, Pakistan agreed to make available to India 4,000,000 bales of raw jute and 450,000 bales of raw cotton. India on its part pressed for as larger provision of cotton textiles for export to Pakistan as possible so that the necessary balance in the trade could be achieved. India also agreed to supply 80,000 tons of iron and steel to meet the requirements of Pakistan for railway stores, electrical steel sheets, ferro-silicon and ferro-manganese. India was itself dependent on the import of iron and steel from hard currency countries for making up its own total domestic requirements. India further agreed to a substantially larger supply of coal than in the previous year, the actual figure being 1,70,000 tons a month to be increased by a further 30,000 tons provided transport arrangements could be satisfactorily made.

Table 2: Coal Export to Pakistan, 1949

Month (1949)	*Supply in tons*
July	180,423
August	206,949
September	168,559
October	198,569
November	222,180

Source: Government of India, White Paper 1950.

Another trade agreement was entered into in March 1953. Under the terms of this agreement, the Government of Pakistan was to withdraw the licence fee of Rs. 2.50 per maund on exports of raw jute to India and reduce the export duty on loose jute bales each weighing 328 lbs[14] to the same level as the export duty on bales each weighing 400 lbs. The Government of India agreed to reduce the price of coal supplied to Pakistan to the level of the price which was charged to Indian customers. The Pakistani authorities agreed to levy at the same rate the import duty on exposed cinematographic films imported into Pakistan from India as may be leviable on imports from other countries.[15]

Imports into India

During the five years ending 1954-55, India's imports from Pakistan decreased from Rs. 440 million to Rs. 194 million. Imports by sea and air decreased by 86.4 per-cent and imports by land decreased by 53.3 per-cent. Imports of raw cotton became nil from Rs. 2.7 million in the base year. Imports of fodder, bran and pollard as well as spices became negligible. Imports of raw jute decreased by 52.8 per-cent; grains, pulses and flour by 95 per-cent; raw hides and skins by 95 per-cent and of fruits and vegetables by 61 per-cent. But imports of fish, poultry and eggs increased by 140 per-cent.[16] It appears that the demand for fish and eggs in West Bengal was highly elastic.

Exports from India

Exports of jute manufactures and tobacco decreased from Rs. 32 million and Rs. 22 million to about nil. Those of vegetable oils and fats decreased by 96.5 per-cent and of cotton textiles by Rs. 64 per-cent. Exports of fruits and vegetables decreased from Rs. 22.5 million to Rs. 0.25 million. Those of coal decreased from Rs. 44 million in 1949-50 to Rs. 1.5 million in 1950-51, but increased to Rs. 30.5 million in 1952-53. Coal exports to Pakistan from India amounted to Rs. 25 million in 1954-55.[17]

Second Period-1955-56 to December 1959

The significant events during this period are:

- devaluation of Pakistani rupee by 30.5 per-cent with effect from 1st August 1955;
- enforcement of export bonus scheme in Pakistan with effect from January 1959; and
- signing of trade agreements between India and Pakistan in July 1955 and January 1957 and the Limited Payments Agreement in December 1959.[18]

By the middle of 1955 Pakistan's reserves of foreign exchange dwindled considerably and necessitated the devaluation of its rupee. This devaluation necessitated an export boron schemes in January 1959. However, in 1955, itself Pakistan and India notched yet another trade agreement.

As per the provisions of the July 1955 trade agreement, India agreed to export to Pakistan 78,000 tons of coal per month, 3100 tons of stone boulders per week and up to 20,000 lbs. of betel leaves per day. India also agreed to export 5,000 tons of hardwood, 10,000 tons of softwood, 500 tons of mica, 1600 tons of bauxite and 300 tons of barytes (white). India was to export books and periodicals of the value of Rs. 0.2 million, Ayurvedic and Unani medicines of Rs. 1.5 million and lime and limestone of Rs. 0.5 million. In return, Pakistan agreed to export to India 1.8 million bales of raw jute, 1.2 million pieces of raw hides and skins and 1000 tons of saltpeter, 1 million tons of rock salt, 20,000 lbs. of betel leaves per day and books and periodicals of the value of

Rs. 0.2 million. Some specified quantity of raw cotton was to be exported from Pakistan. Pakistan agreed to export fish and poultry of the value of Rs. 20 million, bark of walnut of the value of Rs. 50,000 and betelnuts of the value of Rs. 0.5 million to India.[19] In order to facilitate trade in border areas—East Pakistan on the one hand and West Bengal, Bihar, Assam and Tripura on the other—it was agreed that persons holding "A" Category visas could carry small specified quantities of various commodities of daily requirements such as fresh fruits and vegetables, fish, poultry, eggs, firewood, chillies, kerosene oil, washing soap, milk, tea, spices, salt, earthenware, fodder, etc. free from customs duties. Tenants, including Ziratia tenants[20] residing within a ten-mile belt of the border were allowed under this agreement to take across the border within a reasonable period after harvest 40 maunds of paddy per family or total produce of such lands which were cultivated by them whichever was less. It may be noted that similar facilities were not provided with regard to trade by land between West Pakistan and India.

Under a Limited Payments Agreement signed in December 1959, payments were to be made in Indian rupees and the total value of the commodities to be exchanged between India and Pakistan was Rs. 20 million either way. This was the beginning of payments in Indian rupees for a part of the trade between the two countries. India was to export fresh fruits, fruit plants, seeds and bulbs of the value of Rs. 3 million, bidi leaves and cement of the value of Rs. 7 million and other commodities such as limestone, salt and books of the value of Rs. 10 million. Pakistan was to export to India fresh fruits, fruit plants, seeds and bulbs of the value of Rs. 3 million, raw cotton of the value of Rs. 7 million and other commodities like eggs, poultry, paper and books of the value of Rs. 10 million. For the exclusive purpose of facilitating payments, the National Bank of Pakistan opened a separate clearing account with the State Bank of India. A swing limit of 2.5 million on either side was allowed. When the outstanding amount exceeded this swing limit, the country running an import surplus could suspend imports temporarily, while the country which was running an import deficit should take steps to expedite imports so that the imbalance was rectified.[21]

India's imports from Pakistan increased from Rs. 193.8 million in 1954-55 to Rs. 271.1 million in 1955-56. But India's exports to Pakistan decreased from Rs. 96.4 million in 1954-55 to Rs. 83.0 million in 1955-56. In subsequent years both imports and exports decreased continuously and reached the lowest level in 1959 i.e. imports of Rs. 54 million and exports of Rs. 62.9 million.

Imports into India

Imports from East Pakistan decreased from Rs. 184.7 million in 1954-55 and Rs. 256.6 million in 1955-56 to Rs. 50.5 million in 1959. Imports from West Pakistan increased from Rs. 9 million in 1954-55 to Rs. 14.6 million in 1955-56 and Rs. 22.8 million in 1957, but decreased in the following year to Rs. 3.6 million and Rs. 4.1 million in 1959.[22]

Exports from India

During the period from 1954-55 to 1959 exports to East Pakistan decreased from Rs. 47.9 million to Rs. 34.0 million i.e. by 29 per-cent, while exports to West Pakistan decreased from Rs. 48.5 million to Rs. 28.9 million, i.e. by 40.4 per-cent. From Rs. 23.2 million of cotton textiles became almost nil. Exports of spices increased a little. Vegetable non-essential oils decreased by 36 per-cent, drugs and medicines and chemicals by 45 per-cent, while exports of cement by about 73 per-cent. On the other hand, exports of fruits and vegetables increased by 167 per-cent and machinery and millwork by 116.5 per-cent.[23]

Third Period-1960 and Subsequent Years

Representatives of the Governments of India and Pakistan entered into trade agreements in March 1960 and in September 1963. The two Governments recognizing the needs and requirements of each other in the context of their developing economies undertook to explore all possibilities for expansion and promotion of trade between the two countries on the basis of mutual advantage. In the 1960 agreement,each government agreed to accord to the commerce of the other country a treatment no less favorable than that accorded to the commerce of any third country.[24] Under this agreement, India agreed to export to Pakistan fresh fruits, fruit plants, seeds and bulbs to the value of Rs. 12 million, coal of Rs. 41.7 million and miscellaneous items such as limestone of Rs. 34.5 million. Pakistan agreed to export to India fresh fruits, fruit plants, seeds, bulbs and fresh vegetables worth Rs. 12 million, raw cotton Rs. 66 million, jute cuttings Rs. 24 million and other commodities of Rs. 34.5 million, making a total of Rs. 136.5 million.[25] The swing limit of the self-balancing account with the State Bank was raised to Rs. 5 million on both sides. The payments of this barter were in Indian rupee. Under the Protocol of the agreement, India agreed to export to Pakistan 130,000 tons of coal per month, 3,000 tons of hardwood and 2,000 tons of softwood per year. Pakistan agreed to export to India jute cuttings, the quantities of which India was to intimate in September every year.[26] The two governments further agreed to enter into such special arrangements relating to border trade as may be considered by them to be necessary from time to time during the period of the validity of this agreement to facilitate the movement of goods from one country to the other.

The trade agreement of 1963 provides for general trade and contains a protocol under which India agreed to supply to Pakistan 130,000 tons of coal per month and 50,000 tons of stone boulders including Pakur (grinding) stones per year, while Pakistan agreed to supply to India raw jute and jute cuttings and raw cotton, the quantities of which would be intimated by India in September and October each year. Under Protocol II signed in July 1964 a special arrangement was made for the exchange of fresh fruits to the extent of Rs. 5 million by each country on a self-balancing basis. Payments were to be made in non-convertible Indian rupees after the State Bank of Pakistan opened a "Special Fruit Account" with the State Bank of India, which allowed over draft facilities in the said account up to Rs. 2 million. In July 1964 and January 1965 two Protocols were issued providing for import of 120,000 tons of rice valued at Rs. 62.5 million against export of coal, bidi leaves, railways equipment, spices, limestone, etc. of the same value. It was agreed that payments should be made by both the countries in non-convertible Indian rupees, and the National Bank of Pakistan opened the "Special Rice Account" with the State Bank of India. It was the intention of the two parties to complete these transactions by 10th January 1966.[27]

Table 3: India's Trade with Undivided Pakistan

(Rs. lakhs)

Year (April – March)	*Exports to Pakistan*	*Imports from Pakistan*	*Balance of Trade*	*Total Trade Turnover*
1948-49	7,668	10,738	-3,070	18,406
1949-50	4,330	4,405	-75	8,735
1950-51	3,060	4,387	-1,327	7,447
1951-52	4,525	8,750	-4,225	13,275
1952-53	3,090	2,188	+902	5,278
1953-54	801	1,928	-1,127	2,729
1954-55	975	1,938	-963	2,913
1955-56	830	2,711	-1,881	3,541
1956-57	792	1,576	-784	2,368
1957*	668	1,342	-674	2,010
1958*	732	631	+101	1,363
1959-60	721	859	-138	1,580
1960-61	951	1,401	-450	2,352
1961-62	945	1,386	-441	2,331
1962-63	940	1,667	-727	2,607
1963-64	717	936	-219	1,653
1964-65	978	1,575	-597	2,553
1965-66	488	565	-77	1,053

*Calendar years.

Note: The trade statistics for the year 1947-48 have not been taken here as that was an abnormal year. Owing to the partition, the trade for 1947-48 excludes the direct foreign sea-borne trade of the Pakistan Provinces of Sind and East Bengal with effect from 1 August and 15 August 1947, respectively. Figures for 1947-48 also exclude India's sea-borne trade with Pakistan upto February 1948, as Pakistan was declared to be a separate foreign territory for the purpose of trade and customs in March 1948 only. Also in 1949 India devalued her currency while Pakistan refused to do so. The year of devaluation is also thought to be inappropriate to study trade trends. Therefore, 1950-51 is taken as the base year to study trade trends.

Source: Government of India, Ministry of Commerce and Industry (New Delhi), *Indo-Pakistan Trade Statistics 1951-52,* and *Review of the Trade of India, 1947-52: Annual Reports of the Ministry of Commerce,* Government of India, New Delhi; *Monthly Statistics of the Foreign Trade of India* (various issues). For details see: Ranjit Singh Ghuman, *Indo-Pakistan Trade Relations,* Deep and Deep Publications, New Delhi, 1986, pp. 56-73.

The trade agreement of 1960 was in force for more than three years. In respect of imports of raw jute into India the agreement was implemented satisfactorily throughout the three years. In spite of increasing demand for raw jute within Pakistan from her expanding jute manufacturing industry, Pakistan could fulfil the agreement to an appropriate extent. Table 3 depicts the volume of India's trade with undivided Pakistan. The total trade during 1948-49 was of the order of Rs. 18,406 lakhs and was an all-time record in the first two decades of independence from British rule. During the next two years the volume of trade went down substantially. It again picked up in 1951-52 when it rose to Rs. 13,275 lakhs. Thenceforth, there has been a continuous downward trend.

Table 3 clearly shows that in spite of agreements, trade between India and Pakistan gradually decreased from 1948-49 to 1965-66. The agreements indicate that the governments of the two countries had recognised mutual needs and agreed to accord to the commerce of the other country a treatment no less favourable than accorded to the commerce of any third country. But all the agreements were not enforced fully and properly.

In addition to economic causes, there were socio-cultural and political factors which played a major role in inhibiting the expansion of Indo-Pak trade. During the period from 1947-1965 India and Pakistan had abnormal political relations. The 1948 war over Kashmir was followed by mutual hostility and suspicion. The main point to be noted here is that though the partition was accepted by the Indian leaders without any reservations, there was, in their acceptance an inherent aversion to any close and friendly relations with a leadership which had led the people of Pakistan "astray" and thrown the process of history "backwards".[28] The India-Pakistan conflicts are too deep-rooted to be eliminated by simple gestures of friendship or by concessions in the settlement of disputes. The fact of the matter is that since independence, both countries have been looking upon each other as potential enemies and in their external relations, the "friends" of one country were taken as "enemies" by the other. In less than five months after independence, the two countries were on the verge of war over the issue of three princely states of Junagadh, Hyderabad and Kashmir. In less than a year the war over Kashmir further aggravated the already fragile relations. The issue was discussed at the United Nations Security Council where the representatives of both the countries participated.

Charges and counter-charges for carrying out war propaganda were leveled against each other. It gave rise to graver political tensions between the two countries.[29]

The plain fact is that Kashmir is the rock on which attempts to normalize Indo-Pak relations have foundered again and again. Pakistan always takes up the Kashmir issue whenever there is any talk of expanding trade and further normalizing relations.

Immediately after the outbreak of the Indo-Pak war in September 1965, Pakistan banned all exports to India.[30]Trade in subsequent years was mainly limited to the execution of the earlier contracts or through third countries. The suspension of trade has neither reduced the demand in Pakistan for coal, nor the demand in India for raw jute. India has had to import raw jute from other countries with a high price. Pakistan imported coal from China at a heavy price. Political prejudices were carried to the extent of inflicting economic injury of a permanent nature on both India and Pakistan.

Conclusion

At the time of independence, both India and Pakistan were highly dependent on each other for trade. From 1947 to 1965, the two countries entered into 14 bilateral agreements related to trade facilitation. These agreements covered avoidance of double taxation, trade in goods, food items, trade facilitation, border trade, air services and banking. The spirit of pragmatism at this time led to an arrangement under which Pakistan exported grain from Sindh to deficit provinces of India, and India exported flour to East Pakistan. Both India and Pakistan had bank branches in each other's country. In 1965, there were nine branches of six Indian banks operating in Pakistan. Pakistan's Habib Bank had a branch in Mumbai. But all this changed abruptly. In 1965, war broke out between the two countries and trade and economic relations became causalities of war. On the fateful morning of September 6, customs officers at Wagah post near Lahore became the first civilian prisoners of war, and banks in both countries were seized as enemy properties. After the 1965 war, both countries tried to reduce their dependence on one another. Trade resumed on a limited scale after the 1972 Simla agreement. But till date, the bilateral trade remains far below the actual potential. Politics overwhelms economic logic and Kashmir is still the bone of contention between the two countries.

Surrounded by lofty Himalayan ranges and in absence of road fit for wheeled carriage, the Kashmir valley was till the end of the nineteenth century difficult to access. This geographical factor was responsible for restricted flow of trade with the rest of India or even with its neighboring regions.[31] During the middle and later part of nineteenth century, the region enhanced its trade ties with other areas that surrounded it. In 1847, the routes mainly used were:

- The Imperial road from Bhimber to Srinagar leading over the PirPanjal Pass.
- Route from Jammu to Srinagar over the Banihal pass.
- Route following river Jhelum and leading to Muree.
- Route over the Zoji-la to Ladakh and thence to Lhasa and Yarkand.
- Route over the Burzil-la to Gilgit, Hunza, Nagar and Shinshinaki republics.[32]

The most important route connecting Kashmir with the rest of the world was the Jhelum Valley road. It was used for trade, people to people contacts and served as an important link for social and cultural influences. The partition of India in 1947 and the subsequent division of Jammu and Kashmir between India and Pakistan has pushed it into a "secluded periphery".[33] Although the cross-LoC trade between the Indian and Pakistan administered parts of Jammu and Kashmir was started via the Srinagar-Muzaffarabad and Poonch-Rawalakotc routes on October 21, 2008 but it has not really picked up after that. Twenty-one items were identified for duty free passage from each side. Most of the items in the trading list are agricultural commodities, which makes it more of a commodity trade rather than a free trade between the two regions. It is still a barter trade. There is no communication link between the traders on either side. Besides, over the years the number of items for trade has been reduced to around twelve.

The above discussion clearly reveals that the north-western region of India has high stakes in the India-Pakistan trade. The state governments of Punjab, Haryana, Delhi, Jammu and Kashmir, Gujarat and Rajasthan must prevail upon the central government to normalize trade relationship with the neighboring country. It will bring peace and socio-economic prosperity to the region.

References

1. Tridivesh S Maini and Manish Vaid, "Indo-Pak Trade: A Visit to Historical Relations", Briefing Paper, No. 5/2012, *CUTS International,* 2012.
2. C.N. Vakil and G. Raghava Rao, *Economic Relations between India and Pakistan: Need for International Cooperation,* Vora& Co., Bombay, 1968, p. 154.
3. *Ibid.*
4. Naema Sultan Begum, "Indo-Pakistan Trade Relations" in Verinder Grover and Ranjana Arora, *World Community and Indo-Pak Relations: 50 Years of Indo-Pak Relations-2,* Deep & Deep Publications, New Delhi, 1999, p. 160.
5. C.N. Vakil and G. Raghava Rao, op.cit., p. 156.
6. *Ibid.*
7. *Ibid.*
8. The year of devaluation (1949) cannot be an appropriate base year as well to study trends in Indo-Pak trade. There were adverse effects of India's decision to devalue her currency while Pakistan refused to do so. For these reasons, 1950-51 is taken as the base year for studying India-Pakistan trade relations.
9. Sreedhar, "India-Pakistan Trade: Problems and Prospects" in Verinder Grover and Ranjana Arora, *World Community and Indo-Pak Relations: 50 Years of Indo-Pak Relations-2,* Deep & Deep Publications, New Delhi, 1999, p. 209.
10 *Ibid.*
11. Government of India, *White Paper on Indo-Pakistan Trade Relations,* G.O.I. Press, 1950, New Delhi, pp. 3-4.
12. *Ibid.,* pp. 5-9.
13. *White Paper*, op.cit., pp. 49-53.
14. The pound or pound-mass (lb) is a unit of weight equal to 16 ounces (453.592 grams.
15. C.N. Vakil and G. Raghava Rao, op.cit., p. 158.
16. *Ibid.*
17. *Ibid.*
18. *Ibid.,* p. 160.

19. C.N. Vakil and G. Raghava Rao, op.cit., p. 161.
20. At the time of partition in 1947, the Maharaja of Tripura was the landlord of an enormous estate covering over 1,500 villages in the Pakistan borderland. Inhabitants of these villages also had land across the border in Tripura state and, in that capacity, were known as ziratia tenants.
21. C.N. Vakil and G. Raghava Rao, op.cit., p. 162.
22. *Ibid.,* 163.
23. *Ibid.*
24. Trade Agreement between the Government of India and the Government of Pakistan, New Delhi, 21 March 1960. Retrieved from:

    file:///C:/Users/sajad_p/Desktop/Important%20Trade%20Papers/1960%20TRADE%20AGREEMENT%20BETWEEN%20THE%20GOVERNMENT%20OF%20INDIA%20AND%20PAK.htm
25. *Ibid.*
26. C.N. Vakil and G. Raghava Rao, op.cit., pp. 166-167.
27. *Ibid.*
28. Sisir Gupta, "India's Policy towards Pakistan", *International Studies,* Vol. 8, 1966-67, p. 38.
29. Government of India, *White Paper on Indo-Pakistan Relations,* correspondence between the Prime Ministers of India and Pakistan, (15 July to 9 August 1951), New Delhi.
30. Sreedhar, op.cit., p. 210. Also see, Pakistan Ministry of Finance, *Pakistan Economic Survey,* 1964-65, Rawalpindi, pp. 82-83.
31. PNK Bamzai, *Socio-Economic History of Kashmir: 1846-1925*, Gulshan Books, Srinagar, 2007, pp. 78-82.
32. A. Kira, "Cross-LoC trade in Kashmir: From Line of Control to Line of Commerce", *Indira Gandhi Institute of Development Research, Mumbai,* September 2011.

    Retrieved from: http://www.igidr.ac.in/pdf/publication/WP-2011-020.pdf
33. N. Baba, "Peace Process and Imperatives of Resolving the Kashmir Problem" in Amitabh Mattoo, Kapil Kak and Happymon Jacob, ed., *India & Pakistan: Pathways Ahead,* KW Publishers, New Delhi, 2007, p. 215.

Chapter - 13

Need for Humane Governance in North India: A Study of Urban Kashmir

— ***Prof Gull Mohammad Wani***

Abstract

The beginning of the second half of twentieth century in South Asia witnessed -among other things three developments- the birth of new nations, population explosion and fast urbanization. Srinagar-the capital city in Kashmir and Varanasi in Uttar Pradesh happen to be oldest cities in India. Srinagar city for the last twenty five years witnessed phenomenal expansion due to migration of people particularly the middle class from rural Kashmir and also people wanting a better future for their children. This was necessitated due to political violence that struck the state in 1990 and continues in one or the other form. The Babri Mosque/Ram Mandir dispute in the biggest state of Uttar Pradesh fuelled communal disturbances leading to the decline of the civic consciousness of the people. The violence in Punjab equally led to migration and rupture of law and order in many parts of the state. Much of northern India is also caught in the vortex of caste violence which inhibits the civic sense of the people and hence challenges to sustainable urbanization. The state and government machinery remains obsessed with law and order and governance gets neglected giving rise to dysfunctional urbanization. It is only in recent years that there is re-thinking over entire urban governance with focus on smart cities. "Greater Srinagar" concept and "compact townships" can be mechanisms for arresting migration and creating better infrastructure in small towns. Additionally, in Kashmir there is need for humane governance with focus on decentralized democracy, corruption free administration and positive peace which can lead to sustainable urbanization.

Introduction

Different states in northern India carry the historic baggage of misgovernance on account of caste oppression, communal tension and acute political problems having an impact upon political regimes and also developmental goals. The Ram janambhomi dispute continues to fuel communal tension and political class for reasons of short political and electoral goals allows primordial tendencies to grow. This obviously kept the virtues of good governance and civic consciousness submerged. The former union home minister Mr. P Chidhambaram aptly put it at one time that India is poor more because of the northern part and southern India has greatly contributed to the development of modern India. It is the southern India which attracted more and more foreign investment and some of the urban centers/cities like Bangalore turned into hubs for new knowledge economy. The post 1990 economic liberalization did provide an opportunity for northern states to shed their historic baggage in order to move forward and focus upon development of modern infrastructure. It is in this context that one can understand the significance of the 73rd &74th constitutional amendment Acts mandating the devolution of regional and urban planning functions to district planning committees /metropolitan planning committees and urban local bodies respectively. Jammu and Kashmir government enacted Municipal act in 2000 in conformity with the 74th constitutional amendment Act. Srinagar Municipal Council became a corporation in 2003. Under the new Act municipal elections were held in 2005. Electoral process unfortunately again had a collision with political violence and new bodies have not been in place. It is expected that the devolution process will create a template for new stakeholders like youth to play a more meaningful role in the urban futures of twenty first century.

States in the Indian union are partners in the endeavor of "cooperative federalism". The State of Jammu and Kashmir cannot realize its full potential unless it sees opening with its neighboring states and surrounding sovereign countries particularly those with whom it has deep civilization and cultural relations. This can ensure peace and development essential for reaping benefits of new Asian century. Kashmir can easily become Singapore if it can make a transition to humane governance parameters. Singapore has demonstrated that you don't have to be western to be modern and how a poor country can become a rich one in one generation. Kashmir like Singapore needs strategic thinking in sectors viz tourism, education, urban productivity, house ownership, job creation and much more.

India's urban population is low and process of urbanization slow compared to even several developing countries. In census 2011 the urban share of population was 31.16 percent up from 27.81 percent in 2001.There is a definition of "urban" which entails a municipality, a corporation, a cantonment board or a notified town area committee. These are statutorily defined towns. In general terms a habitation is urban if it has a population that is more than 5000, at least 75 percent of male workers are engaged in non-agricultural pursuits and the population density is at least 400 per square kilometers. These are census towns. In case of statutorily towns, one knows who is responsible for urban governance and the delivery of services. In case of census towns we don't know. In Kashmir the civil strife coupled with higher levels of violence took a heavy toll of basic economic infrastructure. The political and governance institutions suffered decay and credibility deficit. The state managers and political governments remained singularly focused on law and order and security related matters. The Kashmir society suffered a terrible drift. There was not only migration of small minority of pundits to other parts of the country but internal displacement from within Kashmir from the majority community as far as politically connected families were concerned. Most of these people started migrating from rural Kashmir in Srinagar and other smaller towns. The affluent middle class from rural Kashmir moved toward Srinagar city in search of security, jobs and good education for their children. Many of the haphazard private colonies in the periphery of Srinagar city were constructed and habituated by these migrants. This apart from the fact that Srinagar city historically has remained a nerve -centre of trade and commerce .Srinagar also has remained the hotbed of political activities of all hues and most of the political formations have their headquarters located in the city. The rural poor and unskilled workers too moved toward city and towns. They readily found jobs in the construction industry and were able to feed their families back in villages. This led to "urbanization of poverty". The heavy rush of people into city created enormous pressure on wetlands and agricultural land which is already in short supply in Kashmir. The precious wetland, in Bemina and agricultural land in areas like Rawalpora, Hyderpora, Nowgam in Srinagar city has completely become "developer's empire". The growth of slums can also be largely attributed to this phenomenon. The Srinagar city has suffered dysfunctional urbanization where there is gap between growth and development. While new houses, malls and shopping complexes have come up quite recently but there is increasing decline of the urban environment.

In 1956 Srinagar Municipal Committee was made as Srinagar Municipal Council and Council got made into corporation in 2003.The Srinagar city development plan (SCDP) accelerated pace of urban growth of Srinagar and has thrown up a number of challenges making urban development management a complex problem. It has also made urban governance a difficult preposition. The Srinagar city along with other towns has seen haphazard growth. It has also given rise to sanitation, sewerage and other water related problems for the consumers.

Humane Governance in Kashmir

Kashmir needs to be rescued from "high conflict politics" geared towards state security, securitization of territory and geo-political politic. This particular policy focus has resulted in reducing day to day needs of the people to mere triviality resulting in greater urban chaos. There were times in Kashmir when protection to Dal Lake, water bodies and clean drinking water and stray dog menace were considered issues of irrelevance and were counted as anti-political movement distractions. The result was accumulation of urban governance woes which have started now unfolding one after another. The 2014 floods brought into sharp focus many of these issues. It is only in recent years that experts, planners and policy pundits have started challenging the existing narrative and frame all civil, environmental, urban and other issues in the framework of humane governance. The attributes of humane governance constitute viz, humane security, decentralized democracy and sustainable peace.

The rural landscape in Kashmir is plagued with its own set of agrarian and livelihood problems giving rise to migrations. This is equally true of other parts of India as well. The neglect of the problems of youth in rural hinterland and not creating sufficient avenues of employment has led to massive migrations which have led to different problems. The resultant urban chaos cannot be cured without an urban revolution. The PDP/BJP coalition government in Jammu and Kashmir in its "agenda of alliance "has taken note of urban challenges in the twin cities of Jammu and Srinagar and other smaller towns. This (AOA) too is conceived within the paradigm of humane governance.

PDP-BJP Agenda of Alliance

The agenda states that state government will be transformed into a smart government which will be proactive, transparent and accountable. It shall be the mission of the coalition government to be the most ethical state in the country from present day position of being the most corrupt state. For this new governance systems shall be introduced with national support and international expertise to provide honest, effective inclusive governance and service delivery. The government will ensure that powers and decentralization of decision making is in practice devolved to the third tier Panchayats, Municipalities and corporations. The third tier of governance will be empowered to discharge their statutory functions effectively and efficiently by giving them functional roles and fiscal responsibilities. Regional development plans will be formulated to ensure that each region has focused and specific economic activity that spurs development in the sphere of crafts and tourism. Two mega cities: Greater Srinagar and greater Jammu will be developed along with two new satellite cities of "New Srinagar" and "New Jammu". The government will upgrade all towns with population size class of 30,000 to 99,999 into cities. The alliance agenda is dictated and guided by existential realities and contextual factors. It in one sense peeps through missed opportunities and backlog of huge cases which need urgent government attention and informed debate by civil society actors and community leaders. Pertinent to note here is that human security aspect of governance and decentralized democratic governance must involve renewed focus on the following critical concerns:

Kashmiri Youth and the Concept of Ethical City

For smart urbanization to be successful in Kashmir there is need to invest in the priorities of youth, creation of jobs they desperately need and more importantly dialogue and other social spaces they can engage with so as to connect with the city. As already noted that Srinagar city over the decades got flooded by all sorts of migrants from rural Kashmir and youth particularly for reasons of security and educational coaching made Srinagar their second home. We need not measure the smartness of Srinagar and other towns in the valley by metrics of internet connectivity. We need to wise up to the deep -rooted socio-psychological frustrations of young so that they can meaningfully negotiate with urban challenges. The relationship between youth populations, crime and violence are more complex. Just as urban youth populations can perpetuate violence, they are also victims of it and for some violence can be a route to identity and violence. Through 1970,s and 1980,s planners, sociologists, geographers and economists cautioned against the dangers of overcrowding and urged the building of alternatives or counter-magnets to the fatal attractions of the city. Some of the alternatives being discussed were Ring towns, satellite Towns, New towns and townships. In case of Kashmir for reasons of violence no such urban need was addressed and Srinagar saw massive horizontal expansion. Abdou Maliq Simone(US academic) has argued in a powerfully crafted essay "people as infrastructure "that building infrastructure does not mean physically laying down reticulate systems of highways, pipes, wires or cables. By contrast it means creating spaces that individuals will live, work and play in". The aim should be the inclusive urbanization. The digital India initiatives show a strong focus on urban development and a push towards smart cities that prioritizes internet connectivity. The government's motivation is to create world - class cities that will account for 40 percent of country's population and contribute up to 75 percent of its gross domestic product by 2030.These future milestones are important not least because of the growing importance of the urban economy and the opportunities that could bring but also because of the challenge of catering to the needs of urban

India. Eighty percent of the infrastructure required to accommodate urban India in 2030 has not yet been built. There is a demand that Srinagar and Jammu be carved into smart cities and it has lately been accepted by government of India. This should be done keeping in view the needs of the youth. The agenda of alliance of the coalition government rightly talks of rebuilding Shehr-e-Khas (old Srinagar city) as the heritage destination by dovetailing craft heritage and tourism, making Dal Lake the world heritage site. Pertinent to note is the fact that stone-pelting by youth saw its emergence first in this part of the city and many security experts found choked streets as the primary reason responsible for it as the youth had no free spaces for interaction and other sports activities. In the interior of the Srinagar city there are no spaces for youth to play, sing, dance or have other amusement activities and the responsibility of the government lies in creating spaces for youth, old age people and other sections of society so that creative energy is used in productive ways. Hence proper planning should be the goal for the state to take care of the urban mess.

Planning as Urban Mission

For attaining different urban missions it is necessary that planning is given due impetus for attainment of urban goals. The government of India has started many such missions over the years viz Swachh Bharat, smart cities etc can bear fruit only if these are backed by proper planning. The planning process in Srinagar city has multiple tasks to achieve considering heritage status and historicity of the city. Planning must ensure proper land use and housing needs of different sections of the society. The planning mechanisms also need to draw proper lessons from 2014 floods which had impacted the Srinagar and other major towns of the valley. A 2012 study by independent consultants in the course of preparing Srinagar Master plan found that 26 sq kmt (7percent) of the city lands under master plan area are under use by the army and paramilitary forces. Earlier in 1970 for military purposes the construction of Mar Nalla(a city drainage canal) into road deprived the Srinagar of a historic outlet system. Again Doodganga Nallah (tributary of Jhelum) was converted into a concrete building. Further Bemina and Batamallu wetlands were converted into residential colonies. In Kashmir multiple steps may have to be taken to augment the urban planning process. One, that the fiscal domain of the urban local bodies in Jammu and Kashmir is poor due to absence of buoyant sources of income. In the absence of Sate finance commission the transfer of funds to urban local bodies have been done on adhoc basis. Second, the institutional framework is also poor in Srinagar as multiple urban development agencies, institutional and local authorities are engaged for managing local urban affairs. Some of these institutions like Srinagar development authority, Lakes and water ways development authority, roads and buildings, pollution control board and public health engineering work at cross purposes and independent of each other to the detriment of urban development. Third , time has come when margins and urban poor must factor in the planning process so that the menace of urban crime is arrested as many of them thrive in slums laying at the outskirts of the city. Fourth, while new roads are being planned and widening of existing roads takes place, there is need to revisit the transport policy. We need to create space for pedestrians and cyclists who should not be denied space in the process. Lastly, compact regional small towns be established to reduce the attractions of migration to the city. Extreme rainfall due largely to climate change should make us conscious of vulnerabilities. The planning process in case of a heritage city like Srinagar must be multidimensional in its conception and operation. It should also draw from local traditions and innovations and more of that came into public knowledge post 2014 floods. Some of the suggestions for maintaining Srinagar city as the heritage tourist destination and one with a soul can be discussed. As already mentioned the city should also attend to all sorts of livelihood issues for the youth whose identities are interwoven with cities.

Conservation and Community

We need to reflect on a truly Kashmir conservation philosophy. A recognition that the traditional architectural craft techniques used to build our monuments and typical kashmiri shrines may be most suitable to repair these structures is now gaining ground. This has gained prominence after we saw how engineers replaced craftsmen as keepers of our shared built heritage in different parts of the valley. The two world famous shrines at *Chaari Shrief* and *Dastageer sehab* got destroyed in fire and were reconstructed carefully but without that typical Kashmir architectural aura around it. By using stone ,Devidar timber, bamboo and Maharaja bricks -our forefathers build splendid structures. It is only for the last many decades that our design and craft capabilities were lost to materials like cement, steel and glass becoming easily available. Again "Makhdoom Sehab" (famous shrine in Srinagar) ropeway project has proved a huge urban disaster. The project is an act of complete cultural and spiritual insensitivity. Haseeb Drabu, formerly the state culture minister feels that "the ropeway leads to consumerist circuit of tourism to intrude into the only space left for spiritual nourishment of the depleted kashmiri self. He further argues that beautiful original structure rooted in Kashmiri ethos at Hazratbal too was demolished .The quaint structure like many others combined heritage with devotion to represent an aesthetic element of our ethnic identity". It appears that in the shift from traditional to the chief modern we have lost architectural craft skills that had the capability of creating millions of man-days of employment while ensuring that our cities had both a unique identity as well as a higher quality of life. In 1997, on the occasion of the 50th anniversary of India's independence, his Highness, the Agha Khan gifted India a restored Humayun,s Tomb-a designed world Heritage Site. At the Tomb inappropriate past repairs were removed. Stone-carvers, masons and carpenters worked at the Tomb with sandstone and lime mortar prepared with traditional tools as part of a multi-disciplinary team. In Delhi "Urban Art Commission" has mandated that over two percent of building costs be used for artwork and this includes traditional building practices such as stone carving. In Srinagar city major infrastructural projects like flyovers are compromising urban quality and hence future of our past historical legacy needs to be kept in mind.

Stray Dog Menace

Urbanization is an ongoing transformation of traditionalistic rural economies to modern commercial or industrial ones. The high speed urbanization and spread of urban sprawl lead to extensive growth of slums and consequent poverty, unemployment, exploitation ,inequality ,misery and low quality of human life. In fact present mode of urbanization and paradigm of development innately promotes public health and environmental issues and one of them is the menace of stray dogs. Indian cities and towns are home to about 30 million stray dogs and eight million people are forced to take treatment for dog bites every year. Regrettably, 30 to 60 percent of the dog-bite victims are children under the age of 15. In Bengluru it is reported that 45 percent of dog bites are of slum children. In 2012, the WHO states that 30 percent of world rabies case is reported from India. One cannot solve stray dog problem until one solves the local garbage issue. Most of the civic bodies, NGO's and private companies on contract for cleaning and transportation of garbage have largely failed to deliver their objectives. In Srinagar stray dog menace has thrown challenges which need expert handling.

Museums and Antiques

Most museums in India continue to languish in the category of unimportant and irrelevant category. We need to provide due importance to historically oriented museums. These can play a role in changing the social attitudes towards our past. These need to be re-conceptualized from "Ajaib Ghar" a place of wonder to social places where people and particularly school children can meet, eat, shop and also look at art. We need to be mindful of changes taking place due to urbanization and dangers it poses to these places. Further, there is a need that with more urbanization taking place and more rural areas brought into urban fold the archaeological contexts should not be disturbed. The government must find some way to create a domestic market for art and antiquities. This has to be incentivized so that local markets thrive and art dealers can sell their collections. In a historic place like Srinagar where future projects may be undertaken care is to be taken to preserve these antiquities. We can create new museums that can be filled with pottery, coins and artifacts found during the excavations. It is encouraging that after missing several deadlines SPS world class museum was thrown open on world heritage day in Srinagar on April 18, 2017. Touted as one among the best museum buildings, the new complex is designed in a way that a visitor starts his journey with Burzahama Exhibition corresponding to the start of 5000 years of Kashmir history. The visitor then follows the Buddhist, Hindu, Muslim and other eras.

Conclusion

By way of conclusion it can be said that urbanization is posing multidimensional challenges to planners and people in general. As more and more people shift to cities there is lot of pressure on civic amenities and need is to learn more and more about art of conservation. Since increasingly there is scarcity of water we have to pay attention to water harvesting structures in meeting survival needs of the people. Several models exist for the development of community institutions to manage traditional water harvesting systems. The efforts to develop Pani Panchayats in Pune, cascading tank system in Sri Lanka, the Kanaats of Afghanistan and waterways of Colombo are a few points of reference among many that need wider recognition and understanding. We also need to reflect on urban disasters as creative moments. In recent times more and more urban locations face huge disasters due to excessive rain and other things .We need to learn to build on the resilience of the people caught in flood like situations of 2014 and see how innovation was born out of the crisis. Without creativity poor and vulnerable citizens cannot live in our cities. As climate change pushes us into increasing number of disasters failing to learn and make use of them will be a terrible waste.

References

1. The BJP/PDP *Agenda of Alliance in Jammu and Kashmir.*
2. Bibek Debroy, *It pays to be smart,* Indian Express March 29, 2015.
3. AbdouMaliq Simone, *People as Infrastructure: Intersecting Fragments In Jonesburg,*
4. public culture 16(3): 407-429
5. Adil Najam and Moeed yusuf ed, *South Asia 2060: Envisioning Regional Futures*, Anthem Press USA, 2013.
6. Arif Ayaz Parrey, "*A Line that controls : a report on the cross-Loc trade*" Centre for Dialogue and Reconciliation supported by Friedrich Naumann stiftung
7. *''Educational opportunities : Cooperation across the Line of Control In Kashmir''* by Conciliation Resources London, 2009
8. Haseeb Drabu, *Symbolism of the Stairs*, The Greater Kashmir, January 30, 2014.

Chapter - 14

Spatio-temporal Variability of Non-Communicable Diseases in North Western Himalayan region - A Geographical Study of Kashmir Valley

— **Ishtiaq A. Mayer, ** Bashir A. Lone,*
*** Sheraz A. Lone. ** Manzoor A. Wani*

Introduction

Levels of human health vary substantially over space and time both inter and intra regionally. It is therefore, essential to characterize such variations in order to identify areas with health problems for epidemiologic research and design appropriate public health policy measures [Cromley & McLafferty, 2002; Ellioitt et al. 2002]. However, recent advancements in Geo spatial techniques such as geographic information system (GIS) have allowed the application of not only disease mapping, but also spatial analyses, spatial clustering and cluster detection in epidemiological research for better understanding in morbidity pattern and human well being approaches [Rosenberg et al. 1999; Jemal et al. 2002].

Non communicable diseases (NCDs) at present are the major cause of death and disability worldwide and have been increasingly affecting people from developing as well as developed countries [WHO, 2009a].

Non communicable diseases including cardiovascular diseases (CVD), diabetes, cancers, obesity and respiratory diseases account for about 60 per cent of all the deaths worldwide each year, and 80 per cent of these deaths occur in low and middle-income countries (WHO, 2009ab). WHO projects the deaths from communicable, maternal, prenatal and nutritional diseases as the most common cause of death by 2030 [WHO, 2011& Boutayeb, 2006]. Over the coming decades, the burden from NCDs is projected to rise particularly fast in the developing world. Without concerted action, some 388 million people worldwide will die of one or more chronic NCDs in the next 10 years [WHO, 2009b].While there has been an increase in the number of deaths due to NCDs in all regions of the world since 2000, the regions of Africa, South-East Asia, South Asia and Eastern Mediterranean had higher mortality associated with NCDs than other regions (WHO, 2014).

India is also undergoing an epidemiological transition with changing patterns of diseases. According to a report, NCDs accounted for 53 percent of all deaths and 44 percent of the disability adjusted life years (DALYs) lost in India [Srinath et al, 2003].

It is estimated that India accounts for 17 percent of global cardiovascular mortality [WHO, 2005] and this is followed by cancer, chronic respiratory diseases, and diabetes contributing to 7 percent, 7 percent, and 2 percent of the deaths respectively. NCDs have a significant effect on the financial condition of households considering the fact that more than 86 percent of the total expenditure on health care is borne out by individuals in India [Mahal et al; 2010].

Like other states of India, Jammu and Kashmir State, a north western Himalayan region undergoes rapid epidemiological transition as a result of its demographic, economic and social changes and is facing the burden of both communicable and non-communicable diseases (Goli, 2014 and Mayer, I.A. 2007). Lack of accurate data on incidence of diseases, research and cause of deaths is a major hindrance to comprehensive assessment of epidemiological transition. The present study is concerned with examining the spatio-temporal distribution of non communicable disease across Kashmir Valley.

Study Area

The North-Western Himalayan Region (NWHR) comprises three states of the Indian Republic viz., Jammu & Kashmir, Himachal Pradesh and Uttarakhand. Geographically, it extends between 28^0 43'-37^0 05' N latitude and 72^0 40'-810 02'E longitude covering an approximate area of 33 million hectares contributing about 10 per cent of total geographical area of the India. In terms of Population, this Himalayan region contributes about 2.44 per cent of the total Population of India. The region occupies the strategic position in the north and touches the international borders of Nepal, China and Pakistan (Kashyap et al., 2014); it covers the river basins of the Jhelum, Chenab, Ravi, Beas and Sutlej. The Great Himalayan and the Pirpanjal ranges surrounding the Kashmir Valley, the Zanskar, Ladakh and Karakoram ranges to the Ladakh region and the Siwalik range in the south of the Jammu region confer the region with a unique physiographic setting of perennially snow-capped peaks interspersed with valleys and lakes (Rakhecha et al; 1983). North western Himalayan region exhibits one of the most complex climatic patterns. Owing to its extreme diversity in its various sub-ecological locations, elevation, and topography, the region is featured by extreme variants of climate. The climatic conditions vary from hot sub-humid tropical in the southern low tracts to temperate, cold alpine and glacial in the northern high mountains (Bhutiyani, 1992).

The region comparatively shows a thin and dispersed human population due to its physiographic conditions and poor infrastructure development. Agriculture, including livestock continues to be the dominant sector despite the fact that the area is exposed to adverse and harsh geophysical and agro-climatic conditions. This is particularly true to Kashmir Himalaya (Mayer, I.A. 2007). The major natural resources of the Western Himalayas are water, forests, flora and fauna biodiversity. Forests constitute the major shear in the land use of the region covering more than 65 per cent of the total geographical area of the region. The region has unique advantage and competitive edge over the adjoining states in the plains, i.e., Punjab, Haryana, and Uttar Pradesh due to diverse agro-climatic conditions for cultivation of off-season vegetables, temperate fruits, aromatic rice, and medicinal and aromatic plants, besides the huge potential for organic farming. Kashmir valley faces several challenges like poverty, inequality in infrastructure, unbalanced regional development and the problems of linkages in rural and urban economies (Mayer, I.A. 2007).

It is against this back drop that a study at district level was carried out to understand the health conditions of the people of the study area. For governance and administrative purposes Kashmir Valley is divided into ten districts with a cumulative population of 6888475, which turns out to be 54.93 per cent of state population (2011, Census)

Table 1.1: Population statistics of Jammu & Kashmir State (2011)

S.No	*District*	*Total Household*	*%age of Household to Total Household*	*Total Population*	*%age of Population to Total Population*
			Kashmir Division		
1.	Anantnag	153640	7.25	1078692	8.60
2.	Budgam	103363	4.88	753745	6.01
3.	Bandipora	58392	2.75	392232	3.13
4.	Baramulla	152635	7.20	1008039	8.04
5.	Ganderbal	45361	2.14	297446	2.37
6.	Kulgam	73728	3.48	424483	3.38
7.	Kupwara	113929	5.37	870354	6.94
8.	Pulwama	86241	4.07	560440	4.47
9.	Shopian	44411	2.10	266215	2.12
10.	Srinagar	191678	9.04	1236829	9.86
Total				**6888475**	**54.93**
			Jammu Division		
11.	Doda	79636	3.76	409936	3.27
12.	Jammu	314199	14.82	1529958	12.20
13.	Kathua	119583	5.64	616435	4.92
14.	Kishtwar	45209	2.13	230696	1.84
15.	Poonch	90261	4.26	476835	3.80
16.	Rajouri	130401	6.15	642415	5.12
17.	Ramban	55490	2.62	283713	2.26
18.	Reasi	56689	2.67	314667	2.51
19.	Samba	65385	3.08	318898	2.54
20.	Udhampur	99240	4.68	554985	4.43
Total				**5378538**	**42.89**
			Ladakh Division		
21	Leh	21909	1.03	133487	1.06
22	Kargil	18338	0.87	140802	1.12
23	J&K	2119718	100	12541302	100

Source: Census of India, 2011.

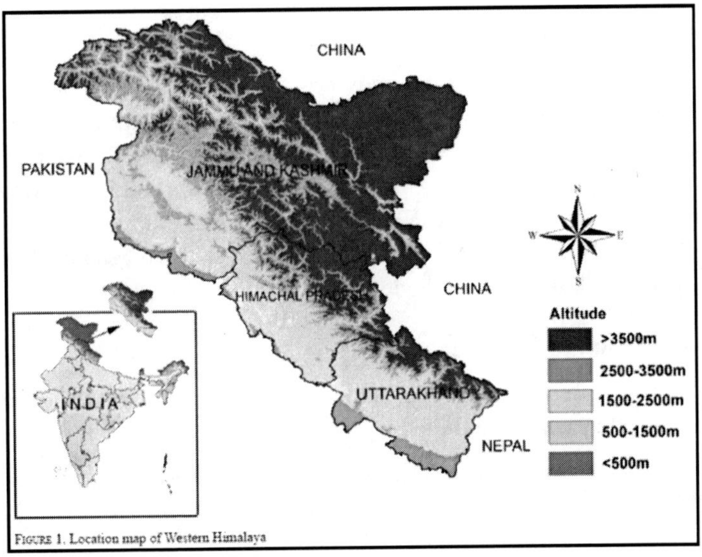

Fig 1.1: Location Map of North Western Himalaya

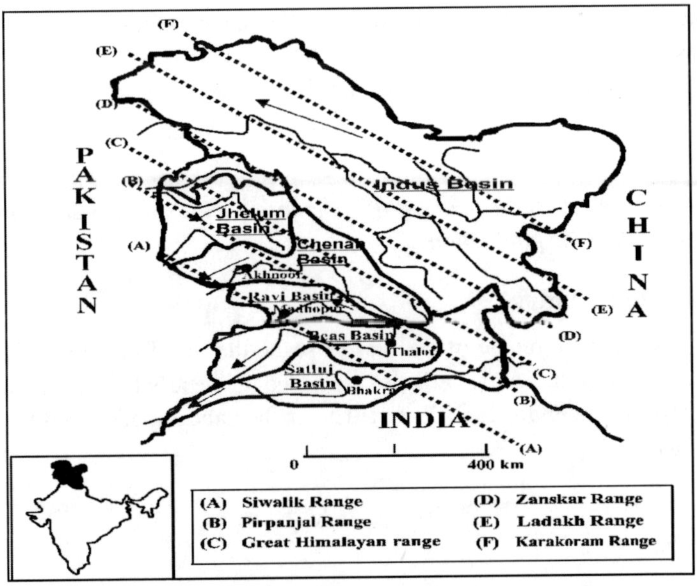

Fig 1.2: Location Map of Study Area.

Materials And Methods

The main purpose of the study was to assess the spatio-temporal variability of non communicable diseases. Therefore, in order to work out the above objective, data was collected from State Surveillance office Srinagar, Directorate of Health services Kashmir and from various district Surveillance offices. The Survey of India Toposheets (1971) on scale 1:50000 was also used in the present study to generate base map. An outline of the methodology used is presented below:

Calculation of Incidence Rate

In the present study, the incidence rate of diseases has been calculated by using the following formula:

$$\mathbf{IR} = \frac{\text{Number of new case of a diseas during a given time period}}{\text{Total population at Risk during the same period of time}} \times 1000$$

Measuring Disease Intensity

For measuring disease intensity of the study area, standardized score (z-score) method has been applied. In the present study, z-score has been extensively used to remove the bias of scale of different variables and for carrying out the levels of disease intensity.

$$z = \frac{x - \mu}{\sigma}$$

*Where, '**μ**' is the mean of the population and 'σ' is the standard deviation of the population*

Composite Index

After the removal of the bias of scale, the transformed or scale free values of the given variables are added up linearly to arrive at the composite index for each district. The mathematical model used is as under:

$$C.I = \sum_{j=l}^{n} \frac{X_{ij}}{X_j}$$

Here, X_{ij} = value of jth variate for i^{th} district; n = number of variables, C.I. = Composite Index

After the construction of composite index, the scored values are classified into three categories (low, medium & high) which show the levels of vulnerability.

Software's used

(i) ERDAS IMAGINE 9.0 ii) Arc GIS 10.3

Statistical Data and its Analysis

Rheumatic Fever

Rheumatic fever (RF) continues to be a major health hazard both in developing as well as in developed economies (Kumar & Tandon, 2013). Rheumatic fever accounts for nearly 25-45% of the acquired heart disease globally (Beheyt et al. 1997). The annual incidence of rheumatic fever is 100-200 times greater than that observed in developed countries and fluctuates between 100-200 per 1,00,000 children of school age (5 years to 18 years). Prevention and control measures for rheumatic heart disease include reduction of household crowding, timely diagnosis and appropriate antibiotics for bacterial pharyngitis (Gupta et al. 2013). The distribution and incidence of rheumatic fever is uneven across the districts of the Kashmir valley. From (table 1.2), it is clear that the incidence of rheumatic fever has increased in all the districts of Kashmir division with few exceptions. In the Kashmir province, the incidence rate of rheumatic fever has increased from 1.13 persons/1000 in 2011 to 3.5 persons/1000 of population in 2015.

Table 1.2: Incidence rate of Rheumatic Fever in Kashmir Division (2011-2015)

District	*Incidence of Rheumatic fever per 1000 persons*					*Change*
	2011	*2012*	*2013*	*2014*	*2015*	*(%)*
Anantnag	4.39	3.00	4.73	5.44	7.03	**2.64**
Baramulla	2.59	2.13	3.49	2.54	3.92	**1.33**
Budgam	2.54	3.12	5.18	5.67	3.93	**1.39**
Ganderbal	1.12	0.54	0.23	2.63	1.41	**0.29**
Kulgam	0.59	2.34	0.01	1.30	1.82	**1.23**
Kupwara	0.29	3.04	0.14	0.72	1.01	**0.72**
Shopian	0.82	1.45	0.06	0.10	0.34	**-0.48**

(Contd...)

Srinagar	7.01	5.12	8.02	7.81	9.95	**2.94**
Bandipora	2.37	4.78	2.57	3.58	2.85	**0.48**
Pulwama	1.60	2.31	3.12	5.97	3.01	**1.41**
Total	**1.13**	**2.78**	**2.75**	**3.58**	**3.5**	**1.20**

Source: State Surveillance office, Srinagar.

Srinagar has the maximum rate of incidence (9.95 persons/1000), followed by Anantnag (7.03 persons/1000) and Budgam (3.93 persons/1000). The minimum incidence rate was observed in Kupwara district (1.01 persons/1000), followed by Ganderbal (1.41 persons/1000) and Kulgam (1.82 persons/1000). The change from 2011 to 2015 showed almost an increasing trend among all districts of Kashmir Valley except district Shopian with an average change of 1.20 percent. The highest change was found in Srinagar fallowed by Anantnag. However, negative change prevails in Shopian (fig. 1.3&1.4).

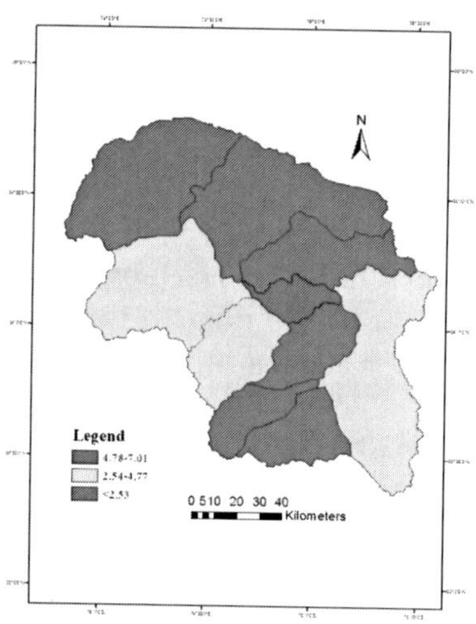

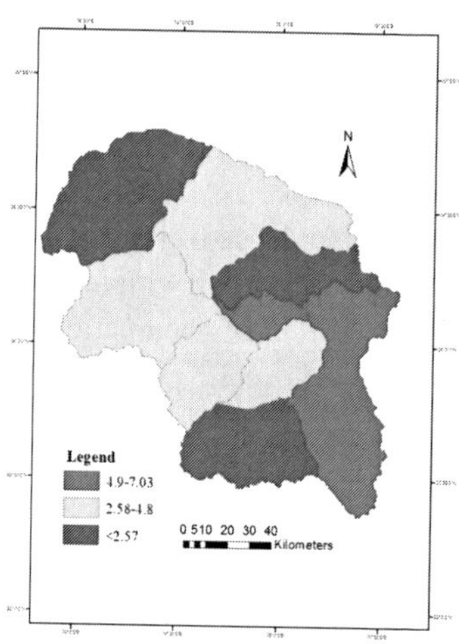

Source: Generated from table 1.2

Fig. 3: Incidence Rate of Rheumatic Fever (2011).

Fig. 3: Incidence Rate of Rheumatic Fever (2015).

Hypertension

Globally cardiovascular disease accounts for approximately 17 million deaths annually and of these, complications of hypertension account for 9.4 million deaths (Boutayeb & Boutayeb, 2005). The Global Burden of Disease study (2005) has ranked hypertension in south Asia as second only to child underweight for age. In an analysis of worldwide data for the global burden of HTN, 20.6 % of Indian men and 20.9 % of Indian women were suffering from HTN in 2015. The rates for HTN in percentage are projected to go up to 22.9 and 23.6 for Indian men and women, respectively by 2025. Recent studies from India have shown the prevalence of HTN to be 25% in urban and 10% in rural people in India (Patil & Durairaj, 2015).

The distribution and incidence of hypertension is uneven across the districts of the Kashmir division. From (table 1.3), it is clear that the incidence of hypertension has increased in all the districts of Kashmir division with few exceptions. In the Kashmir province, the incidence rate of hypertension has increased from 21.46 persons/1000 to 29.04 persons/1000 of population though there are regional variations. Srinagar has the maximum rate of incidence (52.01 persons/1000), followed by Anantnag (47.61 persons/1000), and Baramulla (39.89 persons/1000). The minimum incidence rate is observed in Shopian district (7.16 persons/1000); followed by Ganderbal (14.98 persons/1000) and Kulgam (17.67 persons/1000). The incidence rate is depicted in (fig.1.5&1.6).

Table 1.3: Incidence rate of Incidence of Hypertension in Kashmir Division (2011-2015)

District	*Incidence of Hypertension per 1000 persons*					*Change*
	2011	*2012*	*2013*	*2014*	*2015*	*(%)*
Anantnag	31.29	18.21	31.89	32.04	47.61	**16.32**
Baramulla	26.68	27.14	22.31	31.00	39.89	**13.21**
Budgam	28.20	37.43	43.12	52.73	37.07	**8.87**
Ganderbal	15.25	29.71	26.89	28.44	14.98	**-0.27**
Kulgam	12.28	25.02	17.98	24.17	17.67	**5.39**
Kupwara	17.46	25.56	15.24	10.89	18.89	**1.43**
Shopian	7.23	7.13	6.95	14.74	7.16	**-0.07**
Srinagar	29.67	33.56	38.02	37.42	52.01	**22.34**
Bandipora	22.26	11.03	15.10	25.25	19.03	**-3.23**
Pulwama	24.27	14.45	15.72	27.69	36.09	**11.82**
Total	**21.46**	**22.92**	**23.32**	**28.44**	**29.04**	**7.58**

Source: State Surveillance office, Srinagar.

The total change was 7.58 percent. Higher change was found in district Srinagar fallowed by Anantnag while as negative change prevails in Bandipora.

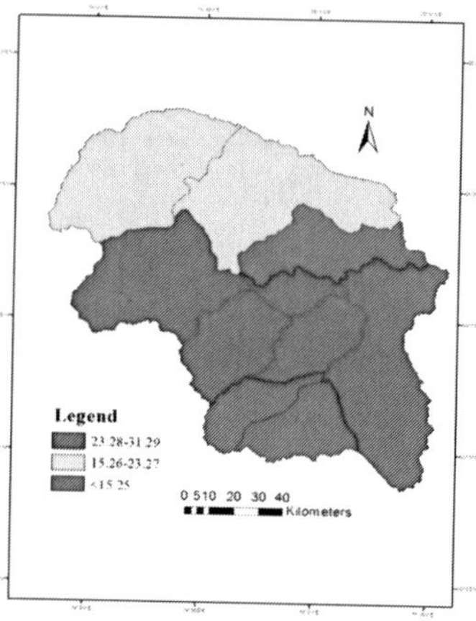

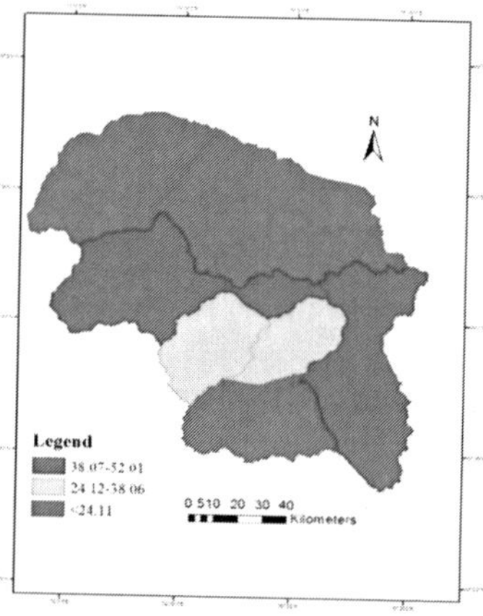

Source: Generated from table 1.3.

Fig. 5: Incidence Rate of Hypertension (2011).

Fig. 6: Incidence Rate of Hypertension (2015).

Ischemic Heart Disease

Ischemic heart disease (IHD) is the generic designation for a group of closely related syndromes resulting from myocardial ischemia, an imbalance between the supply (perfusion) and demand of the heart for oxygenated blood (Armstrong, 2011). The distribution and incidence of ischemic heart diseases is uneven across the districts of the Kashmir division. From (table 1.4), it is clear that the incidence of ischemic heart diseases has increased in all the districts of Kashmir division with few exceptions. In the Kashmir province, the incidence rate of ischemic heart diseases has increased from 1.68 persons/1000 to 12.97 persons/1000 of population though there are regional variations.

Srinagar has the maximum rate of incidence (29.74 persons/1000), followed by Anantnag (18.09 persons/1000), and Baramulla (17.05 persons/1000). The minimum incidence rate is observed in Bandipora district (4.67 persons/1000); followed by Shopian

Table 1.4: Incidence rate of Ischemic Heart Diseases in Kashmir Division (2011-2015)

District	*Incidence of Ishematic Heart Diseases per 1000 persons*					*Change*
	2011	*2012*	*2013*	*2014*	*2015*	*(%)*
Anantnag	0.82	5.90	7.09	12.75	18.09	**17.27**
Baramulla	2.06	7.86	5.04	11.12	17.05	**14.99**
Budgam	0.71	5.09	3.08	8.90	10.67	**9.96**
Ganderbal	5.99	11.54	10.91	16.26	10.56	**4.57**
Kulgam	2.03	10.72	7.32	10.86	9.09	**7.06**
Kupwara	1.46	6.32	4.68	10.23	8.98	**7.52**
Shopian	0.06	2.07	1.34	6.14	5.91	**5.85**
Srinagar	1.28	8.19	13.75	10.59	29.74	**28.46**
Bandipora	0.43	4.95	5.32	9.14	4.67	**4.24**
Pulwama	1.94	11.08	8.51	13.79	14.93	**12.99**
Total	**1.68**	**7.37**	**6.70**	**10.98**	**12.97**	**11.29**

Source: State Surveillance office, Srinagar.

(5.91 persons/1000) and Kupwara (8.98 persons/1000). The change from 2011 to 2015 showed an increasing trend among all districts of Kashmir Valley with an average change of 11.46 percent. The highest change were found in Srinagar (28.46 percent) followed by Anantnag while as lowest change was found in Bandipora followed by Shopian (fig. 1.7 & 1.8).

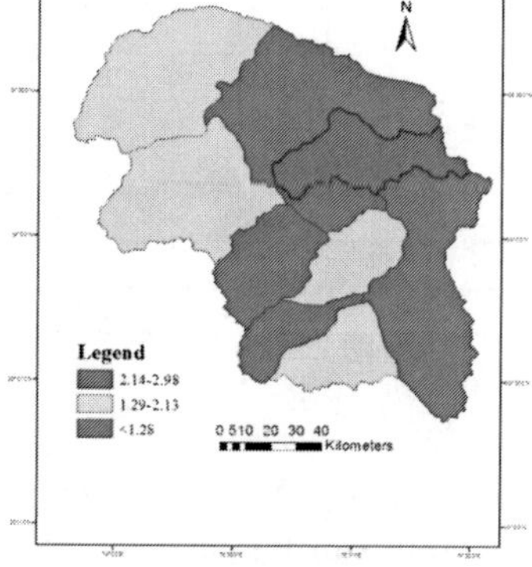

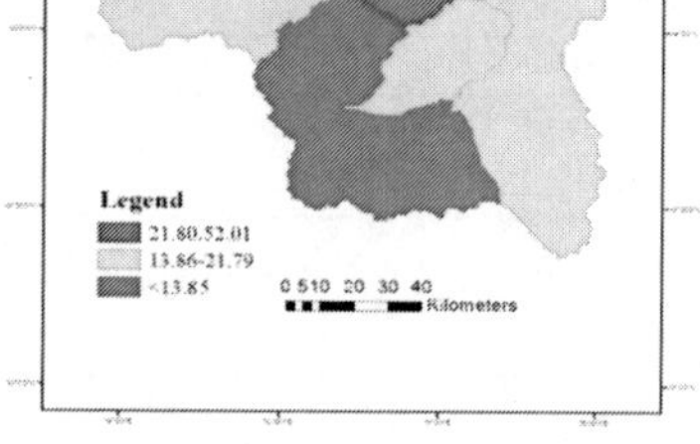

Source: Generated from table 1.4.

Fig 7:Incidence Rate of Ischematic Heart Disease (2011).

Fig 8: Incidence Rate of Ischematic Heart Disease (2015)

Diabetes

Diabetes prevalence has been rising more rapidly in middle- and low-income countries than in high-income countries (Lim, et al. 2007). Diabetes is a major cause of blindness, kidney failure, heart attacks, nerve damage, stroke and lower limb amputation (Forbes & Cooper, 2013). Diabetes is an important cause of blindness and occurs as a result of long-term accumulated damage to the small blood vessels in the retina. Diabetes is among the leading causes of kidney failure (Mealey & Ocampo, 2007).

The distribution and incidence of diabetes mellitus type - I is uneven across the districts of the Kashmir division. From (table 1.5), it is clear that the incidence of diabetes mellitus type - I has increased in all the districts of Kashmir division with few exceptions. In the Kashmir province, the incidence rate of diabetes type - I has increased from 4.94 persons/1000 to 10.56 persons/1000 of population though there are regional variations.

Table 1.5: Incidence rate of Diabetes Mellitus Type - I in Kashmir Division (2011-2015)

District	*Incidence of Diabetes Mellitus Type - I per 1000 persons*					*Change*
	2011	*2012*	*2013*	*2014*	*2015*	*(%)*
Anantnag	9.05	7.57	12.08	15.20	21.15	**12.10**
Baramulla	7.91	6.87	14.43	10.03	17.93	**10.02**
Budgam	1.94	2.86	5.94	1.69	3.01	**1.07**
Ganderbal	0.69	3.68	0.30	0.29	0.46	**-0.23**
Kulgam	2.73	4.46	7.92	3.18	4.67	**1.94**
Kupwara	4.04	5.71	3.09	0.07	9.03	**4.99**
Shopian	3.27	7.06	0.00	9.37	5.91	**2.64**
Srinagar	11.74	17.55	21.58	21.60	29.05	**17.31**
Bandipora	1.46	0.23	2.44	1.42	0.38	**-1.08**
Pulwama	6.62	12.42	10.52	13.39	14.01	**7.39**
Total	4.94	6.84	7.83	7.62	10.56	**5.62**

Source: *State Surveillance office, Srinagar*

Srinagar has the maximum rate of incidence (29.05 persons/1000), followed by Anantnag (21.15 persons/1000), and Baramulla (17.93 persons/1000). The minimum incidence rate is observed in Bandipora district (0.38 persons/1000); followed by Budgam (3.01 persons/1000) and Kulgam (4.67 persons/1000). The change detection of diabetes mellitus type-I from 2011 -2015 shows a total change of 5.98 percent. Higher change was found in district Srinagar fallowed by Anantnag while as negative change prevails in Bandipora (fig. 1.9 & 1.10).

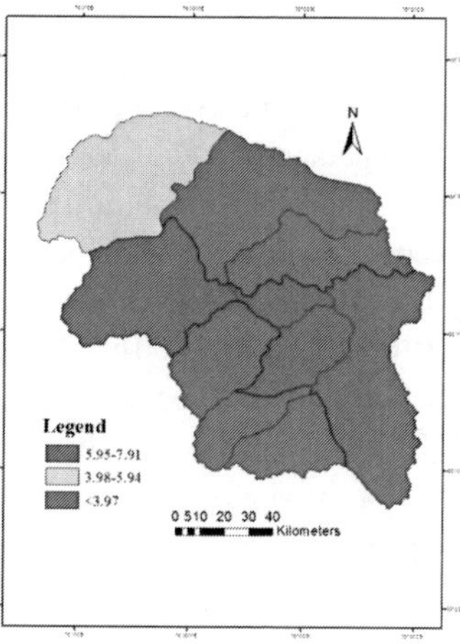

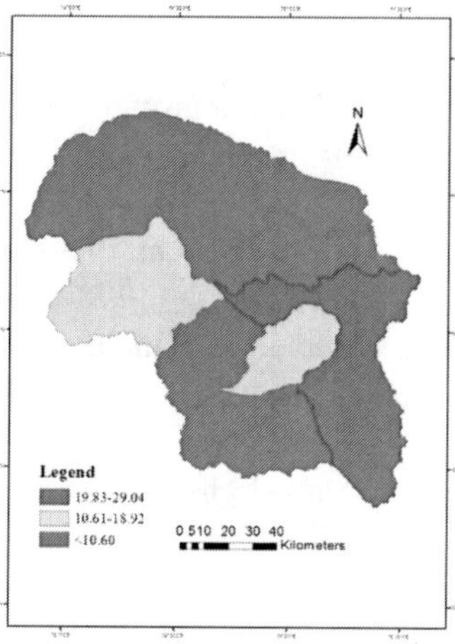

Source: Generated from table 1.5.

Fig 9: Incidence Rate of Diabetes - I (2011).

Fig 10: Incidence Rate of Diabetes - I (2015)

The distribution and incidence of diabetes mellitus type-II is uneven across the districts of the Kashmir division. From (Table 1.6) it is clear that the incidence of diabetes mellitus type - II has increased in all the districts of Kashmir division with few exceptions.

Table 1.6: Incidence rate of Diabetes Mellitus Type - II in Kashmir Division (2011-2015)

District	*Incidence of Diabetes Mellitus Type - II per 1000 persons*					*Change*
	2011	*2012*	*2013*	*2014*	*2015*	*(%)*
Anantnag	5.39	7.55	4.51	15.87	10.51	**5.12**
Baramulla	5.99	12.26	11.09	9.06	14.73	**8.74**
Budgam	4.32	3.90	1.56	0.42	6.91	**2.59**
Ganderbal	3.45	2.11	5.34	3.90	7.26	**3.81**

(Contd...)

Kulgam	0.52	1.03	1.90	2.98	3.05	**2.53**
Kupwara	4.65	5.49	4.50	9.13	9.21	**4.56**
Shopian	0.85	3.04	4.57	7.52	6.51	**5.66**
Srinagar	7.62	9.35	8.26	11.88	19.01	**11.39**
Bandipora	1.87	1.06	2.43	2.98	0.51	**-1.36**
Pulwama	3.88	7.61	11.38	14.57	7.93	**4.05**
Total	**3.85**	**5.34**	**5.55**	**7.83**	**8.56**	**4.71**

Source: State Surveillance office, Srinagar.

In the Kashmir province, the incidence rate of diabetes type-II has increased from 3.85 persons/1000 to 8.56 persons/1000 of population though there are regional variations. Srinagar has the maximum rate of incidence (19.01 persons/1000), followed by Baramulla (14.73 persons/1000), and Anantnag (10.51 persons/1000). The minimum incidence rate is observed in Bandipora district (0.51persons/1000); followed by Kulgam (3.05 persons/1000) and Shopian (6.51persons/1000). The change detection from 2011 -2015 shows an overall change as 4.51 per cent. Higher change was found in district Srinagar fallowed by Baramulla while as negative change prevails in Bandipora (fig. 1.11 & 1.12).

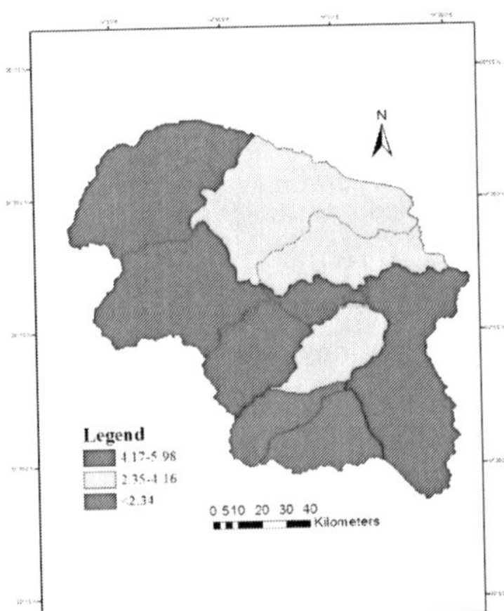

Source: Generated from table 1.6

Fig 11: Incidence Rate of Diabetes - II (2011).

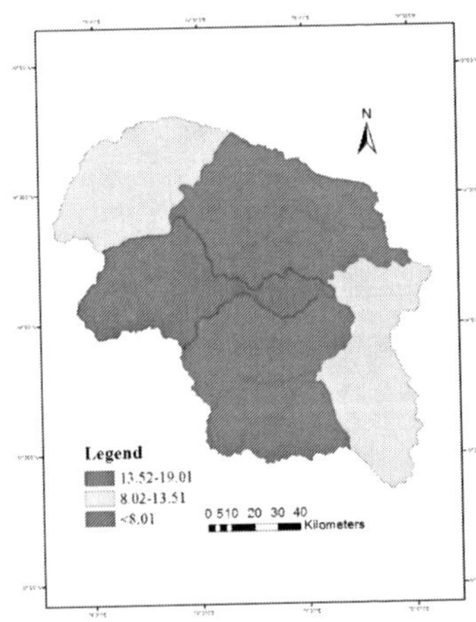

Fig 12: Incidence Rate of Diabetes - II (2015)

Bronchitis

Bronchitis is an inflammation of the air passages between the nose and the lungs, including the windpipe or trachea and the larger air tubes of the lung that bring air in from the trachea (Baroody & Canning, 2003). Bronchitis can either be of brief duration (acute) or have a long course (chronic). Infants, young children, and the elderly are more likely to get the disease because people in these age groups generally have weaker immune systems. Smokers and people with heart or other lung diseases are also at higher risk of developing bronchitis. Individuals exposed to chemical fumes or high levels of air pollution also have a greater chance of developing bronchitis (WHO, 2009).

The distribution and incidence of Bronchitis is uneven across the districts of the Kashmir division. From table 1.7, it is clear that the incidence of Bronchitis has increased in all the districts of Kashmir division with few exceptions. In the Kashmir province, the incidence rate of Bronchitis has increased from 8.64 persons/1000 to 13.36 persons/1000 of population though there are regional variations (fig. 1.13 & 1.14). Baramulla has the maximum rate of incidence (23.85 persons/1000), followed by Srinagar (21.51 persons/1000), and Anantnag (16.01 persons/1000).

Table 1.7: Incidence rate of Incidence of Bronchitis in Kashmir Division (2011-2015

District	Incidence of Bronchitis per 1000 persons					Change (%)
	2011	2012	2013	2014	2015	
Anantnag	11.53	8.01	10.91	13.06	16.01	**4.48**
Baramulla	17.95	11.71	18.01	15.82	23.85	**5.90**
Budgam	9.81	10.03	11.15	14.94	15.91	**6.10**
Ganderbal	5.32	19.58	12.76	7.48	9.53	**4.21**
Kulgam	6.02	3.96	7.56	8.25	9.59	**3.57**
Kupwara	4.14	5.10	4.01	1.99	10.09	**5.95**
Shopian	5.63	1.03	4.22	7.87	8.31	**2.68**
Srinagar	14.98	9.53	15.44	17.24	21.51	**6.53**
Bandipora	4.25	6.91	10.64	7.78	6.81	**2.56**
Pulwama	6.81	5.31	7.52	10.01	12.05	**5.24**
Total	**8.64**	**8.12**	**10.22**	**10.44**	**13.36**	**4.72**

Source: State Surveillance office, Srinagar.

The minimum incidence rate is observed in Bandipora district (6.81persons/1000); followed by Shopian (8.31 persons/1000) and Ganderbal (9.53 persons/1000). The change detection of Bronchitis from 2011-2015 across all districts was 4.72 percent. Higher change was found in district Srinagar followed by Kupwara while as lowest change prevails in Bandipora and Shopian.

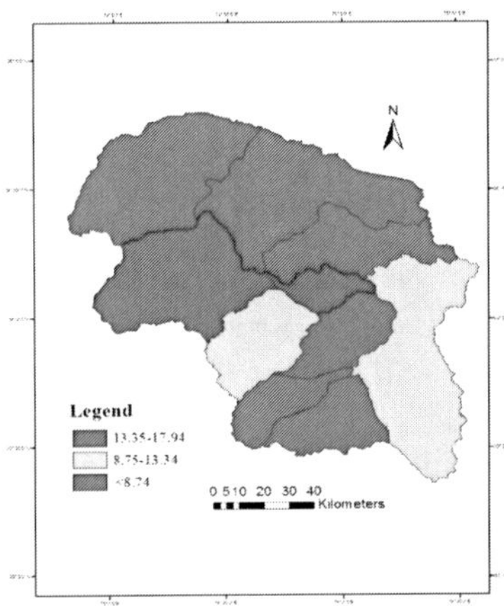

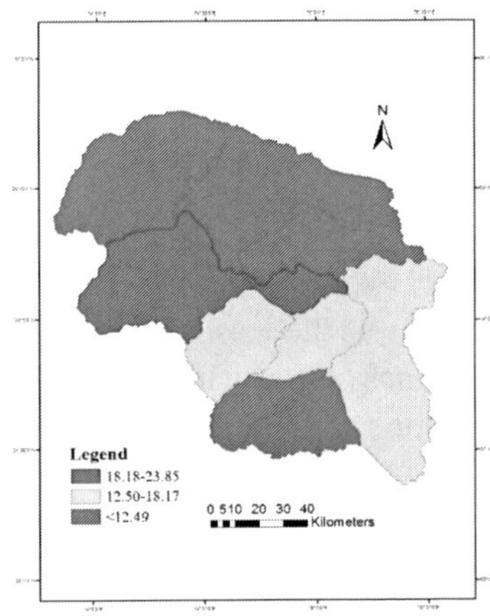

Source: Generated from table 1.7.

Fig 13: Incidence Rate of Bronchitis (2011).

Fig 14: Incidence Rate of Bronchitis (2015)

Asthma

There has been a sharp increase in the global prevalence, morbidity, mortality, and economic burden associated with asthma over the last 40 years, particularly in children and elderly (Braman, 2006). WHO estimates that 334 million people of all ages and all ethnic backgrounds worldwide currently suffer from asthma and its prevalence increases by 50% every decade (Asher & Pearce, 2014). It is estimated that the number of people with asthma will grow by more than 100 million by 2025. Asthma is the 14th most important diseases in terms of extent and duration (Oberg *et al.* 2011). Asthma accounts for about 1 in every 250 deaths worldwide. Most asthma deaths occur in those > 45 years old and are largely preventable, frequently being related to inadequate long-term medical care or delays in obtaining medical help during the last attack (Ibrahim *et al;*2015*)*.

The distribution and incidence of Asthma is uneven across the districts of the Kashmir division. From (table 1.8), it is clear that the incidence of Asthma has increased in all the districts of Kashmir division with few exceptions.

Table 1.8: Incidence rate of Asthma in Kashmir Division (2011-2015)

District	***Incidence of Asthma per 1000 persons***					***Change***
	2011	***2012***	***2013***	***2014***	***2015***	***(%)***
Anantnag	11.68	5.20	9.62	13.05	12.31	**0.63**
Baramulla	9.42	4.57	12.15	13.82	10.97	**1.55**
Budgam	4.06	2.95	2.19	5.26	7.71	**0.65**
Ganderbal	7.35	18.35	11.20	4.47	5.31	**0.96**
Kulgam	5.25	4.78	3.03	6.71	7.01	**1.76**
Kupwara	6.95	5.41	4.46	2.65	7.98	**1.03**
Shopian	3.61	2.50	2.30	2.81	4.31	**0.70**
Srinagar	0.56	0.47	0.62	0.36	0.21	**-0.35**
Bandipora	3.90	8.31.	3.40	5.28	4.71	**0.81**
Pulwama	3.38	5.17	5.17	5.86	3.91	**0.53**
Total	**5.62**	**5.49**	**5.41**	**5.73**	**6.44**	**0.83**

Source: State Surveillance office, Srinagar.

In the Kashmir province, the incidence rate of Asthma has increased from 5.62 persons/1000 to 6.44 persons/1000 of population though there are regional variations (fig. 1.15 & 1.16). Anantnag has the maximum rate of incidence (12.31 persons/1000), followed by Baramulla (10.97 persons/1000) and Kupwara (7.98 persons/1000). The minimum incidence rate was observed in Srinagar district (0.21 percent); followed by Pulwama (3.91 persons/1000) and Shopian (4.31 persons/1000). The change from 2011 to 2015 showed almost an increasing trend across different districts of Kashmir Valley except Srinagar (-0.35 percent) with an average change of 0.83 percent. The highest change were found in Kulgam (1.76 percent) followed by Baramulla while as lowest change was found in Pulwama followed by Anantnag and Budgam.

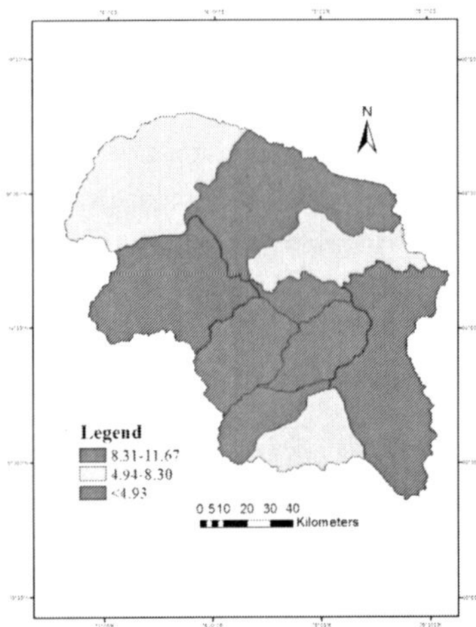

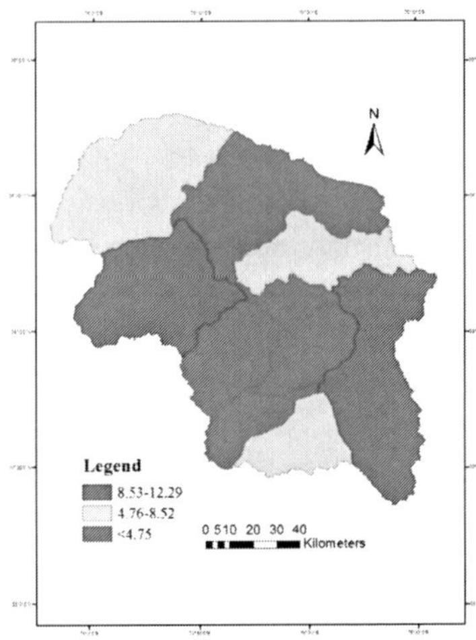

Source: Generated from table 1.8.

Fig 15: Incidence Rate of Ashtama (2011).

Fig 16: Incidence Rate of Ashtama (2015)

Cancer

Cancer affects all nations and therefore it is an endemic disease with considerable variation in frequency according to the site incidence. The geographical differences in total and site incidences have provided clues of causative factors and especially in separating environmental and ethnic factors from intrinsic factors. The total world incidence shows the enormous health problem caused by cancer, which is recognized as the second killer disease in humans (Stewart and Kleihues, 2003). In Japan cancer of the stomach is the most common malignant tumor in both men and women in marked contrast to other countries (Tominaga, 1985). The high incidence of cancer of the mouth in India is well-known and has led to the identification of habit of chewing tobacco with betel nut as a risk factor (Gupta, 1999).

The distribution and incidence of Cancer is uneven across the districts of the Kashmir division. From (table 1.9), it is clear that the incidence of Cancer has increased in all the districts of Kashmir division with few exceptions (fig. 1.17 & 1.18). In the Kashmir province, the incidence rate of Cancer has increased from 0.76 persons/ 1000 to 0.93 persons/1000 of population though there are regional variations. Srinagar has the maximum rate of incidence (0.31 percent persons/1000), followed by Anantnag (0.26 persons/1000) and Budgam (0.19 persons/1000). The minimum incidence rate is observed in Bandipora district (0.04 percent); followed by Ganderbal (0.06 persons/1000) and Kupwara (0.07 persons/1000).

Table 1.9: Incidence rate of Cancer in Kashmir Division (2011-2015)

District	*Incidence of Cancer per 1000 persons*					*Change*
	2011	*2012*	*2013*	*2014*	*2015*	*(%)*
Anantnag	0.17	0.14	0.08	0.13	0.26	**0.09**
Baramulla	0.09	0.11	0.06	0.00	0.14	**0.05**
Budgam	0.12	0.09	0.02	0.11	0.19	**0.07**
Ganderbal	0.04	0.07	0.01	0.00	0.06	**0.02**
Kulgam	0.05	0.40	0.02	0.03	0.09	**0.04**
Kupwara	0.02	0.00	0.05	0.00	0.07	**0.04**
Shopian	0.10	0.05	0.09	0.05	0.13	**0.03**
Srinagar	0.27	0.21	0.29	0.08	0.31	**0.04**
Bandipora	0.03	0.03	0.03	0.07	0.04	**0.01**
Pulwama	0.07	0.08	0.07	0.10	0.11	**0.03**
Total	**0.76**	**1.17**	**0.72**	**0.57**	**0.93**	**0.04**

Source: State Surveillance office, Srinagar.

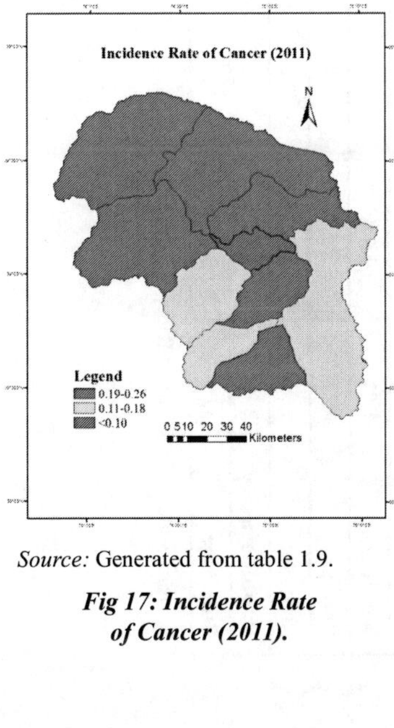

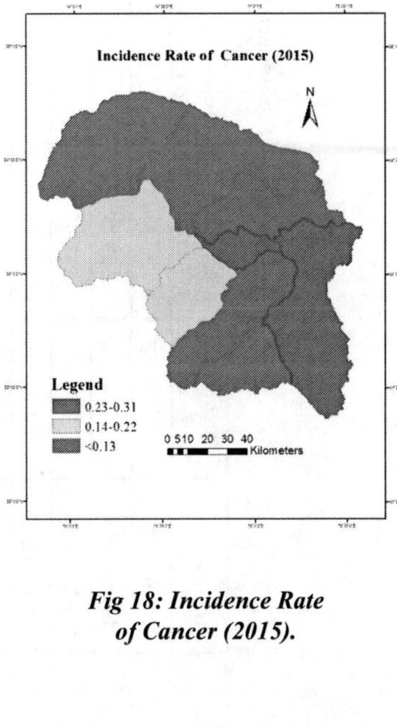

Source: Generated from table 1.9.

Fig 17: Incidence Rate of Cancer (2011).

Fig 18: Incidence Rate of Cancer (2015).

Table: 1.10: Incidence rate of diseases in Kashmir valley

District	*Rheumatic fever*	*Hyper Tension*	*Ishematic heart disease*	*Diabetes mellitus type i*	*Diabetes mellitus type ii*	*Bronchitis*	*Asthma*	*Cancer*
Anantnag	7.03	47.61	18.09	21.15	10.51	16.01	12.31	0.26
Baramulla	3.92	39.89	17.05	17.93	14.73	23.85	10.97	0.14
Budgam	3.93	37.07	10.67	3.01	6.91	15.91	4.71	0.19
Ganderbal	1.41	14.98	10.56	0.46	7.26	9.53	8.31	0.06
Kulgam	1.82	17.67	9.09	4.67	3.05	9.59	7.01	0.09
Kupwara	1.01	18.89	8.98	9.03	9.21	10.09	7.98	0.06
Shopian	0.34	7.16	5.91	5.91	6.51	8.31	4.31	0.13
Srinagar	9.95	52.01	29.74	29.05	19.01	21.51	0.21	0.31
Bandipora	2.85	19.03	4.67	0.38	0.51	6.81	4	0.04
Pulwama	3.01	36.09	14.93	14.01	7.93	12.05	3.91	0.11

Source: State Surveillance office, Srinagar.

Table 1.11: Ranking of Diseases in Kashmir valley

District	*Rheumatic fever*	*Hypertension*	*Ishematic heart disease*	*Diabetes mellitus type i*	*Diabetes mellitus type ii*	*Bronchitis*	*Asthma*	*Cancer*	*Aggregate Rank*
Anantnag	9	9	9	9	8	8	10	9	**71**
Baramulla	7	8	8	8	9	9	9	7	**65**
Budgam	8	7	6	3	4	7	5	8	**48**
Ganderbal	3	2	5	2	6	3	8	4	**33**
Kulgam	4	3	4	4	2	4	6	3	**30**
Kupwara	2	4	3	6	5	5	7	2	**34**
Shopian	1	1	2	5	3	2	3	6	**23**
Srinagar	10	10	10	10	10	10	1	10	**71**
Bandipora	5	5	1	1	1	1	4	1	**19**
Pulwama	6	6	7	7	7	6	2	5	**46**

Source: Compiled by authors.

different districts of Kashmir Valley with an average change of 0.04 percent. The highest change were found in Anantnag (0.09 percent) fallowed by Budgam while as lowest change was found in Bandipora followed by Ganderbal.

Disease Intensity

Study of disease intensity is useful in understanding the distributional pattern and intensity of diseases in an area because it provides an idea of the relative dominance of different diseases in order of importance (Sharma, 1985). In the Present study Kendal's ranking method has been applied for prevalent diseases on the basis of their relative incidence rate. It may be pointed here that higher the composite index means higher the diseases intensity and lower the composite index means lower disease intensity.

Table 1.10 and 1.12 depict noticeable regional imbalances not only in incidence rate and ranking but also in the intensity of diseases across different districts in the study area. For the sake of delineation of diseases intensity regions of the study area, the diseases composite score has been applied and the values, which varies from 71 in district Srinagar and Anantnag to 19 in district Bandipora, have been put in three categories i.e. high diseases intensity zone (Anantnag, Baramulla, Srinagar), medium diseases intensity zone (Kulgam, Pulwama) and low diseases intensity zone (Bandipora, Kupwara, Budgam, Ganderbal, Shopian) (fig. 1.19).

Table 1.12: District Wise Intensity of Diseases in Kashmir Valley

Districts	*CI*	*DiseasesIntensity*
Anantnag Baramulla Srinagar	**53.7-71.1**	**High Intensity**
Kulgam Pulwama	**36.3-53.6**	**Medium Intensity**
Bandipora Kupwara Budgam Ganderbal Shopian	**<36.3**	**Low Intensity**

Source: Compiled by authors.

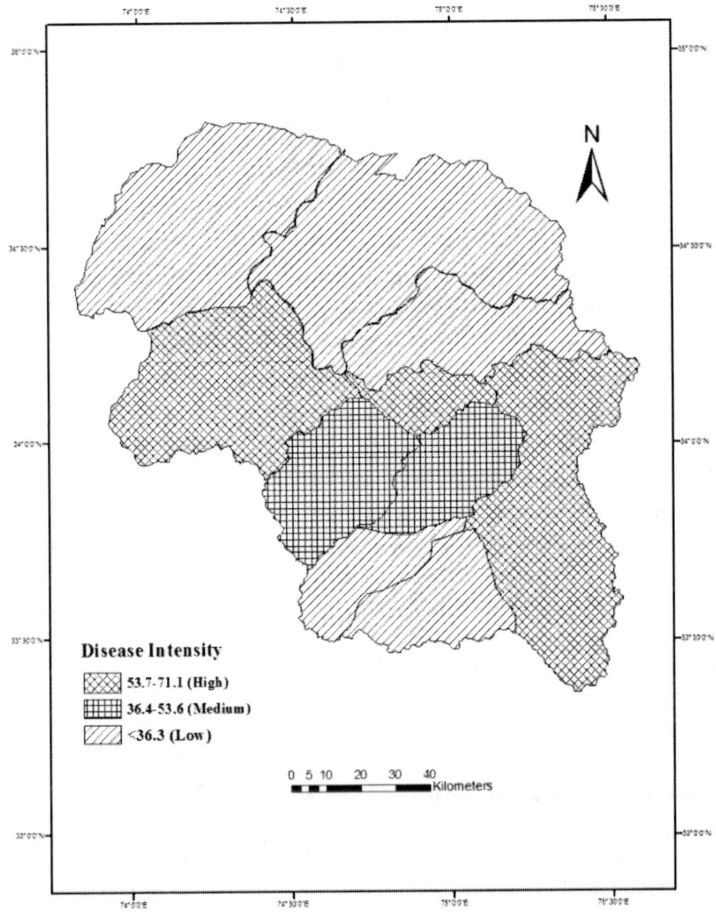

Source: Generated from SOI Toposheets1971 and Secondary data

Fig 1.19: Diseases Intensity Map of Kashmir Valley

Conclusion and Suggestions

The distribution and prevalence of non-communicable is uneven across the districts of the Kashmir valley. The prevalence of non-communicable diseases have been reported from all the districts of Kashmir valley but the incidence rate is observed high in developed districts (in terms of socio-economic conditions) and low in under developed districts. The study shows that Anantnag, Baramulla and Srinagar districts falls under high rate of disease intensity (53.7-71.1-CI), however, Bandipora, Kupwara, Budgam, Ganderbal and Shopian fall under the low (<36.3-CI) category of disease intensity while others are in moderate category.

Disease surveillance and establishing of disease data bank needs to established on priority in order to understand the disease pattern of the area which would help in health care planning and allocation/ location parameters. There should be need to maintain and develop effective public health policies which address the social, economic, environmental and behavioural determinants of health with a particular focus on reducing health inequities. There is an urgent need to develop efficient preventative strategies to halt the growing trend of non-communicable diseases through the control of risk factors like smoking, alcohol, diet and inactivity, and environmental factors in general.

References

Armstrong, E. J., Armstrong, A. W., & Rocco, T. P. (2011). Integrative Cardiovascular Hypertension, Ischemic Heart Disease, and Heart Failure. Principles of Pharmacology: The Patho physiologic Basis of Drug Therapy, 437.

Asher, I., & Pearce, N. (2014). Global burden of asthma among children. The international journal of tuberculosis and lung disease, 18(11), 1269-1278.

Baroody, F. M., & Canning, B. J. (2003). Comparative anatomy of the nasal and tracheal/bronchial airways. LUNG BIOLOGY IN HEALTH AND DISEASE, 181, 1-43.

Beheyt, P., Lintermans, J., Taelman, H., & Kagame, A. (1997). Cardiovascular diseases. Health in Central Africa since 1885; past, present and future.

Bhutiyani MR. 1992. Avalanche problems in Nubra and Shyok valleys in Karakoram Himalaya, India. Journal of Institution of Military Engineers of India 3: 3–5.

Boutayeb A. (2006). The double burden of communicable and non-communicable diseases in developing countries. Trans R Soc Trop Med Hyg. 100:191–9.

Boutayeb, A., & Boutayeb, S. (2005). The burden of non communicable diseases in developing countries. International journal for equity in health, 4(1), 2.

Braman, S. S. (2006). The global burden of asthma. Chest Journal, 130(1_suppl), 4S-12S.

Cromley EK, McLafferty S.L. (2002), GIS and public health New York. Guilford Press.

Ellioitt P, Wakefield JC, Best NG, Briggs DJ: Spatial epidemiology New York: Oxford University Press; 2000.

Forbes, J. M., & Cooper, M. E. (2013). Mechanisms of diabetic complications. Physiological reviews, 93(1), 137-188.

Goli, S. (2014). Demographic convergence and its linkage with health inequalities in India.

Gupta PC. Mouth cancer in India: A new epidemic? J Indian Med Assoc 1999; 97:370-3.

Gupta, A., Yadav, C., Gupta, S., & Dwivedi, A. (2013). Rheumatic heart disease, acute rheumatic fever. SPECTRUM OF RADIOGRAPHIC MANIFESTATIONS IN RHEUMATIC HEART DISEASE, (650).

Ibrahim, W. H., Suleiman, N. N., El-Allus, F., Suleiman, J., Elbuzidi, A. A., Guerrero, M. D & Suliman, S. (2015). The burden of adult asthma in a high GDP per capita country: the QASMA study. Annals of Allergy, Asthma & Immunology, 114(1), 12-17.

Jemal A, Kulldorff M, Devesa SS, Hayes RB, Fraumeni F: A geographic analysis of prostate cancer mortality in the United States, 1970–89. Int J Cancer 2002, 101:168-174.

Kashyap,S.D; Dagar,J.C; Pant and Yewale,A.G.(2014).Soil Conservation and Ecosystem Stability:Natural Resource Mamagement through Agroforestry in North-western Himalayan Region. Springer India. DOI:1007/978-81-322-1662-9

Kumar, R. K., & Tandon, R. (2013). Rheumatic fever & rheumatic heart disease: the last 50 years. The Indian journal of medical research, 137(4), 643.

Lim, S. S., Gaziano, T. A., Gakidou, E., Reddy, K. S., Farzadfar, F., Lozano, R., & Rodgers, A. (2007). Prevention of cardiovascular disease in high-risk individuals in low-income and middle-income countries: health effects and costs. The Lancet, 370(9604), 2054-2062.

Mahal, A. Karan, A. and Engelgau, M. (2010). The Economic Implications of Non-Communicable Diseases for India, World Bank, worldbank.org/ healthnutritionandpopulation/ Resources/281627 1095698140167/ EconomicImplicationsofNCDforIndia.pdf.

Mayer, I. A. (2007), Medical Geography, A. P. H. Publishing Corporation, Ansari Road, New Delhi.

Mealey, B. L., & Ocampo, G. L. (2007). Diabetes mellitus and periodontal disease. Periodontology 2000, 44(1), 127-153.

Oberg, M., Jaakkola, M. S., Woodward, A., Peruga, A., & Pruss-Ustün, A. (2011). Worldwide burden of disease from exposure to second-hand smoke: a retrospective analysis of data from 192 countries. The Lancet, 377(9760), 139-146.

Patil, M., & Durairaj, M. (2015). Risk factors of hypertension among adult men: Evidence from a real world outcomes investigation in a Western Indian population. International Journal, 3(7), 274-282.

Rakhecha PR, Kulkarni AK, Mandal BN, Dhar ON. 1983. Winter and spring precipitation over the northwestern Himalaya. Proceedings of the First National Symposium on Seasonal Snow Cover, New Delhi, 175–181.

Rosenberg MS, Sokal RR, Oden NL, DiGiovann D: Spatial autocorrelation of cancer in Western Europe. Eur J Epidemiol 1999, 15:15-22.

Srinath K. Reddy, B. Shah, C. Varghese, and A. Ramadoss, Responding to the threat of chronic diseases in India," The Lancet, vol. 366, no. 9498, pp. 1744–1749, 2005.

Stewart BW & Kleihues P (2003).World Cancer Report. Lyon: IARC Press.

Tominaga S. (1985). Cancer incidence in Japanese in Japan, Hawaii, and western United States. Natl Cancer Inst Monogr, vol-69:83-92.

World Health Organization (2005). The impact of chronic disease in India: Facing the factsreport.Available from:www.who.int/chp/chronic_disease_report/media/india.pdf.

World Health Organization (2009a). Global health risks: mortality and burden of disease attributable to selected major risks. http://www.who.int/healthinfo/global_burden_disease/GlobalHealthRisks_report_full.pdf. Accessed 18 May 2016.

World Health Organization (2009b). Key messages on non-communicable diseases and injuries which have emerged from discussions at ECOSOC during the first half of 2009.Available from: http://www.who.int/nmh/publications/ecosoc_summary_en.pdf.

World Health Organization (2011). Report on Healthy Lifestyles and non-communicable diseases control. Moscow Declaration.

World Health Organization (WHO). (2014). Global status report on non-communicable diseases 2014. Geneva: WHO.

World Health Organization. (2009). Global health risks: mortality and burden of disease attributable to selected major risks. World Health Organization.

Index

D

E

F

G

K

L

M

T

U

V